Off the

WESTERN CANADA

Pam Hobbs, Joanna Ebbutt & Michael Algar

MOORLAND PUBLISHING

The Globe Pequot Press

Published by:
Moorland Publishing Co Ltd,
Moor Farm Road West, Ashbourne,
Derbyshire, DE6 1HD England

ISBN 0 86190 611 X (UK)

The Globe Pequot Press,
6 Business Park Road,
PO Box 833, Old Saybrook,
Connecticut 06475-0833

ISBN 1-56440-955-4 (USA)

© Pamela Hobbs, Joanna Ebbutt &
Michael Algar 1996

All rights reserved. No part of this publication may be reproduced, stored in a retrieval system, or transmitted in any form or by any means, electronic, mechanical, photocopying, recording or otherwise without the prior permission of the publisher. Requests for permission should be addressed to Moorland Publishing Co Ltd, Moor Farm Road West, Ashbourne, Derbyshire DE6 1HD in the UK, or The Globe Pequot Press, 6 Business Park Road, PO Box 833, Old Saybrook, Connecticut 06475-0833 in North America.

Front Cover: Maligne Lake, Alberta
(*Michael Algar*)

Colour origination by
GA Graphics, Stamford

Printed in Hong Kong by:
Wing King Tong Co Ltd

MPC production team:
Editorial & design: J. A. Robey
Cartography: M. Usher

The right of Pamela Hobbs, Joanna Ebbutt & Michael Algar as authors of this work has been asserted by them in accordance with the Copyright, Designs and PatentsAct, 1988.

Dedicated to the children in our lives — Sarah Tishauer, Hayley and Madelaine Burgess, Samuel and Rhys Lynch. May they be fortunate enough to see it all.

British Library Cataloguing in Publication Data:
A catalogue record for this book is available from the British Library.

US Library of Congress Cataloging-in-Publication Data

Hobbs, Pam,
Off the beaten Track. Western Canada/Pam Hobbs, Joanna Ebbutt & Michael Algar
p. cm. — — (Off the beaten track series)
Includes index.
ISBN 1-56440-955-4
1. Canada, Western — Guidebooks. I. Ebbutt, Joanna. II. Algar, Michael. III. Title. IV. Series.
F1060.4.M83 1996
917.1204'3 - -dc20

96-2473
CIP

Contents

	Maps	4
	Introduction	17
	British Columbia	
1	Vancouver & Excursions From The City	34
2	Pacific Islands & The Sunshine Coast	45
3	By Gold Rush Trails To The Yellowhead	61
4	The Fabulous North	74
5	Through Okanagan Orchards To The Rockies	81
6	Discovering The Kootenays	92
	The Far North	
7	The Legendary Yukon	103
8	Adventuring In The Northwest	114
	Alberta	
9	Alberta's Fabled Rockies	127
	The Prairies	
10	Cattle, Oil & Dinosaurs	142
11	Land Of The Big Sky	162
12	Fossils, Flowers & Desert Sands	180
13	Winnipeg — Where The West Was Born	198
	Accommodation and Eating Out	216
	Canada Fact File	236
	Index	250

Western Canada
Hudson Bay
0 200 400 miles
0 200 400 600 km
CANADA
USA
ALASKA
YUKON
NORTHWEST TERRITORIES
BRITISH COLUMBIA
ALBERTA
Coronation Gulf
Tukloyakuk
Inuvik
Gjoa Haven
Fort Good Hope
Fort Norman
Dawson
Else
Beaver Creek
Haynes Junction
Whitehorse
Watson Lake
Fort Simpson
Rae
Yellow-knife
Hay River
Fort Smith
Fort Chipewyn
Churchill
Thompson
Stewart
Fort St John
Hazelton
Prince Rupert
Queen Charlotte Islands
Prince George
Quesnel
Bella Coola
Jasper
Edmonton
Red Deer
Drumheller
Calgary
Kamloops
Kelowne
Penticon
Vancouver Island
VANCOUVER
Medicine Hat
Swift Current
Moose Jaw
Regina
Yorkton
Prince Albert
Dauphin
Portage la Prarie
Brandon
Selkirk
WINNIPEG
N
S
E
W

Chapter 1

Vancouver & Environs

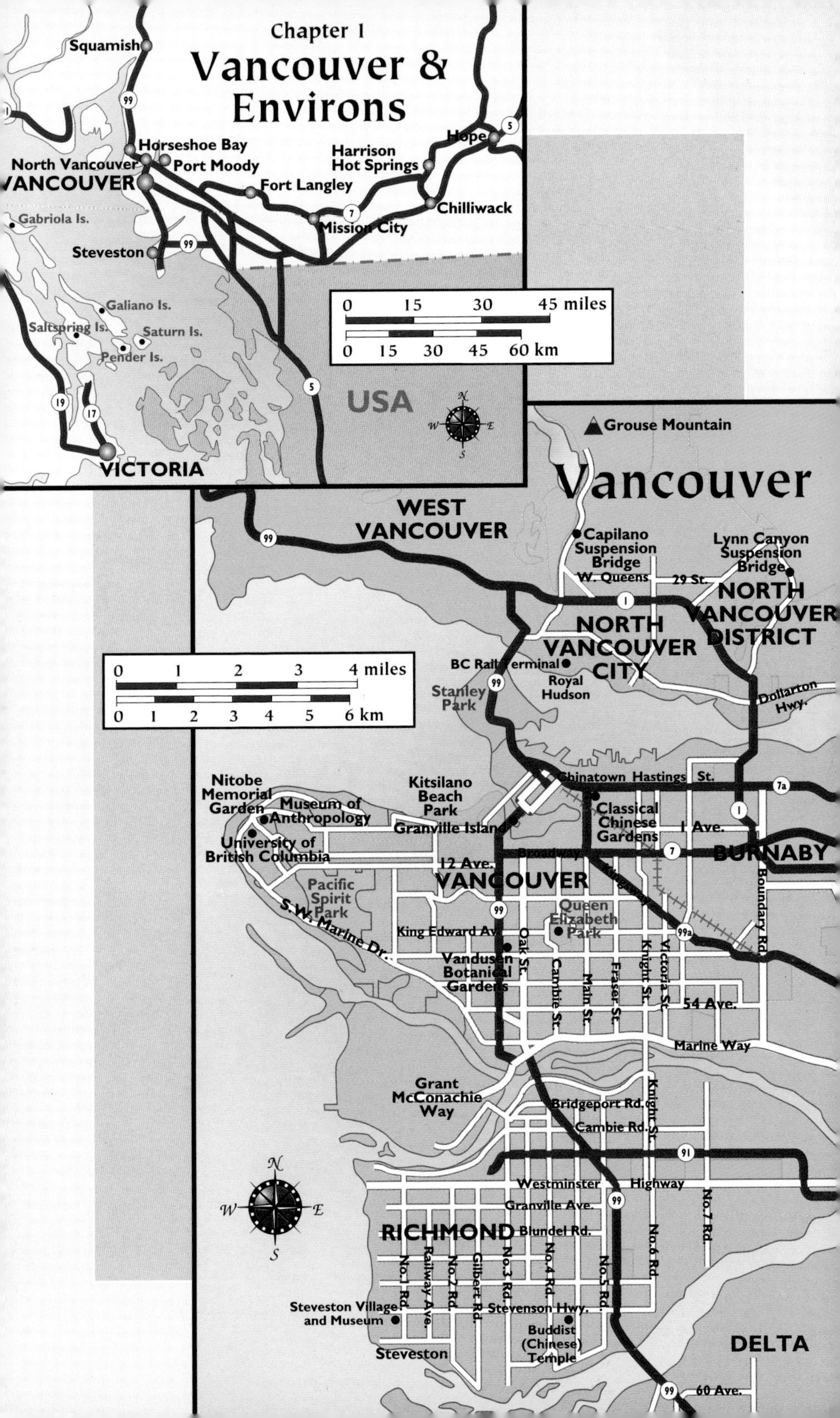

GRAHAM ISLAND
N
W
E
S
Queen Charlotte
Prince Rupert
Port Edward
MORESBY ISLAND
PITT ISLAND
Chapter 2
British Columbia Coast
0 15 30 45 60 miles
0 30 60 90 km
Cape Scott Park
Port Hardy
VANCOUVER ISLAND
QUADRA ISLAND
Strathcona State Park
Campbell River
Tofino
Comox
Powell River
Ucluelet
Port Alberni
BROKEN GROUP ISLANDS
Parksville
Nanaimo
Sechelt
Pacific Rim National Park
Lake Cowichan
Gibsons
VANCOUVER
Duncan
VICTORIA
SEATTLE
U.S.A.
Prince George
Wells
Bowron Lake Park
Tête Jaune Cache
Quesnel
Barkerville
Mount Robson Park
Wells Gray Park
To Tweedsmuir Park and Bella Coola
Williams Lake
150 Mile House
Clearwater
100 Mile House
0 15 30 45 60 miles
0 30 60 90 km
Sicamous
Cache Creek
Kamloops
Salmon Arm
Shalath
Lillooet
D'Arcy
Logan Lake
Spences Bridge
Lytton
Whistler
Hell's Gate
Garibaldi Park
Boston Bar
Hell's Gate
VANCOUVER
Hope
Chilliwack
USA
Chapter 3
Fraser Valley & South Central British Columbia

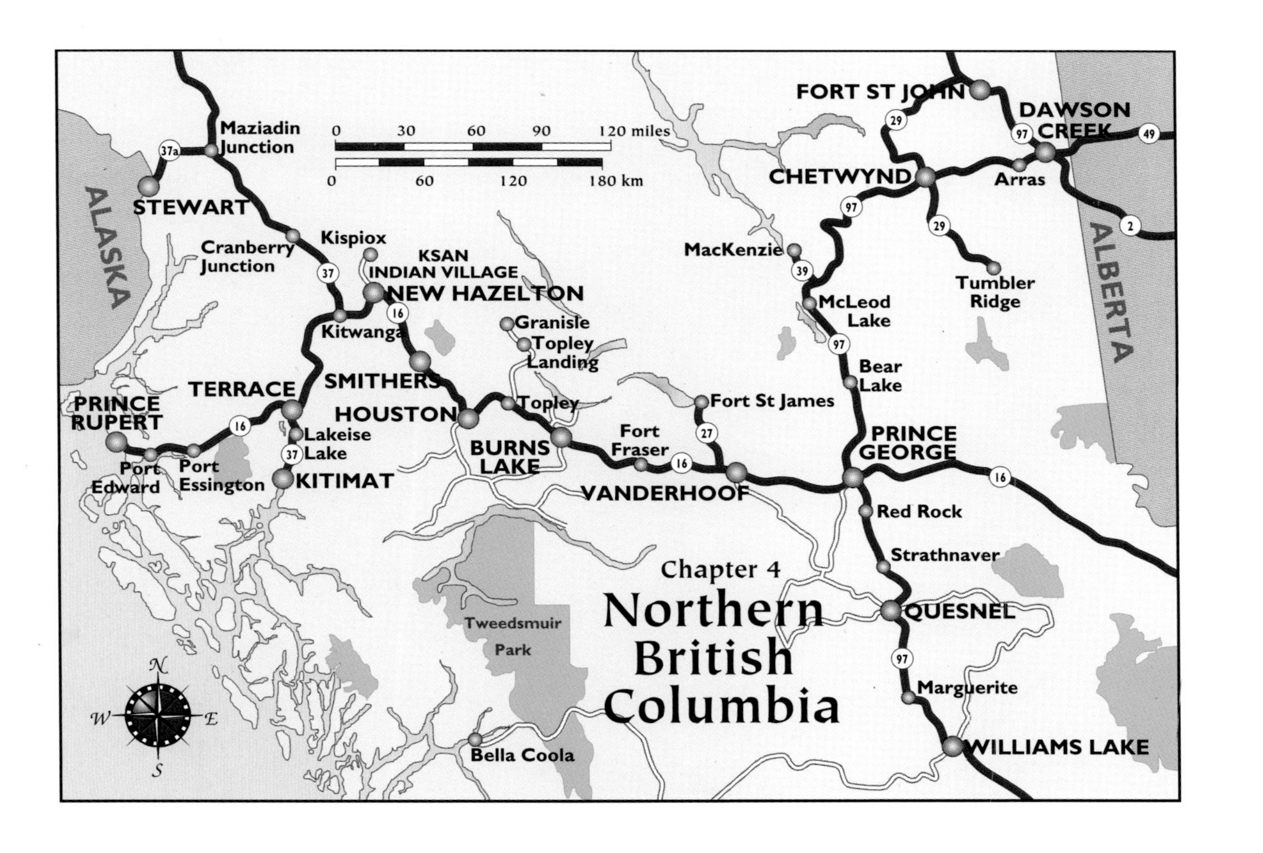
Chapter 4
Northern British Columbia
ALASKA
ALBERTA
0 30 60 90 120 miles
0 60 120 180 km
FORT ST JOHN
DAWSON CREEK
CHETWYND
Arras
Tumbler Ridge
MacKenzie
McLeod Lake
Bear Lake
PRINCE GEORGE
Red Rock
Strathnaver
QUESNEL
Marguerite
WILLIAMS LAKE
Fort St James
VANDERHOOF
Fort Fraser
Granisle
Topley Landing
Topley
BURNS LAKE
HOUSTON
SMITHERS
KSAN INDIAN VILLAGE
NEW HAZELTON
Kispiox
Kitwanga
Maziadin Junction
STEWART
Cranberry Junction
TERRACE
PRINCE RUPERT
Port Edward
Port Essington
Lakeise Lake
KITIMAT
Tweedsmuir Park
Bella Coola
37a
37
16
97
29
39
27
49
2
N
W
E
S

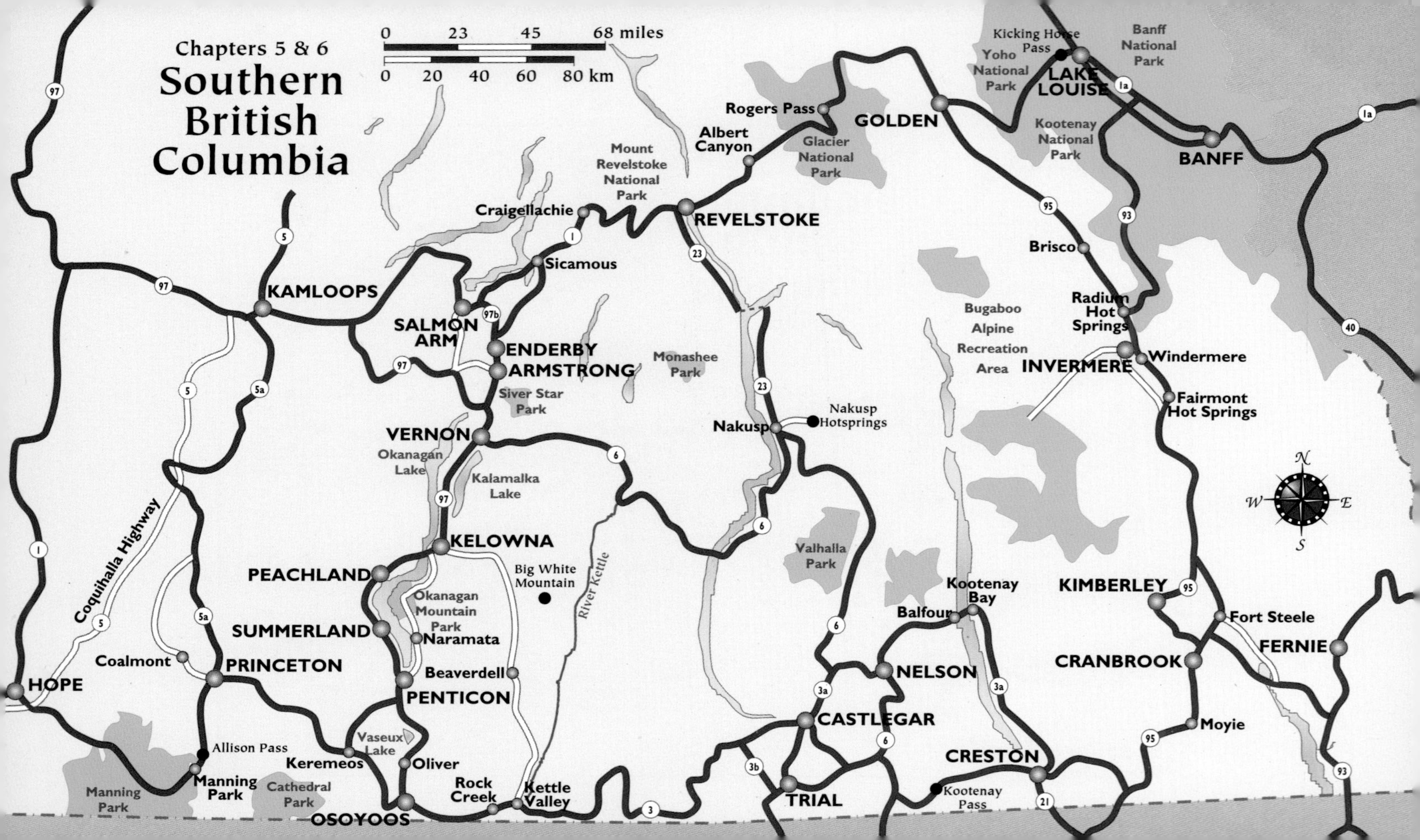
Chapters 5 & 6
Southern British Columbia
0 23 45 68 miles
0 20 40 60 80 km
Kicking Horse Pass
Yoho National Park
Banff National Park
LAKE LOUISE
Kootenay National Park
BANFF
GOLDEN
Rogers Pass
Albert Canyon
Glacier National Park
Mount Revelstoke National Park
REVELSTOKE
Craigellachie
Sicamous
KAMLOOPS
SALMON ARM
ENDERBY
ARMSTRONG
Monashee Park
Siver Star Park
VERNON
Okanagan Lake
Kalamalka Lake
Nakusp
Nakusp Hotsprings
Brisco
Radium Hot Springs
Bugaboo Alpine Recreation Area
INVERMERE
Windermere
Fairmont Hot Springs
KELOWNA
PEACHLAND
Big White Mountain
River Kettle
Okanagan Mountain Park
Naramata
SUMMERLAND
Coquihalla Highway
Coalmont
PRINCETON
HOPE
Beaverdell
PENTICON
Vaseux Lake
Allison Pass
Keremeos
Oliver
Manning Park
Cathedral Park
Rock Creek
Kettle Valley
OSOYOOS
Valhalla Park
Kootenay Bay
Balfour
NELSON
CASTLEGAR
TRIAL
CRESTON
Kootenay Pass
KIMBERLEY
Fort Steele
FERNIE
CRANBROOK
Moyie
N
W
E
S

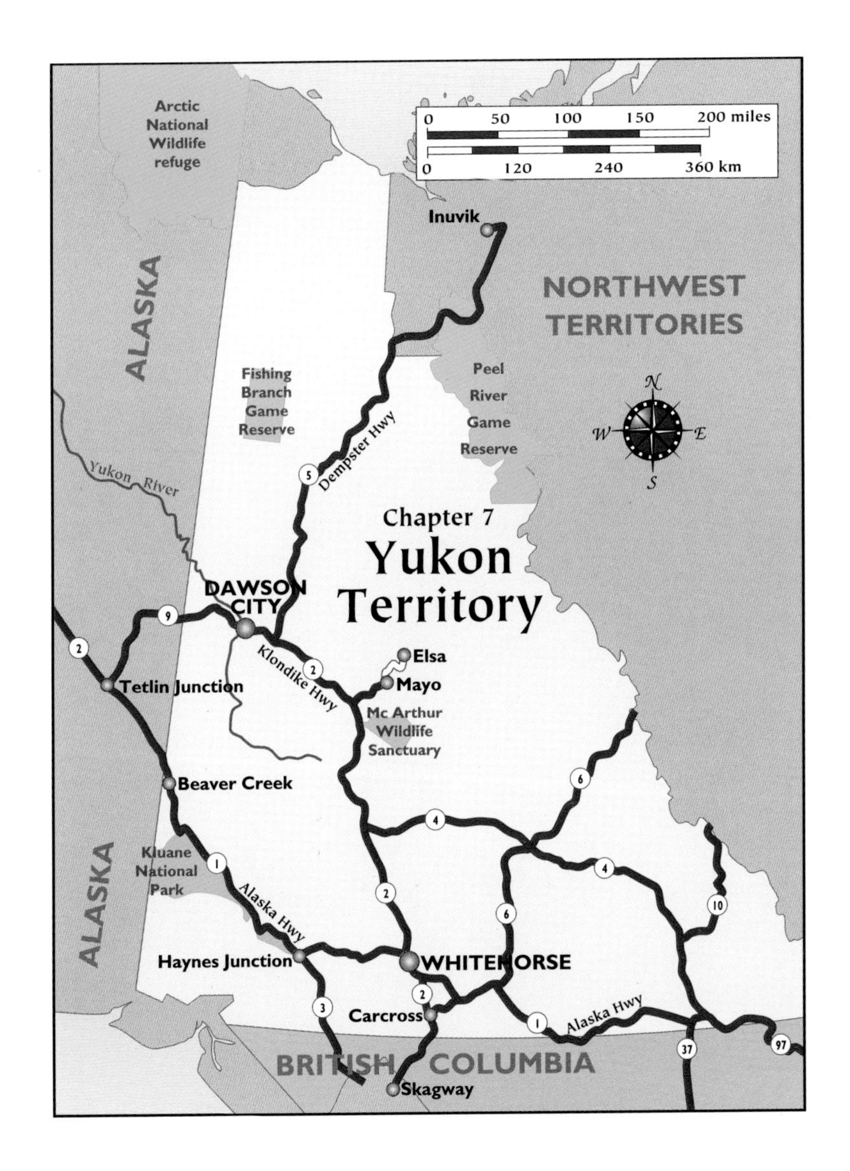
Arctic National Wildlife refuge
0 50 100 150 200 miles
0 120 240 360 km
Inuvik
NORTHWEST TERRITORIES
ALASKA
Fishing Branch Game Reserve
Peel River Game Reserve
N
W
E
S
Dempster Hwy
Yukon River
Chapter 7
Yukon Territory
DAWSON CITY
Klondike Hwy
Elsa
Mayo
Tetlin Junction
Mc Arthur Wildlife Sanctuary
Beaver Creek
Kluane National Park
Alaska Hwy
ALASKA
Haynes Junction
WHITEHORSE
Carcross
Alaska Hwy
BRITISH COLUMBIA
Skagway

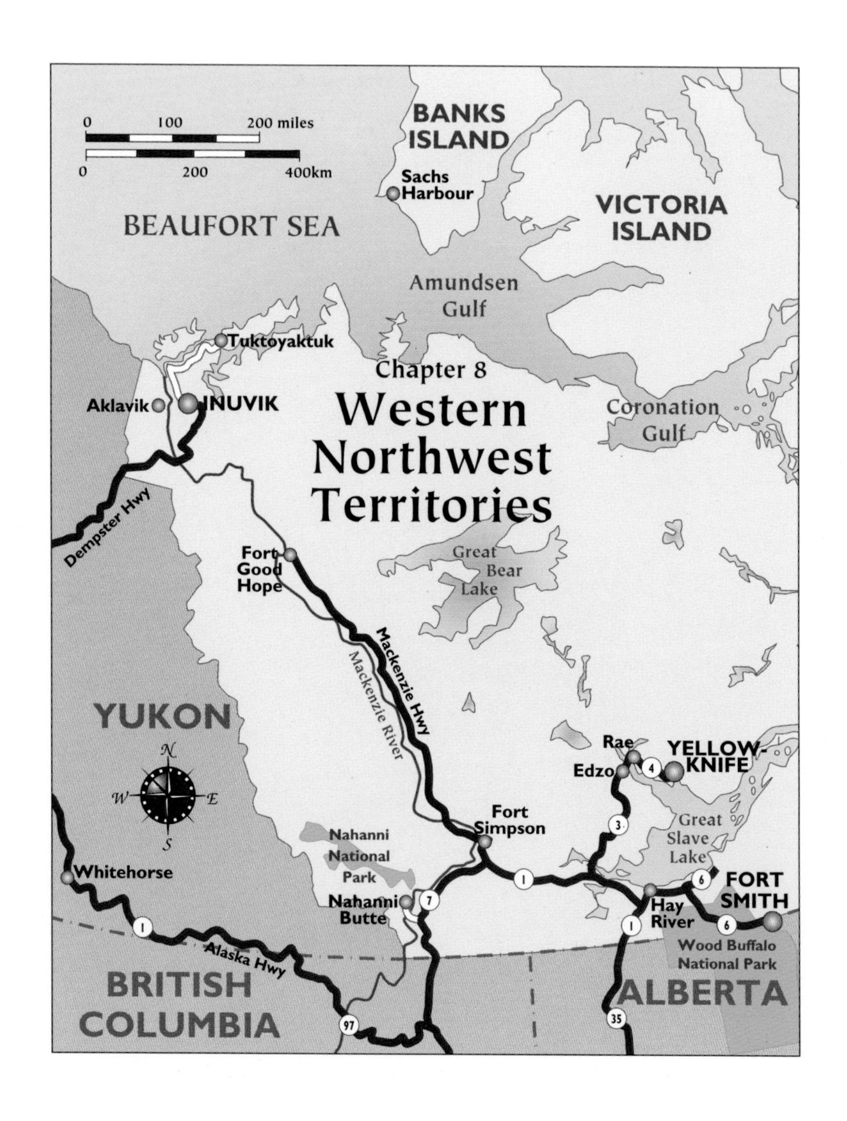
0
100
200 miles
0
200
400km
BANKS ISLAND
Sachs Harbour
VICTORIA ISLAND
BEAUFORT SEA
Amundsen Gulf
Tuktoyaktuk
Chapter 8
Western Northwest Territories
Aklavik
INUVIK
Coronation Gulf
Dempster Hwy
Fort Good Hope
Great Bear Lake
Mackenzie Hwy
Mackenzie River
YUKON
N
W
E
S
Rae
Edzo
YELLOW-KNIFE
Fort Simpson
Nahanni National Park
Great Slave Lake
Whitehorse
Nahanni Butte
FORT SMITH
Hay River
Alaska Hwy
Wood Buffalo National Park
BRITISH COLUMBIA
ALBERTA

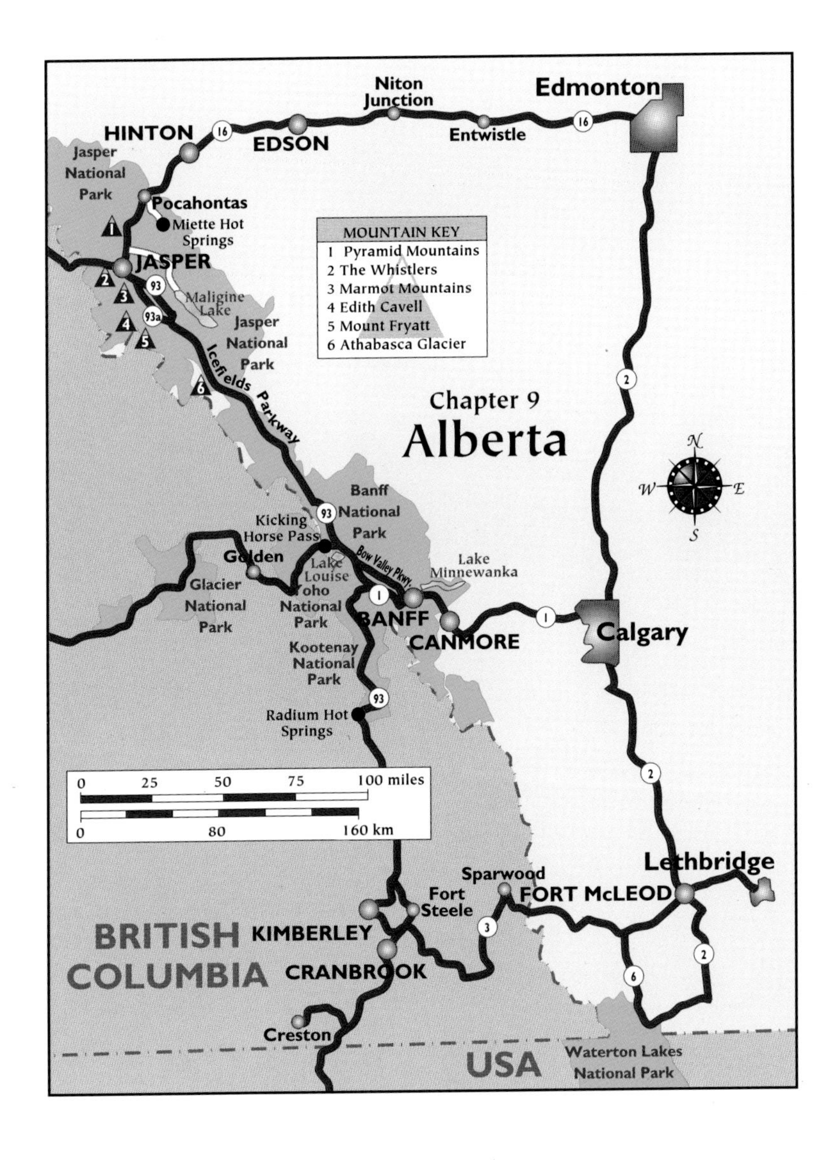
Edmonton
Niton Junction
HINTON
EDSON
Entwistle
16
Jasper National Park
Pocahontas
Miette Hot Springs
JASPER
93
93a
Maligine Lake
Jasper National Park
Icefields Parkway
MOUNTAIN KEY
1 Pyramid Mountains
2 The Whistlers
3 Marmot Mountains
4 Edith Cavell
5 Mount Fryatt
6 Athabasca Glacier
Chapter 9
Alberta
2
N
W
E
S
Banff National Park
Kicking Horse Pass
Golden
Lake Louise
Bow Valley Pkwy.
Lake Minnewanka
Glacier National Park
Yoho National Park
BANFF
CANMORE
1
Calgary
Kootenay National Park
Radium Hot Springs
0
25
50
75
100 miles
0
80
160 km
Lethbridge
Sparwood
Fort Steele
FORT McLEOD
3
6
BRITISH COLUMBIA
KIMBERLEY
CRANBROOK
Creston
USA
Waterton Lakes National Park

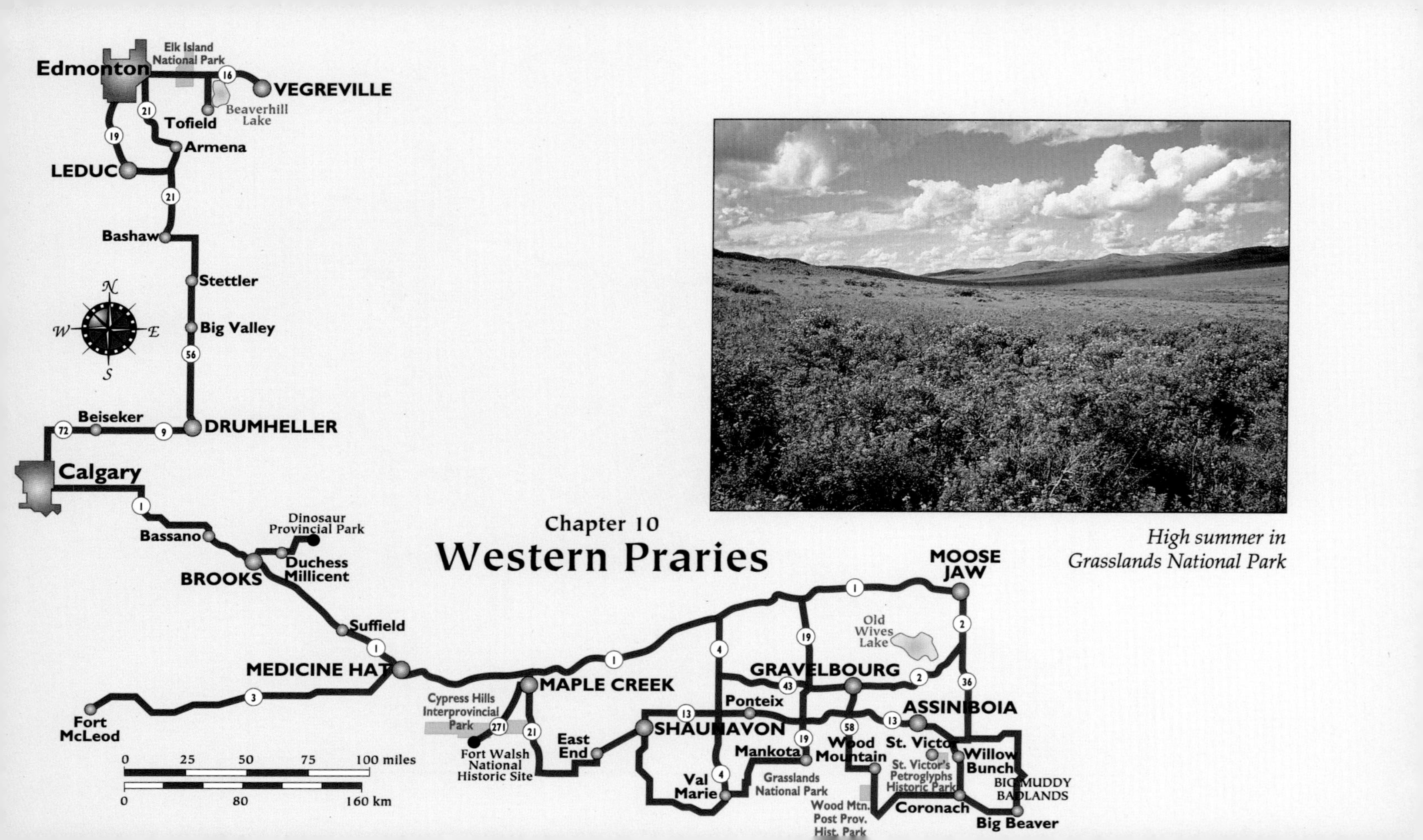

Chapter 10

Western Praries

High summer in Grasslands National Park

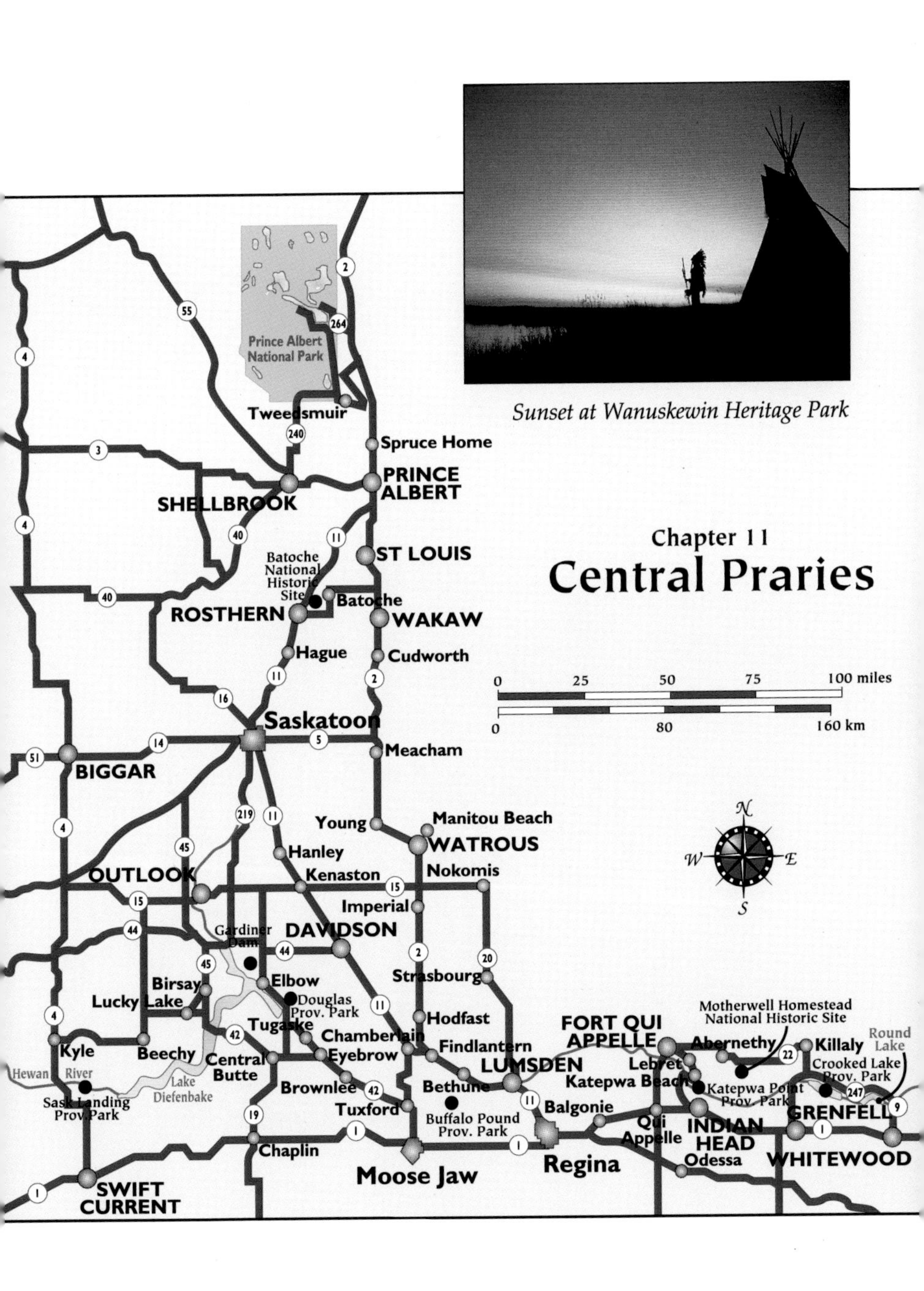

Sunset at Wanuskewin Heritage Park

Chapter 11
Central Praries

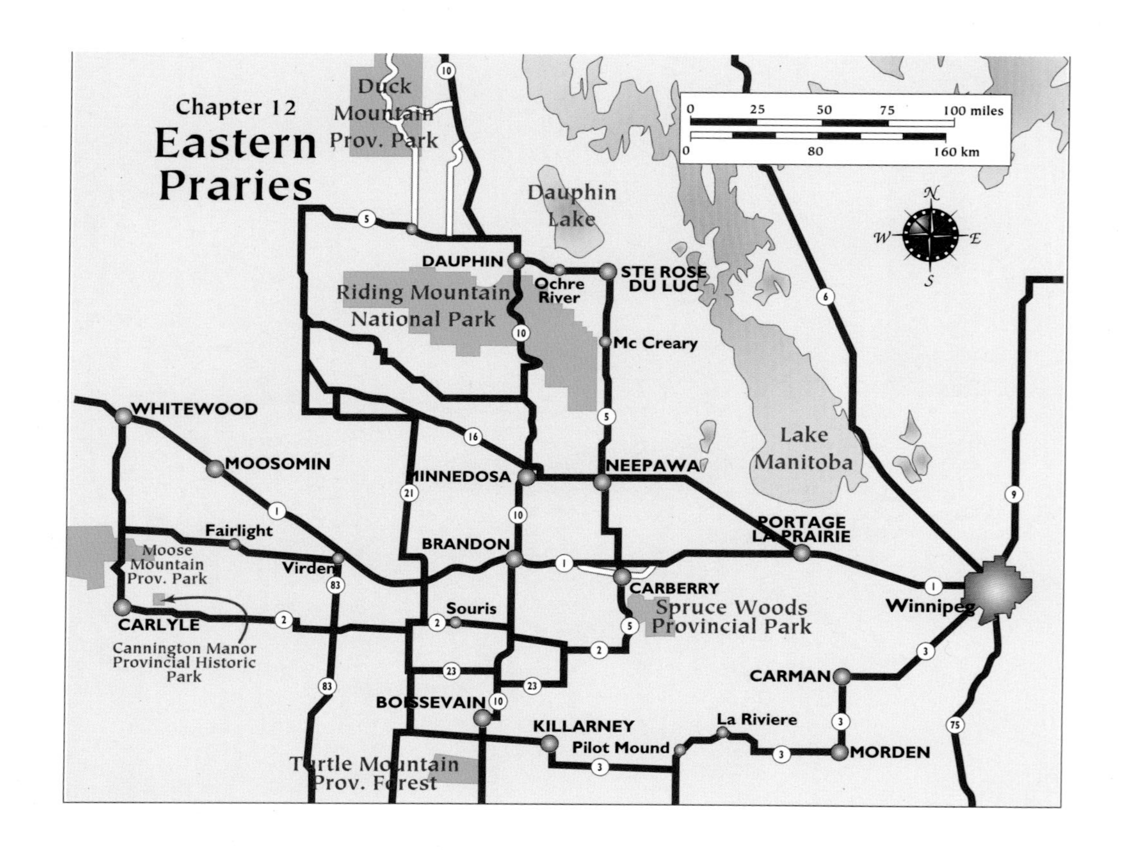
Chapter 12
Eastern
Praries
Duck
Mountain
Prov. Park
0
25
50
75
100 miles
0
80
160 km
N
W
E
S
Dauphin
Lake
DAUPHIN
Ochre
River
STE ROSE
DU LUC
Riding Mountain
National Park
Mc Creary
WHITEWOOD
MOOSOMIN
MINNEDOSA
NEEPAWA
Lake
Manitoba
Fairlight
Moose
Mountain
Prov. Park
Virden
BRANDON
PORTAGE
LA PRAIRIE
CARBERRY
Winnipeg
Souris
CARLYLE
Spruce Woods
Provincial Park
Cannington Manor
Provincial Historic
Park
CARMAN
BOISSEVAIN
KILLARNEY
La Riviere
Pilot Mound
MORDEN
Turtle Mountain
Prov. Forest

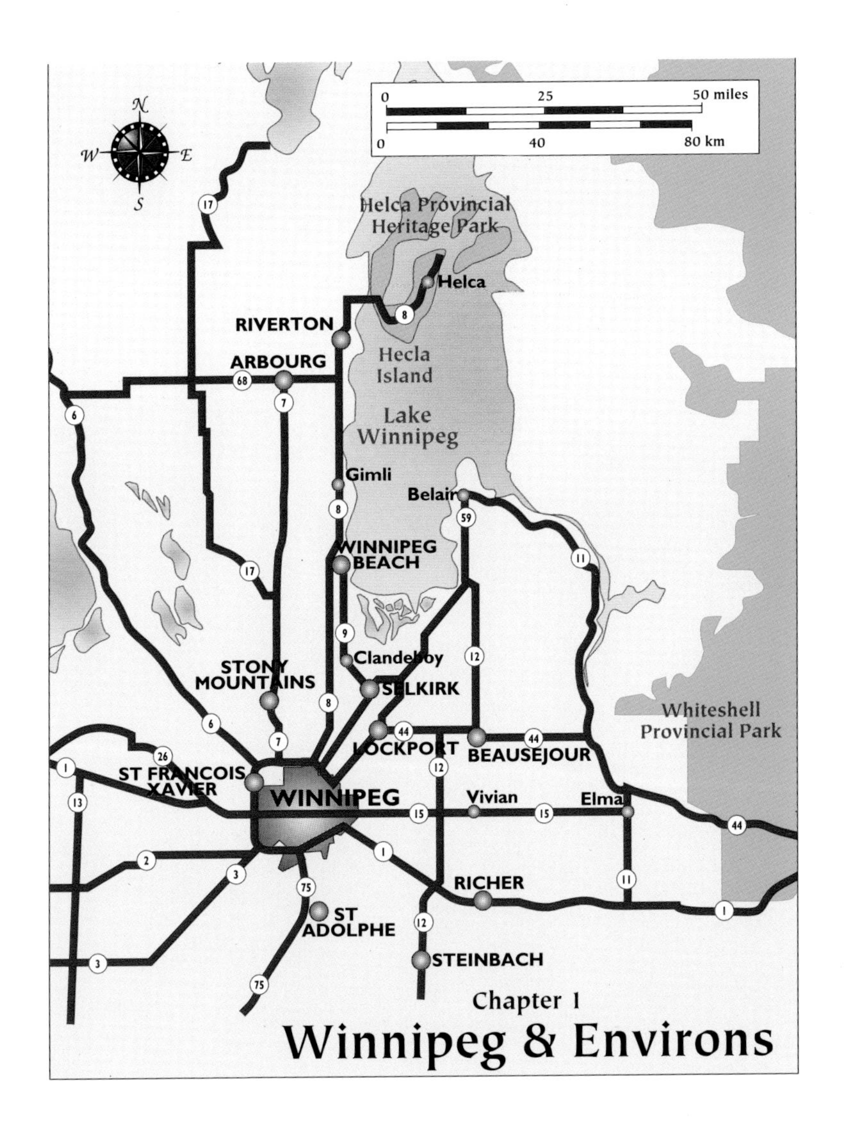

Chapter 1

Winnipeg & Environs

Cyclists in Jasper National Park (Chapter 9)

Introduction

The powerful beauty, the wilderness, the wide open spaces — the sheer magnitude of western Canada is what brings *Off the Beaten Track* travellers to this part of the world time and again. No other country can boast such natural abundance, the visual grandeur of its Rockies, the countless pristine lakes and forests. Fields of golden wheat stretch forever to meet a broad prairie sky. Rivers can be so thick with salmon, fishermen almost always bag their limit. Waterways carry vacationers for hundreds of miles along routes of early traders. Foot trails lead to natural wonders so virginal you could believe no human has come this way before.

For the purposes of this guide, western Canada is a region spread over five million square kilometres (two million square miles) from the Pacific coast of British Columbia north to the Yukon and western Northwest Territories, then east through Alberta, Saskatchewan and Manitoba to the Ontario border. The distance, were you to drive from the west coast to Ontario, is approximately 2,700km (1,700 miles). The terrain, the wildlife, and even the cultures are so diverse it is as if you are travelling through half a dozen different countries. Moreover, these are prosperous regions where millions of dollars go to preserving the past, and the environment, and making them accessible to present and future generations.

Considering all they offer to visitors, many areas are remarkably untravelled. Eighteenth- and nineteenth-century explorers returned to Europe with tales of natural phenomena. A century ago British travel agent Thomas Cook organized 'Adventure Vacations' for a wealthy few who would come from Europe by ship and rail. Once here they stayed at luxurious castle-style railway hotels, in newly developed cities and in the most spectacular of wilderness sites. Mountain climbers, skiers, hunters, naturalists and seekers of solitude trickled in during the first half of the twentieth century. But it took world expositions to put western Canada in the global arena of tourism.

Following Vancouver's Expo '86, the Winter Olympics held in

Calgary in 1988, and the 1994 Commonwealth Games in Victoria, it is as if a gentle giant has been prodded awake from a long sleep. Now tourism is one of Canada's leading industries, earning $6 billion annually. Promotional campaigns are proving effective. The favourable exchange rate helps too, as Americans find their tourist dollars buying a lot more north of the border than at home. European and Japanese visitors are in awe of the open spaces. Even Canadians, who for years flocked south, are now appreciating their own country as a vacation destination. The surprise is that it took so long for word to get around, and for Canadian tour operators to get organized with home-front itineraries. Now they have done just this, so that in western Canada you can ride a helicopter to a mountain plateau for a picnic beside alpine lakes as clear as polished glass. You can be taken by float-plane for a day or a week to fish in lakes beyond all roads. You can canoe where snow-capped mountains are mirrored in emerald green water, ride on a glacier and make snowballs in July. Golf at midnight above the Arctic circle. Watch whales cavorting off the Pacific coast, and polar bears that wander through town in Manitoba. Follow the routes of the early explorers, fur traders and prospectors heading for the 1888 Gold Rush, and camp where dinosaur bones are still being found.

Modern adventurers can ride horseback on week-long safaris, with a group or on their own using gear rented from an outfitter. They can visit the far north, land of the Inuit and Dene, to learn about their ancient cultures, travel by dog sled, and watch the Northern Lights (aurora borealis) at their best. If all this sounds too rugged, there are exciting day trips from comfortable lodges and resorts. Or easy-to-navigate houseboats that will get you onto the waterways, with stops at uninhabited islands and beaches and small markets for supplies.

Western Canada has national, provincial and territorial parks designated to preserve unique terrain and natural phenomena. Many have cottage and lodge accommodation as well as serviced and wilderness campgrounds. And yet a short walk from a central hub brings you into that other world, where noise is a bird's song and splash of a paddle dipping into still waters.

Historical landmarks are well remembered at rebuilt trading posts, and battle sites, and at pioneer settlements staffed with costumed 'residents' who demonstrate how it used to be. You can see where the North West Mounted Police (later the Royal Canadian Mounted Police) were established, and hear about their heroes. Aboriginal encampments are restored to the era of buffalo hunts, and traditional pow-wows attract participants from across the continent. And although the world's most famous stampede in downtown Calgary is definitely *On* the Beaten Track, there are more rodeos in small communities where contestants are working cowboys from local ranches.

In western Canada just about everything outside the city cores can be considered *Off the Beaten Track*. For some it will be a few hours spent in the recreated gold mining town of Barkerville in central British Columbia. Others will want to follow the arduous route taken by nineteenth century prospectors. Hikers can encounter primitive beauty in Banff National Park within minutes of leaving its paved roads. Or they may choose to go further, for the heady experience of pitching a tent in splendid isolation on a wilderness river bank. Whatever your choice you will find it in *Off the Beaten Track*. So bring your walking shoes and binoculars, your mountain bike or canoe. Basic cook-ware and a cooler can be useful too, since you may find yourself far from food outlets even on one-day excursions. In Western Canada *Off the Beaten Track* is as near or far as you want. And that is the pleasure of it.

Geography & Environment

Canada is the world's second largest country. (Only Russia is bigger.) Covering approximately 10 million square kilometres (3.9 million square miles) it occupies most of the northerly part of the North American continent, bounded by the Atlantic, Arctic and Pacific Oceans, and the United States of America to the south. It has more freshwater lakes than any other country and a population of roughly 31 million.

The country is divided into ten provinces between the west and east coasts, and two territories north of the 60th parallel in the west and the continental coastline in the east. In the south the border with the United States is formed by the 49th parallel, dipping down a little to take in all of Vancouver Island. In the northwest, a long straight frontier separates the state of Alaska, with the Alaska panhandle stretching south down the coast.

British Columbia takes in the area between the Pacific coast and a line along the peaks of the Rocky Mountains. Approximately 700km (435 miles) across, this is Canada's share of the huge cordillera system of mountain ranges, valleys and plateaus which stretch all the way down the Americas. The coastline is mountainous, indented by fjords and with thousands of islands. Largest of these are Vancouver Island and the Queen Charlotte Islands to the north.

Ocean currents bring a pleasant climate to the coastal regions; prevailing winds blowing from the Pacific Ocean cause heavy rain west of the Coast Mountain range, while the sheltered eastern side may receive very little. Except for the province's large northern plateau, this same pattern is repeated inland among the Columbia, Monashee, Selkirk and Rocky Mountain ranges. The result is an environment as varied as lush rain forests and semi-arid grazing lands, and valleys of rich farmland often enhanced by commercial irrigation.

Most of British Columbia's population lives in the southwest corner along the coastal regions and in the lower Fraser River valley. Coastal fisheries are very productive; lumbering and forest products along with mining and agriculture are other major industries. Hydro-electric plants provide relatively inexpensive power for local manufacturing.

British Columbia has everything a vacationer could possibly want. There are islands steeped in native lore, where walking trails lead to stunning ocean and mountain views. You can climb mountains, experience whitewater rafting at its best, and soak in hot springs. Heli-hiking and mountain biking demand no special skills in return for their thrills. The coastal ferry system is so extensive it will take you from Vancouver Island northward through the fabled Inside Passage for your connection with another ferry service bound for Alaska.

Its scenery is so grand, British Columbia has no less than six national parks, more than 300 provincial parks and recreational areas. Even the cities are uncrowded. Vancouver is recognized as one of the world's most beautiful places, for its Pacific shoreline, downtown parks and mountains on its doorstep. Victoria is known as Canada's most British city because of its flower displays in bloom by early March, double-decker buses, dampish weather and a large population of British descent.

The terrain of the **Yukon Territory** is similar to that of northern British Columbia. Here, the coastal regions are warm, but mountain ramparts inland seal off moderating breezes from the Pacific Ocean making the interior climate dry, and in winter very cold. Twice the size of the United Kingdom, larger than Washington and Oregon states combined, it has a population of about 32,000, most of whom work in government offices or mining.

Although it is possible to drive to the Yukon, many visitors arrive by cruise ship via Alaska, and continue through the Yukon by tour bus. Others fly here and then rent a car or camper.

Until commercial quantities of gold were discovered in 1896, native groups and fur traders lived here in beautiful isolation. But then the find at Bonanza Creek, and subsequent Yukon Gold Rush of 1897-8, brought thousands of prospectors into the area. Fortunes were made. In 12 years no less than $100 million was taken from Yukon gold fields and this history makes it one of Canada's most fascinating destinations.

Construction of the Alaska Highway in 1942 resulted in more changes, and this road is now an essential part of the territory's economy. Although there is still some gold, important resources these days are copper, zinc and lead. The far north's inhabitants continue to live closely with the outdoors. Natives still learn and practise skills essential for survival in the bush. They hunt and fish and can generally live off the land in summer and winter. Acting as guides, they happily share these skills with visitors who come for the trophy-sized game, unrivalled fishing, astonishing tundra where wild flowers carpet the landscape beneath a sky in which the summer sun sets only briefly.

The Yukon River system which stretches for close to 1,125km (700 miles) provides access to the territory's southern and western regions. Highways, bus services and a rail line provide access to the more populated sections. Experienced hikers can enjoy former Indian, trapper and miners' trails, including the 51km (32 mile) Chilkoot Trail used by 1890s prospectors. Canoeists love the many rivers and streams. Whitewater rafting can challenge even the most daring.

The Northwest Territories are about as *Off the Beaten Track* as you can get in Canada. They are accessible by road from Edmonton, Alberta, or Prince George, BC but are most often reached by air. This is the country's least populated region.

Occupying one third of Canada and spread over 3.4 million square kilometres (1.3 million square miles), it has a population of less than 64,000. At present the Northwest Territories comprise the mainland east of the Yukon from the 60th parallel to the North Pole, as well as the Arctic Islands. It is expected that the territories will be divided into two territories, each with a new name, on 1 April 1999.

In most areas outside Yellowknife, aboriginals are in the majority and a number of native languages are officially recognized. There are few roads other than the two major highways. The Dempster Hwy from the Yukon continues north to Inuvik, while the Mackenzie Hwy which connects with Alberta, follows the Mackenzie River to Fort Good Hope just below the Arctic Circle. Domestic transportation is by efficient commuter air services.

In this guide the western region of the Northwest Territories extends across the top of Canada, from the Yukon eastward to Hudson Bay. Sensational scenery, wildlife and rare bird species bring summer tourists. Even if you go little further than Yellowknife you will have a good sense of the true north. The city itself has modern hotels and government buildings, and the Old Town dating to times when bush pilots were the north's true heroes, and a pioneering spirit was a requisite of new arrivals.

Wilderness landscapes are overwhelming in their size and beauty. Two of the Northwest Territory's national parks are designated UNESCO World Heritage Sites. The legendary Nahanni in the Mackenzie Mountains provides canoeists, hikers and naturalists with compelling scenery. Wood Buffalo National Park straddling the border with Alberta is a vast tract of forest, lakes and rivers, with remarkable salt plains that attract herds of buffalo. Big game hunting is permitted on a quota basis, so you can (for a price) take home a polar or grizzly bear, moose or caribou. Fishing is superb. Half and full day fishing trips from Yellowknife include use of all gear, and cooked shore lunch or dinner.

As in the Yukon, outfitters here can furnish you with guides and gear for just about every outdoor pursuit. They will fly you into a remote fishing camp to do your own thing, or take you to wilderness lodges for excursions from which you return to a comfortable bed and prepared meals at the end of the day. Camping is idyllic. You can carry your own tent, or hike and paddle to fixed-site canvas accommodation set up by your outfitter. Winter visitors come for the Northern Lights and to dog-sled, snow-shoe and ice fish.

The western boundary of **Alberta** is formed by the Continental Divide in the Rocky Mountains, where rivers on the west side flow into the Pacific and those on the east drain into the Arctic and Atlantic Oceans. The flat, often undulating plains that stretch from the Rocky Mountains as far as the Ontario border, are divided more or less equally into the provinces of Alberta, Saskatchewan and Manitoba. The prairies, grasslands which are now largely devoted to growing cereal crops and cattle ranching, take up the southern portions of these provinces, while their northern regions comprise sparsely populated areas of forest, grasslands and innumerable lakes. In addition to agriculture, oil and gas discoveries have made Alberta one of Canada's most prosperous provinces.

This is the picture-postcard province that so often inspires visitors to 'think Canada' for their vacations. The snow-capped mountains, fairytale castle hotels, turquoise lakes, legends of pioneers who tamed this land and photos of wildlife all combine to attract vacationers. The greatest appeal for many is its chain of Rocky Mountains in all seasons. Veteran travellers are quick to agree that the Icefield Parkway connecting Banff and Jasper is one of the world's most extraordinary drives, hemmed in by snow-draped mountains with glaciers from the Columbia Icefield reaching almost to the highway, as mountain goats and bighorn sheep stare down at motorists.

Mountain climbers, skiers, hikers, hunters and fishermen are naturally drawn to Alberta. There are organized horseback safaris for experienced and novice riders. Some trips depart from hotels and ranches for an hour or two. Others have you sleeping under the stars, bathing in natural pools, eating meals cooked over a campfire. You can even fish in glacial lakes accessible only on foot or horseback.

In Alberta, rafting, canoe and kayak excursions are geared to various levels of fitness and experience. Mountain bike trails lead to emerald lakes and hot springs far from roads and highways. Alpine paths can be reached by cablecar, or better yet a helicopter will deposit you on a remote peak for a walkabout. Alberta has Canada's oldest national park (Banff) and three more, along with nearly a hundred provincial parks and other preserves of natural beauty.

Edmonton, the provincial capital, has gone from trading post to modern metropolis in approximately 200 years. A vibrant city, it has more parklands per capita than any other city in Canada, including some that stretch for miles along the picturesque North Saskatchewan river valley.

Saskatchewan, east of Alberta and west of Manitoba, is universally known as Canada's Bread Basket, conjuring visions of nothing but fields of wheat stretching forever. They are here, but in reality this province's approximately 652,000 sq km (251,000 sq miles) is one-eighth water. It has 100,000 lakes, two national parks and over twenty provincial parks. Agriculture, though, is the largest single source of income, a fact you won't dispute when driving past a pale gold sea of wheat interrupted by neat farm buildings and traditional grain elevators on railway sidings.

The capital city, Regina, was known to early inhabitants as Pile o'Bones, due to the remains of buffalo slaughtered there. An important agricultural centre, it became the provincial capital at Saskatchewan's birth in 1905 and now visitors marvel at the city fathers' foresight in preserving 930 hectares (2,300 acres) around a scenic lake in the city core.

Gateway to Saskatchewan's north country, Prince Albert National Park has all essential visitor amenities as well as wilderness trails and remote lakes. In the south, a stretch of original Prairie along the Frenchman River valley is preserved to provide a safe habitat for grassland creatures.

Saskatchewan has more museums per capita than any other province. Some of the largest detail the development of the Prairies to the present day and one shows how the Royal Canadian Mounted Police as the North West Mounted Police was established to bring order to the Prairies.

Proud of their colourful past, Saskatchewan natives are known for their strong opinions. Historically, they have led the way in industrial reforms, and were in the vanguard of the trade union and cooperative movements. Their inclination to be different is often obvious. For example, this is the only province in Canada which, for assorted reasons, declines to use daylight saving time to keep in synchronization with the Greenwich time zones.

Exciting adventures abound here. Ride a covered wagon, pioneer style, for an hour, day or week. Follow historic routes reliving the dreams and dramas of early settlers. Rent a houseboat, stay on a working farm, enjoy a northern fishing camp far away from 'civilization', or soak in spa water with more mineral content than the Dead Sea. The options are endless, and often surprising.

Manitoba is Canada's heartland, a Prairie province with so many lakes (100,000 at last count), that some have never been fished. Close to 700,000 sq km (250,000 sq miles), its terrain is not quite what you would expect either, ranging from great forests and plains to a desert where cacti bloom and powdery sand beaches more readily associated with the Atlantic provinces. You do not have to travel far, even from Winnipeg — its southern-based capital — to encounter the Canadian wilderness, and perhaps watch the Northern Lights dance through the nighttime sky.

One-sixth of Manitoba's surface is covered by inland waterways. For starters, over 100km (62 miles) of rivers zigzag through Winnipeg. In the north, the province has its own Arctic coastline — 645km (400 miles) of Hudson Bay shore with the port of Churchill connected to the south by railway. The province's early history was shaped by the waterways. Hudson's Bay Company explorers, traders and the voyageurs from Quebec travelled the river systems, founding such trading centres as Fort Garry and Fort Rouge on the site of present day Winnipeg. Indeed, the province's name has a watery connection. The pounding waves of Lake Manitoba were said to sound like the drums of the Indian Manitou, or 'great spirit'.

When the province was carved out of the North West Territories in 1870, it was a small chunk of the lands once controlled by the Hudson's Bay Company, 13,928 square miles in comparison with today's 250,950. Due to its shape and size, it was nicknamed the Postage Stamp Province. In 1881, after a long drawn-out dispute with Ontario over its eastern limits, Manitoba was enlarged, and a final extension of the province took place in 1912.

Manitoba has outstanding parks, one national and ten provincial. One of the finest, and most accessible, is Whiteshell Provincial Park. On summer weekends Winnipeggers flock there to enjoy the campgrounds, resorts, beaches, fishing and golfing. Also within commuting distance, Birds Hill Provincial Park, just 20km (12 miles) northwest of Winnipeg, is a big draw for birdwatchers. Riding Mountain National Park offers a real wilderness experience with creature comforts conveniently close at hand, and Grand Beach has been voted one of North America's most beautiful. Clear Lake, so named because of the ease with which you can see the lake's floor, 10.7m (35ft) below, provides a clear advantage to would-be trophy hunters in search of trout.

Besides a wealth of possibilities for outdoors enthusiasts, Manitoba has rich potential for culture buffs. Over the years the province has spawned countless writers, artists and musicians who have gone on to achieve both national, and international fame. In addition to countless ethnic heritage celebrations, there's a strong tradition of literary and other artistic pursuits that also finds expression in schools and community centres across the province. And for anyone with intellectual leanings, there is no dearth of stimulation in Winnipeg with its constant cultural offerings in a wide range of areas, year-round.

Western Canada's History

Although this guide concentrates on western Canada we must refer briefly to all of Canada when talking of its history, because earliest signs of European habitation are from tenth-century Vikings who settled in northern Newfoundland. In the fifteenth century European explorers arrived on the east coast, and soon after this fishermen discovered the rich cod fisheries off Nova Scotia and Newfoundland.

In the early 1600s trappers and traders catering to European demands for beaver pelts were penetrating the wilderness, travelling waterways that carried them north and west. As Britain and France competed for the fur trade, France created the colony of New France and embarked on a series of ambitious annexations. Britain's Charles II chartered the Hudson's Bay Company, giving it rights to exploit resources in all lands draining into Hudson Bay. The entire area was known as Rupert's Land.

Battles between these two countries seemed never ending during the seventeenth and eighteenth centuries. Then on an early September morning in 1759 the British were victorious in a decisive battle on the Plains of Abraham in Quebec City , and borders were virtually settled. Next came the American Revolution and the invasion of 1775. Although their forces captured Montreal they were defeated at Quebec City and made to retreat. One outcome of the Revolution was the migration of some 50,000 United Empire Loyalists into Nova Scotia and parts of the St Lawrence River valley.

As these conflicts raged in the east, fur traders travelled further west. Explorer Alexander Mackenzie reached Bella Coola on the Pacific shore in 1779, one year after Captain James Cook landed there having sailed across the Pacific Ocean. In 1792, Captain George Vancouver came to study the coast in more detail. Travelling overland in 1808, Simon Fraser descended the river which bears his name, and in 1811 David Thompson followed the Columbia River from its source to the ocean.

The Hudson's Bay Company ruled its northwest fiefdom of Rupert's Land into the nineteenth century, establishing fur trading posts which grew into permanent settlements. Lord Selkirk (a Hudson's Bay Company partner) led a group of Scottish pioneers escaping the Highland Clearances back home to create a community on the banks of the Red River. Surviving all odds, including floods, droughts, disease, plagues of grasshoppers, as well as the hostility of fur traders, this became the city of Winnipeg. The Hudson's Bay Company established trading posts throughout the west and on the Pacific coast. Fort Langley, near Vancouver was established in 1827, Fort Victoria on Vancouver Island in 1843.

In 1846 the 49th parallel was established as the frontier between Canada and the United States. All of Vancouver Island was included in Canada, and became a crown colony. On the mainland, discovery of gold near the Fraser River and in the Cariboo attracted thousands of fortune seekers, making this western Canada's most populated area. The need for an orderly administration led to the creation of the colony of British Columbia in 1858. Mining towns such as Barkerville and Quesnel Forks were founded, and in 1862 British military engineers built a road through the fearsome Fraser Canyon to the gold mining region.

In the 1870s, after the easily extracted gold was exhausted, the stampede came to an end and residents started to leave. To reduce administrative costs, the colonies of Vancouver Island and British Columbia were amalgamated as British Columbia in 1866, with Victoria as capital. Five years later residents agreed to be part of the Canadian Confederation, conditional upon the federal government building a railway to join east and west within ten years. (Between 1857 and 1860, the Palliser Expedition had explored the west and its discoveries greatly influenced development, including the building of this railway.)

As promised the Canadian Pacific Railway forged west. In May 1887, the first passenger train from Montreal steamed into the terminus at Port Moody. When the small village of Granville, 20 km (12 miles) to the west, was seen to be sited on one of the continent's finest harbours in North America, the line was extended here and the community renamed Vancouver.

By the dawn of the twentieth century, British Columbia's mining companies were exploiting silver, lead, zinc, copper and coal instead of gold. Lumbering and fishing became primary industries. Farm lands opened up on Vancouver Island and in the lower Fraser River Valley, Okanagan Valley and other inland areas. Migrants poured in from eastern Canada, the United States, Europe and Asia. Meantime Vancouver and Victoria had become cities with five and six storey buildings, good shops and hotels and a public transportation system

On the prairies the railway received large tracts of government land along its right of way, and could anticipate handsome revenues from shipment of goods and farm produce. Some of the region's migrants became farmers. Others settled in communities which had sprung up along the railway line. Life was particularly hard for isolated farming families, who usually had to live in sod huts for the first two or three years. Many eventually prospered as the world demand for wheat increased. Winnipeg, Regina, Edmonton and Calgary grew into prosperous cities. More towns were established around railway stations and depots.

The tiny province of Manitoba had been created from the old Red River Colony in 1870. With increased settlement, boundaries were expanded until 1912 when the province reached its present size. In 1905, Alberta and Saskatchewan were formed from sections of the North West Territories. Modern usage simplifies the territories' name to 'Northwest'.

The First Inhabitants

When Europeans arrived on this continent the aboriginal population is believed to have numbered two or three hundred thousand. Exactly when their ancestors crossed from Asia to North America is in some dispute, but scientists agree that the earliest major human occupation of this continent began about 12,000 years ago. Migrants are believed to have travelled across the Bering land bridge, down the western side of the continent through present-day Alaska and British Columbia. Some groups branched out to the north and east, while others continued south to eventually populate North and South America. The Inuit are believed to have come across the Polar regions from Siberia about 5,000 years ago.

At the time Europeans were introduced to the west coast, as many as a hundred thousand natives lived comfortably in semi-permanent villages along the rivers and bays of coastal British Columbia. The regions between the Rocky Mountains and the Great Lakes were more sparsely populated, as nomadic groups hunted buffalo on the grasslands, caribou and smaller creatures in the northern forests and the barren lands beyond.

From the outset, the arrival of Europeans dramatically changed the lives of Canada's native peoples. Early fur traders from the east brought diseases, including measles and smallpox, against which the natives had no natural resistance. Among the trade goods they exchanged for furs were knives, axes and metal pots which replaced stone-age implements. Traders also introduced them to firearms and alcohol.

The new arrivals enlisted allies among native groups and taught them to fight their rivals with modern weapons. As more Europeans married native women, a new nation was founded. Children fathered by French-speaking traders and voyageurs became Métis. Those fathered by the British were known simply as 'halfbreeds'. They evolved into hunters, traders, carters and part-time farmers and later played an important role in western Canada's history. The depredations of traders among the natives during the mid-nineteenth century highlighted the need for a police force and led directly to the founding of the North West Mounted Police.

Wild descendants of horses brought by sixteenth-century Spanish conquerors far to the south migrated to the prairies, arriving at the same time as firearms became freely available. This combination of horses and guns proved deadly, changing forever the way aboriginals hunted the buffalo upon which they were entirely dependent for food, clothing and shelter. The situation worsened with the arrival of the railway builders who required meat in their diets, causing the buffalo herds to be hunted to virtual extinction.

As settlers took over their lands in the mid 1800s, natives were increasingly confined to reserves established by government treaties. Métis leader Louis Riel led the Red River rebellion of 1869, which brought into being a new province called Manitoba. He was hanged in 1889 for leading the North West Rebellion in the South Saskatchewan River Valley four years earlier. Of five significant battles fought during this rebellion, only Batoche was a victory for the Canadian government. The outcome was disastrous to Métis and Indians alike. Most faced destitution due to the extinction of the buffalo. Now their dependency on the government for food proved a powerful lever used in confining them to reserves.

On the Pacific coast, Europeans arrived at a time when native culture was at the height of its development, and this region had the largest aboriginal population in the country. They lived in houses made up of massive cedar planks, and enjoyed increased leisure time which was spent developing art forms. Religious ceremonies were important. Groups traded among themselves and potlatching (an elaborate exchange of gifts) was an important part of their culture.

As in the east, traders were attracted by furs, particularly those of the sea otters which populated coastal waters. Along with their trade goods, these Europeans brought smallpox and other white men's diseases. By the time fur trading forts closed a century later, disease had wiped out two-thirds of western Canada's original inhabitants.

Bloody conflicts were inevitable. White settlers arrived intent on acquiring land belonging to natives. Christian church lobbies insisted that colonial authorities ban religious and cultural ceremonies. Entire villages were destroyed, signalling the beginning of a systematic destruction of the natives' way of life.

Visitors wanting to learn more about the plight of Canada's earliest inhabitants will find numerous books on this subject. Excellent museums also tell the story well. In western Canada, three of the best are the Manitoba Museum of Man in Winnipeg, Head-Smashed-In Buffalo Jump near Fort Macleod, Alberta, and the Royal British Columbia Museum in Victoria. Equally eloquent are clusters of totem poles, carved by present generations, to replace those destroyed by European religious zealots.

The Fur Trade

While the fifteenth century was an era of discovery, it took a new fashion in mens' hats made from beaver pelts to bring about serious trading in furs. Such headgear became so popular that in 1602 Henri IV of France chartered a fur trading company. Three years later its agent, Samuel de Champlain, established a fortress in Nova Scotia's Annapolis Valley, and befriended Algonquin and Huron Indians who controlled fur trading in the west.

Traders from New France travelled further west in search of furs to exchange for their European goods. Yet when Pierre Esprit Radisson and Médard Chouart des Groseilliers (sometimes described, even in Hudson's Bay Company minutes, as 'Gooseberries') returned to Quebec in 1660 from a northwestern expedition weighed down with furs, they were jailed for leaving New France without permission. For their next trip, they sought backing from a group of wealthy Britons, and in 1668 their ships sailed a more northerly course, bypassing the French-occupied St Lawrence River. They returned with so many furs that in 1670, Charles II granted a charter to 'the Governor and Company of Adventurers for trading into Hudson's Bay' with rights over Rupert's Land, the vast region draining into Hudson Bay.

Over the next century and a half, Hudson's Bay Company employees founded trading posts as far west as the foothills of the Rocky Mountains. Meanwhile explorers from New France continued their own discoveries. In the 1730s, the La Vérendrye family led expeditions westward beyond the Red River and south to the Dakotas, from bases in what are now northern Ontario and Manitoba.

Following the defeat of France in North America, a group of Montreal merchants in 1776 established the North West Company to rival the Hudson's Bay Company. They employed many French and Métis traders and voyageurs who transported goods by canoe and continued the practice of exploring new routes. It was this company's employees, Alexander Mackenzie, David Thompson and Simon Fraser, who first arrived overland at the Pacific coast.

The Hudson's Bay Company absorbed its rival, the North West Company, in 1821. Although the fur trade remained its primary interest, the company also provided government-style administration for settlers in the Red River Colony. In 1840, it established trading forts on the Pacific coast and in 1849 was granted Vancouver Island to be developed as an agricultural colony, with the company's Chief Factor as Governor.

In 1863, controlling interest in the Hudson's Bay Company passed from the original founders' heirs to the International Financial Society. While still connected with the fur trade, it became increasingly involved in real estate ventures and economic development in western Canada. Following Canadian Confederation in 1867, the Dominion government purchased Rupert's Land from the company. On its 300th anniversary in 1970, the company's head office was moved from London, England to Winnipeg. Today, the Hudson's Bay Company is Canada's largest retail company. It also has vast investments in real estate and the petro-chemical industry.

Building of the Railway

When, in 1871, British Columbia agreed to join the new Dominion of Canada it was conditional upon a trans-continental railway being constructed within 10 years. The proposed railway, about 1,600km (1,000 miles) longer than the first trans-continental line built in the United States, was an enormous undertaking for a struggling new country of less than four million people.

It was built in sections. Construction started at Thunder Bay, Ontario, in June 1875, but it was not until July 1882 when the line was approaching Regina (Saskatchewan), that the route through the Rocky Mountains was established. Many of the railway's engineers and builders had learned their trade during the American Civil War. Labourers came from eastern Canada and the United States and as immigrants from Europe. And for the western segments thousands were recruited in China to live in squalid camps and work under the most dangerous conditions.

The North West Rebellion of 1885 provided the necessary spur for the government to finance completion of the difficult northern Ontario section. It joined up with the already-completed prairie segment, which had reached Calgary (Alberta) in August 1883.

In British Columbia, construction started at Yale in April 1879 and by September 1885 had reached from Port Moody on the Pacific coast to Eagle Pass in BC's interior. On 7 November 1885 the last spike in the railway's final section was driven at Craigellachie BC, with considerable fanfare. The first passenger train in what was soon to become a daily service arrived in Port Moody from Montreal on 4 July 1886. In addition to carrying passengers and goods for 4,800km (3,000 miles) across the country in a matter of days, the railway provided telegraph lines to transmit messages between east and west in a few minutes.

Within days of the railway's arrival in Port Moody, ships chartered by the company arrived with goods from Japan. This was the beginning of Canadian Pacific's shipping lines which carried prairie grain, lumber and other natural products to world markets, then returned home with manufactured goods. The company also started building hotels in resort areas and cities along its railway line.

Political intrigues and financial manipulations surrounding the Canadian Pacific Railway's development form some of the most intriguing chapters in Canadian history. As any passenger riding through the Kicking Horse Pass or Fraser Canyon today can readily imagine, construction was enormously difficult. Revelstoke BC, close to the site of the last spike driven at Craigellachie, represents a topical footnote: it was named after Lord Revelstoke, head of Barings, one of the banks that financed the railway.

The Mounties

A need for law enforcement in the newly acquired North West Territories was obvious during the late 1800s. Violence among settlers and Indian uprisings were distinct possibilities and so was the threat of American intervention. However, it was the slaughter of a native band by American whiskey traders at Fort Whoop-up in the Cypress Hills that spurred the government into action.

The force was formed in August 1873 to maintain law and order and to be a visible symbol of Canadian sovereignty in the North West Territories. Between autumn 1873 and spring 1874 some 300 recruits were assembled at Lower Fort Garry, near Winnipeg. Armed with pistols, carbines and small artillery pieces, they wore military-style red tunics instead of blue uniforms traditionally worn by police.

In June 1874 the entire group set out on a gruelling two month march from Lower Fort Garry into what is now southern Alberta, where they warned off the whiskey traders. Half of these men, under Assistant Commissioner James Macleod, set up a permanent post at Fort Macleod; another group marched on to Edmonton and the rest returned to Manitoba. The following year posts were established at Fort Walsh, Fort Calgary and Battleford. During the next 15 years, the force assisted natives in making the transition to life on reserves after treaties were signed. They also helped new settlers, policed sections of the new railway right of way, and provided administration for the Yukon during the gold rush era.

In 1904 'Royal' was appended to their name, and in 1919, the force was merged with the Dominion Police to become the Royal Canadian Mounted Police. Members served overseas in both World Wars, and today they participate in United Nations operations. At this time the RCMP numbers 20,000 men and women, who protect

Granville Island, Vancouver (Chapter 1)

Totems in Stanley Park, Vancouver (Chapter 1)

Dr Sun Yat-Sen Chinese Gardens' Vancouver (Chapter 1)

Capilano Canyon Suspension Bridge, North Vancouver (Chapter 1)

national property and services across the country and provide police services in every province and territory except Ontario and Quebec.

Early years of the North West Mounted Police are recalled in museums at Regina, Fort Macleod and Fort Walsh. A line of highways across the Prairie provinces between Winnipeg and Fort Macleod approximate the route taken by those first mounties in 1874. It has been designated the Red Coat Trail.

Culture

The influx of immigrants in the last 40 years has changed the face of Canada, bringing a wonderful melange of cultures to those already established by original inhabitants and early settlers. All cities, and often smaller communities, have areas where ethnic cultures are kept alive in restaurants and festivals, craft shows and traditional holiday celebrations. A list of regional events from local tourist offices will lead you to ceilidhs, stampedes and sea festivals. In the north you can visit native camps to see how hides are tanned and fish is cured; sample caribou stew and Arctic char, and buy unique arts and crafts.

Museums, often housed in architecturally acclaimed buildings, can be especially exciting when they tell their stories through use of modern technology and imaginative settings. Every dramatic event in Canadian history, it seems, is carefully recorded in recreated settlements, marked battle sites, forts and trading posts and pioneer villages.

Visual and performing arts are alive and well in western Canada, thanks to both private patrons and government funding at provincial and federal levels. In cities you will find some of this continent's finest galleries, while small towns often surprise with the excellence of their folk-art collections. Symphony orchestras, ballet and theatre companies are respected at home and abroad. Summer theatre brings everything from Shakespeare to puppet shows, favourite Broadway musicals, classical, jazz and folk concerts, to western Canada's parks and riverbank locales.

1 • Vancouver & Excursions From The City

An Introduction to British Columbia

Snug between the Pacific Ocean and Rocky Mountains, British Columbia is a glorious start to any tour of western Canada. It is big, bold and beautiful, endowed with a scenic diversity that cannot be matched anywhere else. The climate is relatively mild in the south, where you can be showered with cherry blossoms while the rest of the country is under snow. Fishing and scuba diving are year-round sports, yet skiers can still enjoy mountain peaks in April when there is golfing in the valleys below. You can walk for miles undisturbed on beaches, follow canoe routes and hiking trails once used by early traders and trappers, or prospectors eager to reach the gold fields.

This is Big Country: a land of big ranches, big mountain vistas and vast plateaus, big lakes and rivers (containing big fish) and forests that seem to continue for ever. It is wilderness within a short drive of sophisticated cities; an upbeat province, energetic and rich in natural resources. Visitors soon realize that British Columbians live here because this is where they want to be. Many came for a vacation attracted by the great outdoors, and found reason to stay. They have left careers in the corporate world elsewhere, to become entrepreneurs here. To be transferred to British Columbia is inevitably cause for celebration. BC is the family's favourite child.

Whether you arrive on the west coast by land, air or sea, your first stop will likely be Vancouver, a dynamic city happily wedged between mountains and sea. This metropolis then, and brief excursions from it are the subject of our first itinerary. The second will take you to Vancouver Island, home of Canada's ever-so-British provincial capital of Victoria. Others direct you around the southern Coast Mountains and into the interior, north to Gold Rush territory, and through the farmlands of the Okanagan Valley. Finally, you will be guided 'north by northwest' to regions of awe-inspiring wilderness.

Vancouver & Excursions From The City

On a warm sunny day Vancouver more than lives up to its reputation as being the crown jewel of western Canada. Generously favoured by Nature, it also welcomes visitors with international shops and the second largest Chinatown west of the Rockies, historic Gastown and dramatically modern buildings erected for Expo '86.

Close to downtown, though easily missed by visitors, **Granville Island** can be handily reached on foot, by a No 50 bus or a brief ferry ride from various points on False Creek. Granville was a mere sandbar settlement when railway magnate William Van Horne renamed it after famed explorer Captain George Vancouver. The site was occupied by railway yards, sawmills, machine shops and other industries until it went into decline. Now it is revived as a people's place, housing an arts school, theatres and galleries. A lively food market sells just about everything from stuffed pork hocks to strawberries as sweet as honey, and international snacks. Craft shops, bookstores and boutiques, seafood restaurants, marine suppliers and tour companies all conspire to give you an interesting few hours on Granville Island.

A bonus from the city's temperate, often damp climate is its numerous parks where flowers bloom from early March to late autumn. Even at the height of summer they are islands of tranquility, usually within steps of busy commercial or residential areas. The remarkable **Stanley Park** contains 400ha (1,000 acres) of prime land within 10 or 15 minutes' walk of downtown Vancouver. Bounded by sea on three sides, it has roughly 285ha (700 acres) of primitive forest, with Douglas firs so tall that they disappear into the sky, and so dense that you can walk along trails beneath them in pouring rain and not get wet. About 125ha (50 acres) of formal gardens lead to open fields where children run and tumble. Recreation facilities include tennis courts, playing fields, a harbour for leisure craft, swimming pools and beaches, and miles of trails for pedestrians and cyclists.

Jogging takes on new dimensions, and new enthusiasts, in this park where a paved path follows the sea wall for 11km (7 miles), winding past such notable landmarks as the Nine O'Clock Gun, lighthouses, totem poles and the harbour entrance. For centuries, Salish Indians inhabited this region. Shells from their refuse heaps actually paved the park's first roads, and their trails still criss-cross its central forest. When in 1886 Vancouver became a city, one of its first items of business was a request to make this prime city land a public park. Dedicated by Lord Stanley in 1889 'for the use and enjoyment of all people of all colours, creeds and customs for all time' it is, in spite of constant use, a veritable oasis. Resident swans and ducks must think so, as they nest unperturbed in reeds of the Lost Lagoon, little more than a stone's throw from the city proper. A No 11 bus along Georgia or Pender Streets will get you there in a jiffy. Bicycles, strollers, roller skates, and whatever else you might need for a successful family outing are for rent across from the park entrance.

The second best view in town is awarded to **Queen Elizabeth Park** at Cambie St and W 33rd Ave. (The best is from Grouse Mountain in North Vancouver.) Once a dismal quarry, now surrounded by elegant homes, this is a favourite with older visitors who like to stop and smell the flowers as they walk its paved paths and formal gardens. The Bloedel Conservatory (paid admission) provides a controlled environment for exotic plants and flowers in simulated tropical, rain forest and desert climates. At this, the park's high spot, panoramas of Vancouver laid out before a backdrop of North Shore mountains are magnificent. Come around 10 o'clock on any morning rain or shine, and you will see hundreds of the city's Chinese population performing tai-chi exercises up here. And from a lookout on a clear day you will see Mt Baker, Golden Ears, Mt Seymour and Grouse Mountain. Seasons in the Park Restaurant receives top reviews for its full service meals, while a neighbouring snackbar serves tasty spinach and sausage rolls to have with your mid morning coffee.

On a smaller scale, the **Dr Sun Yat-Sen Classical Chinese Garden** provides an unexpected pool of calm in the heart of frenetic Chinatown. A poem of limestone rockeries and pools, waterfall, trees and plants, it is modelled after private classical gardens in the city of Suzhou during the Ming Dynasty.

The **University of British Columbia** on Point Grey must be envied for its locale, overlooking the Straits of Georgia. An added perk for visitors is that 247ha (610 acres) of the campus is devoted to botany. In consequence you can tour its teaching gardens. One example is the Asian Garden containing 400 species of rhododendrons, vines and shrubs, giant Himalayan lilies as well as countless annual and perennial flower varieties collected in Asia. Another, the very tranquil Nitobe Memorial Garden, is a formal Japanese Garden with flowering shrubs, a teahouse, stone pagoda and curved bridge over a pond filled with contented looking carp. Across the road, the university's Museum of Anthropology has a grand collection of archeological artifacts but is best known for the totems carved by peoples of coastal British Columbia. Often native artists are at work on huge cedar logs here, and willingly pause for a while to talk with visitors. In North Vancouver, 20 minutes by car or bus from downtown, Grouse Mountain has an aerial tramway to the 1,128m (3,700ft) level chalet. An observation deck affords tremendous city views which can extend to Vancouver Island and the Gulf Islands. After dark, with lights winking and blinking way below, the city looks at its magical best. Trails for walking in summer, and winter skiing give you a heady mountain experience without leaving the city.

While in North Vancouver, you will want to visit Capilano Suspension Bridge and Park. This swinging footbridge, 137m (450ft) long spans a spectacular 70m (230ft) deep canyon. Picnic areas and hiking trails, and in summer totem carvers at work, plus a scary walk across the bridge, make this a popular family attraction. There is another, less publicised suspension bridge in North Vancouver's Lynn Canyon Park. It is 83m (272ft) above a canyon and waterfall, alongside quiet walking paths and a natural pool for swimmers.

A pleasant stroll from downtown hotels is to the Harbour Centre Complex with its observation deck, and terraces where you can sit and watch the water traffic. Often a cruise ship or two is in port, docked in the shadow of the grand hotels. Its theatre features a multi-media presentation called 'Vancouver Discovery Show.' Restaurants include one atop the tower. Harbour tours by sternwheeler are available in summer.

In such a cosmopolitan city, dining out is an event whether you choose the ethnic places along Robsonstrasse, some of the 200 Chinese restaurants, or French in Old Gastown. At night the rooftop revolving restaurants are understandably popular, as is the Grouse Nest in the Grouse Mountain Chalet.

Considered the cultural centre of western Canada, Vancouver supports a symphony orchestra and opera company and several theatre groups. Summer concerts and musicals are featured in Stanley Park and at Kitsilano Beach, weather permitting. Numerous festivals are held throughout the year. The Pacific Exhibition in late August celebrates British Columbia and its people.

Short Excursions from Vancouver

Half-day and full-day excursions from Vancouver are such you could be forgiven for straying no further. This would be a pity. On the other hand, if you have only a few spare hours during your city stay the following are well worth your time.

Steveston

City airports are not generally known for their aesthetic locations, but Vancouver-bound air passengers have to be impressed with this one in the pretty suburb of Richmond. Immediately to the south is Lulu Island, named after the American actress Lulu Sweet by the British military engineer Colonel Moodie. A long-time centre of Japanese culture it now has a large Chinese population too, as you will realize when driving the Steveston Highway and come upon the somewhat incongruous sight of a colourful Buddhist Temple with a pagoda-style roof of glittering tiles. Interior sculptures, paintings and embroidery displays make it worthwhile to climb the steps for a closer look. Gardens are typically planted with bonsai, and a smiling Buddha is the recipient of gifts.

Continue along this highway and you will reach Steveston, one of those tucked-away destinations where Vancouverites like to take their guests for a seafood meal. Only 45 minutes from the city, yet reminiscent of a nineteenth-century hamlet, its historic significance is revealed during a self-guided walking tour to a museum, the nineteenth-century Gulf of Georgia Cannery and the Britannia Heritage Shipyard which has some of the oldest remaining structures here on the Fraser River. Waterfront cafes have outdoor seating. The harbour is home to a large fishing fleet and leisure boats with names like *Foolish Pleasure* and *Killing Time*. Relaxation comes easily in Steveston.

Squamish

A longer trip from Vancouver is to Squamish by rail, with a return trip by sea, through picturesque mountain and ocean scenery. Train buffs especially enjoy riding over trestles and through tunnels in the 1940s passenger coaches hauled by the powerful streamlined steam locomotive Royal Hudson. Should you decide to stay over, you will find plenty of outdoor pursuits in Squamish where rock climbing and windsurfing are popular.

The Islands

Vancouverites, especially those who have escaped the hectic pace of life in Toronto, tend to think of themselves as the 'chosen ones'. But even they now and again feel the need for an escape hatch from western Canada's fairest city. That is when they head for the islands.

It is almost shameful to allow only one day for Vancouver Island, though with helicopters from Vancouver's waterfront willing to whip you to Victoria in less than an hour, it is possible to taste a small sampling of the provincial capital in a half day.

Reached from Victoria and from the mainland, the Gulf islands are where city dwellers head for a change of scene and pace. Most of the ferries will take your car, but in summer you should phone ahead to see if they have space. If not, you can manage nicely without a car. The hills can present a challenge for all but the fittest of hikers and cyclists, but with scooters and taxis available you will not be stuck for transportation.

Scattered off Vancouver Island's eastern shore, five islands: Salt Spring, Mayne, the Penders, Galiano and Saturna are the most visited islands in the southern group. Blessed with a Mediterranean climate, calm waters and surprisingly little rain, their bucolic charm has attracted cottagers for over a century. Luckier ones have found ways to become permanent residents. Painters, writers and crafts people are so inspired by these islands that many have chosen to live here, and now a favourite pastime for visitors is to explore the studios and retail outlets for the work of local artists. Maybe you can't move in for as long as you'd like, but even a brief visit will acquaint you with resident birdlife, sea lions, seals and whales. The islands have resorts and inns, B & Bs and self-catering cottages, but it is best to reserve before boarding the ferry. We have listed tourism information centres instead of making individual suggestions.

Only 35 minutes by ferry from Victoria's Swartz Bay terminal, **Salt Spring** is largest and most populous of the Gulf Islands. Almost all of its 7,000 inhabitants live in and around Ganges, a pretty village hugging the harbour. (For handiwork of artists throughout the islands visit Mahon Hall in Ganges. Prices are competitive, variety exciting.) On the south end of Salt Spring, Ruckle Provincial Park is preserved for its natural beauty and 10km (6 miles) of shoreline. Camping, picnicking, swimming, fishing and hiking are happily pursued within the preserve. Activities in the 1920s were a little less lawful, when the park's Beaver Point was a rum-running port for smugglers who brought liquor across the Canada-US border.

Pender is actually two islands connected by a bridge. Their coastline is carved from gentle bays, pebble and sand beaches. North Pender has all the services you could need. Its Driftwood Centre is the commercial hub, with a farmers' market open from May through September for your picnic supplies. This is a great island to explore from the water, with gear rented from any of its several harbours. Often resorts can be reached from docks, making them handy lunch stops for boaters.

Saturna (pop 290) covers only 31 sq km (12 sq miles) and is not as accessible as the others because it calls for a ferry transfer. Some naturalists consider this an advantage, because such inaccessibility has preserved the very essence of its rural character. **Mayne**, at 21 sq km (8 sq miles), is the smallest of the southern Gulf Islands but has a more frequent ferry service than some of the others. Miner's Bay, a few minutes from the terminal at Village Bay, is this island's hub. It was named during the 1858 Gold Rush days when prospectors going from Victoria to the mainland goldfields would stop off here. Its old jail is now a museum. By the turn of this century the island was popular with Vancouverites and already boasted hotels and boarding houses. For your picnic lunch with a view you might head for Georgina Point lighthouse. In the early 1900s a hotel here was focal point for island social life, when people would row over for a pint or two at the pub. Mount Park is a public domain at the top of the island's highest point, but the access road to it is private, so you must walk up (1.6km, 1 mile) from the ferry terminal.

Long and narrow **Galiano Island**, affectionately known as the 'Jewel of the Gulf,' is served by ferry sailings from both Swartz Bay in Vancouver Island and Tsawwassen on the mainland. The beachcombing here is terrific. Fishing charters and sightseeing cruises are available, and kayak trips suited to both the veteran and the beginner give you a real appreciation of the very scenic coastline.

The Lower Fraser Valley

This circular drive from Vancouver takes in a stretch of rich farmlands in the Fraser River Valley. Although it is an enjoyable one-day trip, a more sensible plan is to give it several days and stay at Harrison Hot Springs. In fact, this is a region where families often choose to spend their entire summer vacations. The described loop is a pleasing 300km (190 miles), taking you east through the floodplain between the river's north bank to Hope and the Coast Mountains, then returning along the River's south side.

Leave Vancouver via Hwy 7 (Lougheed Hwy). Soon, a turnoff directs you north to **Port Moody.** There is little to remind you of its beginnings as the Canadian Pacific Railway's first Pacific terminus, so you may choose to keep going. Another possible detour is at an intersection where signs point to **Pitt Polder**, a swamp until the late 1940s when Dutch immigrants dyked it to create prosperous dairy farming land. Here meadows are dotted with European cattle, and names on mailboxes reflect the region's Dutch heritage. City dwellers like to escape for a few hours to this little patch of Holland. They walk or cycle on the dykes, or canoe through neighbouring marshes. Bird-watchers particularly enjoy the area in springtime, when bald eagles, ospreys and rare greater sandhill cranes are just a few of the birds to nest here. The small community of **Maple Ridge** is gateway to **Golden Ears Provincial Park**, a 556 sq km (215 sq mile) preserve dominated by the snow-covered twin peaks of Golden Ears Mountain to the east of Pitt Lake. More hiking trails here, 60km (37 miles) of them, as well as facilities for camping, boating and swimming. The park's northern section is connected in the north with Garibaldi Provincial Park (see pages 61-2).

Continuing east you will reach **Mission**, named after an Indian mission founded in 1860. Here, Westminster Abbey, a community of Benedictine monks, has a retreat centre open to the public. And in summer, all along this stretch of highway, you will see stands heavy with local fruit. In July, their home-grown raspberries are a bargain at any price.

Harrison Lake was once part of the miners' route to the goldfields. According to legend, a trio of prospectors, a little the worse for wear, tipped out of their canoe and found themselves in remarkably warm water. Its natural hot springs source was discovered, the water's therapeutic powers promoted, and soon a resort community grew around the lakeshore. Now **Harrison Hot Springs** is a village of approximately 600 permanent residents. A municipal pool and another within the Harrison Hot Springs Hotel are fed by the springs. A wide sand beach, boat rentals and cruises, interesting restaurants and visitor accommodation all contribute to a very relaxed break during your busy western Canada tour. Neighbouring **Susquatch Provincial Park** is named after the ape-like creatures which supposedly live here. A relative of Bigfoot, sighted in the northwest United States from time to time, the hairy Susquatch is said to be twice the size of any human. When you aren't searching for gigantic footprints you will enjoy scenic hiking paths around the lake, as well as fishing and swimming, and campsites which include some suitable for RVs.

From Harrison Hot Springs, you can drive south to **Agassiz** via Hwy 9 and turn east on Hwy 7 to parallel the Fraser River. Or, continue along Hwy 9 to **Minter Gardens** at the very foot of the Coastal Mountain Range. There are eleven themed gardens spread over 11ha (27 acres). Although they are rather too formal for some tastes, photographers will especially enjoy them from early spring through late autumn.

A further 36km (22 miles) east along Hwy 7 **Hope** is situated at the head of the lower Fraser Valley, surrounded on three sides by the Cascade Mountains. The town dates back to a Hudson's Bay Company post established here in 1848. Whether its name echoes the sentiments of miners as they set off on the next stage of the tortuous pack trail, or hopes that this area would not become part of the United States, is open to conjecture. Certainly the community was laid out in 1858 by Royal Engineers at a time when there was a rush for gold on the river's sandbars. Hope's most visible feature is the huge rock slide which occurred in 1965 when part of Johnson Peak collapsed and buried the highway under 45m (148ft) of rubble. (Often in mountain areas signs warn of falling rocks. If you see one coming in your direction, you can only get out of the way as best you can.) Hope is situated at the lower end of the Trans-Canada Hwy which leads to the Fraser Canyon and is also southern terminus of the Coquihalla Hwy, featured in other itineraries in this guide.

Turning back now, it is 19km (12 miles) westwards along the Trans-Canada Hwy to **Chilliwack**, an agricultural centre with hotels, restaurants and other facilities useful to travellers looking for a good stop-over between Vancouver and the interior. It is also a military base, with connections to those Royal Engineers who built the Cariboo Road (page 65). About 11km (7 miles) south of the highway, **Cultus Lake Provincial Park** is a lovely spot. In summer its beach-trimmed lake is a playground for water-skiers and boaters. Campgrounds are especially busy at weekends and childrens' activities are featured. Every June the park is scene of a large Indian Festival which brings participants from British Columbia and Washington State. If you are in the area then, you will find the festival very worthwhile, especially the war canoe races across Cultus Lake.

Park beaches can get noisy at weekends, but hiking and horseback riding trails will have you at peace with nature any day of the week. North of the park entrance, a road follows the rugged Chilliwack River valley 42km (26 miles) as far as **Chilliwack Lake Park**, where there are more campsites. This stretch of river, renowned world-wide for its challenging white waters, is home to the Canadian Olympic Kayak team.

Closer to Vancouver, Abbotsford (population 14,500) is a prosperous agricultural centre. During the second weekend in August, its large airport is scene of a very well attended air show.

Just 6km (4 miles) north of Langley off the Trans-Canada Hwy, **Fort Langley National Historic Park** is often overlooked by visitors to Vancouver. A recreated Hudson's Bay Company trading post built on this site in 1840, it provided supplies for fur traders, and later gold prospectors in the area. One of its reconstructed buildings is the Big House, in which the proclamation establishing the colony of British Columbia in 1858 was first read.

Abandoned later, the rebuilt fort is now operated by Parks Canada. Costumed interpreters perform chores and talk to visitors about their day-to-day lives as nineteenth-century inhabitants. A little community around the park has pleasant restaurants and cafes, art and craft stores on pretty tree-shaded streets.

Additional Information
— Vancouver & Surrounding Area —

Places to Visit

Chilliwack
Minter Gardens
Trans-Canada Hwy and Hwy 9
Open: daily April to October
☎ (604) 794-7191

Langley
Fort Langley National Historic Park
6km north of Trans-Canada Hwy
Open: daily
☎ (604) 888-4424

Mission
Westminster Abbey
Hwy 7 north of Mission
Open: daily
☎ (604) 826-8975

Vancouver
Capilano Suspension Bridge and Park
Capilano Rd
North Vancouver
Open: daily
☎ (604) 985-7474

Dr Sun Yat-Sen Chinese Gardens
578 Carrall St
Open: daily
☎ (604) 662-3207

Grouse Mountain Tramway
6400 Nancy Green Way
North Vancouver
Open: daily
☎ (604) 984-0661

Lynn Canyon Park
Lynn Valley Rd
North Vancouver
Open: daily
☎ (604) 987-5922

Royal Hudson
Departs 9.00am from North Vancouver Station, 1131 West 1st St, North Vancouver
Available from early June to late September, Wednesday to Sunday
☎ (604) 688-7246 or 1-800-663-1500

UBC Botanical Gardens — Nitobe Memorial Gardens
6408 Northwest Marine Dr
Open: daily
☎ (604) 822-9666

UBC Museum of Anthropology
Northwest Marine Drive
Open: daily in summer, closed Mondays and Tuesdays at some other times of the year
☎ (604) 822-3825

Vandusen Botanical Display Garden
5251 Oak St
Open: daily
☎ (604) 266-7194

Parks

Cultus Lake Provincial Park
11 km (7 miles) south of Trans-Canada Hwy (Hwy 1) at Chilliwack
☎ (604) 858-7161

Golden Ears Provincial Park
10km north of Hwy 7 at Maple Ridge
☎ (604) 929-1291

Susquatch Provincial Park
6km north of Harrison Hot Springs
☎ (604) 858-7161

Ferry Services

BC Ferries
Vancouver
☎ (604) 669-1211

Tsawwassen to Galiano, Mayne, Pender, Salt Spring with connections to Saturna.
Two round trips daily, more on weekends and in summer.

Victoria (Swartz Bay) to Galiano, Mayne, Pender, Salt Spring with connections to Saturna.
At least six sailings daily, more on weekends and in summer.

Tourist Information Offices

Gulf Islands
Saltspring Island Travel InfoCentre
Box 111
Ganges BC
V0S 1E0
☎ (604) 537-5252

Other Islands
Tourism Association of Vancouver Island
302-45 Bastion Square
Victoria BC
V8W 1J1
☎ (604) 382-3551

Southwestern British Columbia
Tourism Association of Southwestern BC
Suite 304
828 West 8th Avenue
Vancouver BC
V5Z 1E2
☎ (604) 876-3088

Vancouver
Vancouver InfoCentre
1055 Dunsmuir St

Write to:

Pavilion Plaza
Four Bentall Centre
PO Box 49296
1055 Dunsmuir St
Vancouver BC
V7X 1L3
☎ (604) 683-2000

2 • Pacific Islands & The Sunshine Coast

For first-time visitors to Vancouver Island this southern excursion is little more than a taster, because there is enough here to keep you for ever. A fairly large island, 405km (252 miles) long and 65-130km (40-80 miles) wide with an area of 32,000 sq km (12,400 sq miles), it is six times the size of Prince Edward Island, one and a half times the area of Wales in the UK, and bigger than either Vermont or New Hampshire in the USA. The winter climate is Canada's mildest, and snow is rare except in the mountains. That means you will see flowers growing outside during winter months — something unheard of elsewhere in Canada. On the down-side, it rains a lot, especially on the west coast, where the central mountain range traps moisture carried by prevailing winds from the Pacific Ocean. Locals have a word of advice on this subject: start the day early, because if rain is on the way it will likely arrive in time for afternoon tea.

Vancouver Island's rugged west coast is swept by wind and rain for most of the year. Not surprisingly then, it is fairly sparsely populated, and in national and provincial parks you can enjoy complete solitude. Because rainfall can be heavy, and the trails are often slippery, it is prudent to bring rainwear and waterproof footwear with good traction. When you venture *Off the Beaten Track*, be sure to heed the rangers' advice, especially on how to avoid bears and cougars.

In contrast, the sheltered east coast has wide expanses of agricultural land, interspersed by small communities. Recreational opportunities abound. Trimmed with long, clean beaches, warm waters offer some of the best fishing, and scuba diving is a year-round pursuit. Sailing, kayaking and golf are popular. So is hiking, camping and mountain climbing. Group tours to view the wildlife, particularly the whales, sea lions and eagles, are readily available. There are sophisticated resorts, motels and comfortable B & Bs. Because so many artists have chosen to live and work on this side of the island, quality artwork and crafts are everywhere. In reality an

OUTDOOR ADVENTURES

As you will have gathered from the text, Off the Beaten Track Canada is great for adventurers. You can canoe and hike, kayak in rivers or on the ocean, climb mountains and dive in pristine waters. You can raft and ride horseback, join a hunt, a fishing expedition or photographic safari. In truth, there is probably as wide a range of outdoors adventures available in Canada as anywhere on earth. Sadly, some visitors meet with misfortune, often because they overestimate their abilities.

Some adventures we describe are simple and totally safe, calling for nothing beyond a willingness to try something new. At the other end of the scale are long treks by land or water into remote and totally unforgiving country. While no responsible outfitter will service or equip anyone clearly unqualified, and no park warden will allow such people into his or her territory, the individual must bear the ultimate responsibility for his actions.

Visitors wanting to learn a new skill will find instructors and companies happy to fill their needs. Those planning strenuous activities requiring specialized skills should make sure they are sufficiently qualified before setting off into Canada's back-country.

east coast vacation is what dreams are made of.

Often in summer delays occur in ferry services to the island from Vancouver, and it is a wise traveller who telephones BC Ferries for up-to-date information. If you are going 'up island' the shortest route is via the Horseshoe Bay (West Vancouver) terminus to Nanaimo. For Victoria, the Tsawwassen-Swartz Bay route is more direct.

The capital of British Columbia, **Victoria** (population 70,000) is not strictly *Off the Beaten Track*, but to avoid it would be a shame when it is such a lovely city. If you go little beyond a stroll around the inner harbour you will capture its essence, including the English, rather genteel character.

Though it can be tacky at times, Victoria came by its British image honestly. Located on the island's southern tip, her climate is similar to that of southern England. Moderate weather has continued to attract British immigrants ever since the early 1900s, when they were joined by retirees from the colonial service in India and the Far East. Here, they can walk by the sea and enjoy a round of golf at any time of the year. They take great pride in their gardens. And wherever they are at mid-afternoon they can stop for tea.

Victoria's roots go back to the 1840s when the Hudson's Bay Company established Fort Victoria in the vicinity of the present Bastion Square. The 1860s saw this as an outfitting centre for prospectors heading towards the Fraser River gold fields. In that same decade the community, with a population then of 2,000, became incorporated as the City of Victoria, capital of the crown colony of British Columbia.

Double-decker buses and sweet-shops selling bullseyes and humbugs aside, Victoria is a compact and attractive city for walkers. On even a brief stay, you will want to visit important buildings around the inner harbour dominated by The Empress, Parliament Buildings and the Royal British Columbia Museum.

Even if you have little inclination for museums visit this one anyway, to gain an understanding of provincial history and culture. A living microcosm of the entire province, it is so comprehensive that an admission ticket is good for two days. Outstanding displays show how Pacific Coast Indians lived before the arrival of Europeans. Others illustrate the evolution of European settlement, with dioramas representing life at various periods. Dynamic displays illustrate the development of the fishing, lumber, mining and agricultural industries to the economy of the present day. The native section is outstanding.

When the 1859 government buildings became inadequate, an architectural competition was held and new Parliament Buildings constructed from the winning design in 1893. The chosen entry was submitted by Francis Mawson Rattenbury, a young man who had moved to BC from Britain a year before and went on to make a name for himself across Canada. At night the domed buildings are outlined with more than 3,300 lights. By day, their grounds make for very pleasant strolling. Free public tours are conducted. Across from here, facing the inner harbour, The Empress is one of Canadian Pacific's best known heritage hotels. Built in the early 1900s, now completely restored and upgraded, it is famous for its afternoon tea, which is so popular that they start serving it at noon.

On leaving Victoria, there are two distinct itineraries which could easily be combined: a fairly short excursion to the Pacific Rim National Park, and a longer trip to the northern tip of the island, with the option of returning via the Sunshine Coast, an enchanting section of the mainland which can only be reached by sea or air.

FRANCIS MAWSON RATTENBURY — ARCHITECT

Rattenbury was a 25-year-old recent arrival from England, when he won the competition to design the BC Legislature Building. He was not present at the new building's 1898 opening ceremonies. Instead, he was in the Yukon with his new bride, establishing a transportation company to supply the Klondike gold fields.

When his Yukon ventures failed, Rattenbury returned to Victoria and resumed an architectural career which included The Empress, first of a number of railway hotels he designed, as well as government buildings, banks and private homes throughout BC. After achieving a reputation as successful architect and businessman, municipal politician and society leader, he shocked Victoria's society by flaunting his young mistress, Alma Packenham. After the death of his wife, he married Alma, but by this time was beset by financially crippling taxes and legal bills.

In 1930, the couple left Victoria to settle into obscurity in Bournemouth, England. In 1935, when Rattenbury was murdered, Alma and her young lover, George Stoner (he was the family chauffeur,) were charged. After a sensational trial, Alma was acquitted, but later committed suicide. Stoner's death sentence was commuted to life imprisonment and eventually he was released from prison.

Excursion to the Pacific Rim

This itinerary calls for at least one or two nights' stay in or near Pacific Rim National Park. With a bit of luck you will stay longer.

Leave Victoria on the Trans-Canada Hwy (Hwy 1), and 60km (37 miles) later you will be in **Duncan**. A major farming and lumbering centre, it is also described as the 'city of totems' for the colourful totems made by local carvers for downtown streets. There is a photogenic collection of native carvings and totems behind the city hall too, and the town has two interesting museums. One, the Native Heritage Centre, beside the Cowichan River, is probably the best of its kind anywhere in the province. It has a longhouse, theatre, and arts and crafts centre. Conducted tours are available; native history and culture are dramatically told in an audio presentation. Craftsmen on site include carvers, bead-workers and knit-

Totems at the Native Heritage Centre, Duncan (Chapter 2)

Award-winning murals at Chemainus (Chapter 2)

Sport fishing harbour on the Powell River (Chapter 2)

The day's catch of a fine halibut at Ucluelet (Chapter 2)

ters. An excellent selection of the distinctive Cowichan woollen products are for sale. The other, the BC Forest Museum, tells the story of logging in British Columbia with an old-time farm homestead and logging camp, operating logging railroad and audio-visual presentations.

A unique community undertaking here is the Cowichan and Chemainus Valleys Ecomuseum. This 1,000 sq km (400 sq miles) 'museum without walls' involves a region taking serious steps to preserve its heritage through a number of individual projects.

A very worthwhile side trip is via Hwy 18 which leads along the Cowichan valley to Lake Cowichan. This valley, blessed by a gentle climate (Cowichan is an Indian word meaning 'warmed by the sun') is cattle and dairy farming country. It produces much of British Columbia's milk and the forest-ringed lake is great for trout fishing.

Chemainus just north of Duncan is one of the island's oldest European settlements. Over the last two decades, it has become famous for its award-winning collection of thirty-two larger-than-lifesize murals. Painted by local artists on the walls of downtown buildings, they celebrate life in the Chemainus Valley, its native peoples and the logging industry. This is a captivating little town, with street upon street of craft and antique shops, art galleries, cafes and restaurants, all of which attract a steady flow of visitors. Rockhounds will enjoy this area as a source of the rare flower-stone, containing flower-shaped quartz crystals.

A further 55km (34 miles) via the Trans-Canada Hwy will bring you to **Nanaimo**. The Hudson's Bay Company established a trading post here in 1849, and discovery of coal led the company to recruit miners in England and Scotland. The Bastion, a wooden blockhouse built to protect those miners is now a museum. Another is the Nanaimo Centennial Museum, where exhibits illustrate more facets of the city's early history. Coal was most important to the economy until deposits were exhausted and the city (current population 48,000) turned to the manufacture of wood products and fishing in the 1950s.

Nanaimo is a popular centre for hikers and campers who explore neighbouring mountains and lakes as well as the offshore islands. Charter companies arrange wildlife tours during the winter and early spring, especially to view bald eagles and sea lions wintering in the area. The Nanaimo Bathtub Race in July is a much publicised event, when enthusiasts race motorized bathtubs and similarly outlandish craft across the 55km (34mile) Strait of Georgia to Vancouver. Nanaimo is served by a daily train from Victoria on weekdays only. It is also a terminal for BC Ferries to Vancouver. Local ferries take you to rustic **Gabriola Island**, where accommodation and campsites are available, and to **Newcastle Island**, a great place for camping or a day's visit to hike, cycle, picnic and watch for wildlife.

Leaving Nanaimo, take Hwy 19 to **Parksville** and then turn inland on Hwy 4 leading to Port Alberni. En route, (about 32km — 20 miles from Parksville) **Macmillan Provincial Park** is good for a short break. Its Cathedral Grove is a wondrous stand of massive Douglas firs which escaped a massive forest fire 300 years ago. Some trees are 800 years old. Plaques along a self-guided tour explain life in the rain forests which once covered most of the island. On a warm day with the sun filtering through the branches, this is a delightfully cool and quiet spot, provided you haven't arrived on the heels of a tour group or two. **Port Alberni** is at the head of Alberni Inlet, named after an eighteenth-century Spanish officer commanding forces which occupied the area. An 1860 sawmill built here founded the still flourishing lumbering industry. With a population of 20,000, this is British Columbia's third largest port. Fishing charters leave the port which (along with a few other island communities) claims to be the 'Salmon Fishing Capital of the World'. The freighter *Lady Rose* carries goods and passengers from Port Alberni to other ports in the area, including some within the Pacific Rim National Park. In summer another ship, the *Frances Barkley* services Ucluelet and the Broken Islands from here.

From Port Alberni it is a 90km (56 mile) drive via Hwy 4, a winding stretch of mountain highway, to the south-west coast and **Pacific Rim National Park**'s Long Beach. The park is comprised of three sections: the Long Beach area between Ucluelet and Tofino, the Broken Island group of islands in Barkley Sound, and the West Coast Trail between Bamfield and Port Renfrew. In all the 510 sq km (197 sq mile) park encompasses varied terrain, from snow-capped mountains and dense rainforests to rugged headlands and islands, river estuaries and 130km (81 miles) of shoreline with long sandy beaches. The park is home to considerable bird-life, ranging from forest-dwellers to shore birds such as puffins, cormorants, geese, ducks and bald eagles. Forests are inhabited by bear and cougar, mink and martens. Seals and sea-lions laze on the beaches. In summer migrating grey whales feed offshore.

In the most developed area of Long Beach leisure time favourites on this 11km (7 mile) scimitar of hard-packed white sand are hiking, swimming and surfing. It is even relaxing to wander the shore observing tiny creatures in the tidal pools. The Wickaninnish Centre explains park features with lectures, slide shows and guided hikes, all aimed at teaching visitors about the region's human and natural history. Descriptive brochures of hiking trails along the shoreline and into the rain forest are available here. The centre's restaurant is first-class by any standards, and the views from its windows are magnificent. Within the park, you will want to take in some interpretive walks to learn more about the environment. The Bog Trail demonstrates how nature uses high water table levels and acidic soil to stunt the 100 year-old shore pines, and so produces her own version of bonsai. The Rain Forest Trail is a must, for its journey through coastal forests as they were before lumbermen and farmers arrived. The 1km (½ mile) walk leads you along a wooden footpath at different levels above the forest floor, past astonishingly beautiful ferns. And all is quiet but for the sounds of birds and dripping water.

South of the park entrance the fishing community of **Ucluelet** (population 1,500 and pronounced 'You-*clue*-let') has a variety of visitor accommodation. Some places offer lodging and charter fishing packages. A unique resort is the *Canadian Empress* where visitor accommodation is aboard a cruise liner that never leaves port. Whale watching in March and April, sport fishing and nature cruises between May and September, are aboard the liner's 13m to 16m (43-52ft) deep-sea cruisers with experienced skippers and guides. Air travel from Vancouver and transfers to the ship can be included in the package. Full and half day fishing trips bring back such giant halibut, ling cod and salmon, locals often gather to watch the boats come in simply to see if records have been broken.

Just west of town, Mandy and Neil Sinclair offer a similar but less costly program with accommodation in the Crow n' Eagle B & B (five bedrooms, two baths). Neil has his own charter boat and will customize fishing and sightseeing tours to suit you. Transfer from the airport is arranged for Crow n' Eagle guests who fly in. Also listed in Additional Information, Majestic West Coast Wilderness Adventures is an organization which provides day-long paddling tours for novices. They offer longer adventures complete with fully-equipped single and double kayaks, wet suits and camping equipment. Sea-kayaking is common all around the coast of British Columbia, and unlike its energetic relative, river kayaking, it is peaceful, and relaxing, and suitable for almost everyone so long as some common-sense rules are followed.

Just beyond the park's northern edge, **Tofino** (population 1,300) is a fishing village with a thriving artists' community and a reputation for an even more relaxed life-style than some of its neighbours. The Pacific Rim Whale Festival, held here each spring, celebrates the whales' migration between the Arctic and waters off Mexico's Baja California. Since some whales are resident year-round, they can be spotted any time. Like Ucluelet, Tofino is a centre for sea-kayaking, scuba diving and fishing charters. We have listed accommodation in and near the village.

The **Broken Group Islands** are an archipelago of more than 100 islands reached only by boat across open water. The freighter service from Port Alberni to **Gibraltar Island** within the group often carries campers, who continue on to other islands by canoe and kayak. Experienced kayakers study charts and weather conditions before setting off, and novices should heed the advice of locals, because dangers await small craft which attempt seemingly direct passages. Some fifty sunken wrecks are popular with scuba divers. The fishing is great, though you may have to compete with bald eagles for your catch. Nature lovers will enjoy this, the world's largest concentration of bald eagles and the colonies of sea lions which have taken over the smaller uninhabited islands.

The park's 77km (48 mile) West Coast Trail is a former footpath carved out of the wilderness so that shipwrecked sailors could reach safety. It should be attempted only by experienced, self-reliant hikers carrying up to a week's supplies. Park authorities describe it as 'one of the most gruelling treks in North America'. Hardened adventurers may differ, but most agree this series of beaches, coves, waterfalls, caves and tidal pools, with the thundering Pacific on one side and the temperate rainforest with its stands of Sitka spruce and lush ravines on the other, is unforgettable.

The northern trailhead is reached through **Bamfield**, a pleasant little community, on 90km (56 miles) of gravel logging road, or by freighter from Port Alberni. There is a marine research station here which offers field trips for interested visitors (write in advance if you want to be included.) Bamfield's boardwalk which hugs the shoreline is a great place to watch the shipping arrive at Port Alberni. The southern trailhead near Port Renfrew is 102km (63 miles) from Victoria via Hwy 14. A National Park campground at Green Point is suitable for RVs, but it is often full so campers may have to look for space at a commercial campground near the park gates.

Access to the West Coast Trail is limited to fifty-two hikers starting each day. A permit is required, current cost of which is $60. Reservations are accepted by telephone for an additional fee of $25.

Vancouver Island North

This journey takes you by road from Victoria to Port Hardy near the northern tip of Vancouver Island, from where you may choose to board a ferry for its 15-hour journey to Prince Rupert on British Columbia's northwest coast. Included are a number of side trips to parks and smaller islands. After staying overnight in the northerly Prince Rupert (perhaps on board the ferry), there are several alternatives: return to Port Hardy; take a different BC ferry to the Queen Charlotte Islands; continue on into the interior of British Columbia by road or Via Rail which is the subject of Chapter 4. It is essential to make reservations for the Port Hardy-Prince Rupert passage well in advance, especially if you are taking a motor vehicle or require a cabin. It is equally important to make ferry reservations for the Queen Charlotte Islands.

From Victoria the 504km (313 miles) to Port Hardy calls for a fairly early start. After reaching Nanaimo via the Trans-Canada Hwy (Hwy 1), follow Hwy 19 north to **Courtenay**. Abundance of game and berries brought Comox Indians to the area before the first European visitors (who were Spanish navigators) arrived here in 1791. The town is named after a British admiral who surveyed this coast in the 1840s. Ten years later the Hudson's Bay Company established a store here, and immigrants began coming from Britain and other parts of Canada in the 1860s. Present day Courtenay (population 9,000) is a prosperous logging, fishing and agricultural centre, well known for recreational opportunities which include both sailing and skiing. One downtown section is particularly pleasant for its cobbled streets, old-fashioned street lamps and flower-filled planter boxes.

The nearby town of **Comox** traces its origins back to the Hudson's Bay Company, which established a farming community here. It is now site of a large military installation and is terminus for the ferry to Powell River on the mainland. It is also the starting point for the scenic alternative return route down the Sunshine Coast to Vancouver described on pages 57-8.

Continuing north to Port Hardy, **Campbell River** was already inhabited by Kwakiutl Indians when Vancouver surveyed the coastline in the early 1790s. By 1900, loggers had settled the area. Now Campbell River (population 16,000) remains a wood-products centre as well as an important salmon-fishing port. Like other Vancouver Island communities, it claims to be 'Salmon Fishing Capital of the World'. Certainly some of the biggest salmon ever caught on a line have been wrestled on board here. Charter boat captains are so confident that they offer money-back guarantees of a catch. The town's Tyee Club awards membership to anyone fishing in a specific area who lands a spring salmon weighing more than 13.6kg (30lb). In July the annual Salmon Festival features fishing competitions and war-canoe races.

Campbell River is the terminal for the hourly 15-minute ferry to **Quadra Island**. This is less built-up than some of the islands to the south, and its four small communities offer a variety of accommodation, including a campground. It is a superb spot for salmon fishing, clam digging, and for exploring deep forests and mountain trails. Some of the best scuba-diving in North America is available at the south end of the island. The Kwagiulth Museum and Cultural Centre at Cape Mudge, 4km (2½ miles) south of the ferry terminal displays the history and culture of the northwest native peoples.

Visitors simply passing through will find Campbell River an enjoyable stop for a waterfront picnic lunch. This should be a refuelling stop for your car too, since there are no more service stations until you reach Port Hardy.

Soon after leaving Campbell River, Hwy 28 leads to two provincial parks. **Elk Falls Provincial Park** is a beautiful little preserve near the highway where the Campbell River drops 27m (89ft) into a deep rocky canyon. It has picnic sites and camping and salmon fishing that is legendary. About 50km (31 miles) further inland the 2,120 sq km (820 sq miles) **Strathcona Provincial Park** offers a complete range of outdoors activities. Centre of the park is Vancouver Island's highest peak, Golden Hinde (2,200m, 7,218ft) and Della Falls (440m, 1,444ft) which is among the world's highest waterfalls. The park is inhabited by wolverine, wolf, cougar and Vancouver Island's last elk herd. There are virgin stands of Douglas fir here, including one 1,000-year-old giant reaching for the sky at 93m (305ft). In springtime clearings are a mass of wild flowers. The Buttle Lake and Forbidden Plateau areas, both accessible by road, have some visitor facilities. The rest of the park is accessible only on foot.

Some 8km (5 miles) south of Port McNeill, a turnoff leads to the coast at **Telegraph Cove**, where there is accommodation and a campsite. The coastal scenery here is a joy to photographers. Fishing, sea-kayaking, diving and whale-watching are popular pursuits. During summer, killer whales can be seen rubbing themselves on the gravel beaches. Only they seem to know why.

Near the northern tip of Vancouver Island, **Port Hardy** (named after the captain of Nelson's HMS *Victory*) is a further 238km (148 miles) from Campbell River. The economy of this community (population 5,000) is based upon copper mining which accounts for 10 percent of Canada's production and is the largest local employer. Lumbering and fishing are also important. As terminus for the ferry to Prince Rupert this is your overnight stop, for which we have listed accommodation suggestions. Port Hardy is a pleasant stopover for an overnight stay. Its harbour is busy with the comings and goings of fishing boats, pleasure craft and float planes, and the Port Hardy Museum details the area's history going back to human habitation 8,000 years ago. Bear Cove (where the ferry terminal is located) is site of the earliest evidence of human occupation discovered in central and northern British Columbia.

From Port Hardy, it is a 67km (42 mile) drive around Vancouver Island's northern tip to 1,507 sq km (582 sq mile) **Cape Scott Provincial Park**. There is trailhead parking, but entry is on foot. This park is situated in a rugged rain forest region with a windswept shoreline which includes 23km (14 miles) of beautiful sandy beaches. Violent storms are frequent and the annual rainfall is about 500cm (200in). Forest undergrowth is so thick, hikers may be obliged to use the gaps made by resident black bears. Needless to say, Cape Scott's challenge is for experienced and well-equipped campers.

The ferry *Queen of the North* leaves Port Hardy at 7.30am on alternate days during summer (less frequently at other times) for her 441km (274 mile) voyage up the Inside Passage. The Inside Passage is one of the world's most scenic natural waterways, as you will see from the constantly changing panorama of deep fjords and islands and densely wooded mountains sweeping down into the sea. Be sure to reserve some film for the narrow Grenville Passage. Ferry passengers can expect to see luxury cruise liners which leave southern oceans to ply this route in summer. Also resident sea lions, dolphins and perhaps cruising pods of orca (killer) and humpback whales.

Queen of the North is a comfortable ship with two-berth overnight cabins, dining and other facilities. While it does carry motor vehicles, many passengers make this a mini-cruise in both directions, leaving their cars in the long-term parking lot for pick up on their return to Port Hardy. Arrival in **Prince Rupert** (see page 74) is at 10:30pm, so hopefully you have booked accommodation in town if you are not staying on board overnight. (The ship will depart for its return to Port Hardy at 7:30 the following morning.) Alaska Marine Highway System ferries sail from here to Alaska, providing access to the Yukon through Skagway. Via Rail has passenger services to Prince George, Jasper and points east.

The Queen Charlottes

BC Ferries operates a service from Prince Rupert to the **Queen Charlotte Islands**, five days a week in summer, three in winter, and the passage takes eight hours. These islands are popular as a vacation destination, and home to nearly 6,000 residents, many of whom are writers and artists totally dedicated to their relaxed lifestyle. Residents include about 1,000 members of the Haida nation, whose ancestors have lived here for at least 6,000 years.

There are 138 islands in this scimitar-shaped archipelago stretching over 250km (155 miles). These islands escaped the recent glaciation that covered most of Canada, leaving some unique rugged landscapes covered by 1,000-year-old rain forests. The islands are unique in other ways too. Often mist-shrouded, they seem remote and mysterious, taking us back to a time when the aboriginal people first arrived, and the human race had a radically different relationship with nature. Geologists, botanists and biologists come to study the islands and their environment; vacationers come simply to enjoy the rugged mountain scenery, Sitka spruce and cedar forests. And the magical shoreline with its deep fjords and colonies of seabirds and sea lions. On Anthony Island, the old Haida village of Ninstints is a UNESCO World Heritage Site for its fascinating collection of Haida mortuary poles, all over 100 years old. It is incorporated in the recently-established Gwaii Haanas National Park Reserve, a step in the creation of the new South Moresby National Park, to protect this environment from logging and other commercial encroachment.

In addition to the ferry service, the islands are served by scheduled air flights from the BC mainland; the larger islands are connected by ferries or boat services. There is a total of only 150km (93 miles) of roads on the two major islands, Graham and Moresby, so visitors may prefer to rely on local taxis, boats, and the tours conducted by Haida elders.

The Queen Charlottes have small hotels and B & Bs as well as campgrounds, and because space is limited it is essential to make advance reservations. We suggest you book through the Islands' Travel InfoCentre, whose address is provided in the Additional Information section.

The Sunshine Coast

For those planning a return journey down the island, there is no alternative route to that already described until you arrive at **Courtenay** and the road leading to **Comox**. This is the terminal for the ferry to **Powell River** on the 'Sunshine Coast', about 150km (93 miles) northwest of Vancouver. Although part of the mainland it is an area accessible only by air or ferry. Despite this, it is a favourite get-away for Vancouverites because of the long sunny days and low rainfall. The only highway (Hwy 101) links Powell River with a group of small communities to the north and south, and from your base in one of these, you will find lots of opportunities for fresh and saltwater fishing. Lakes and rivers are teeming with cutthroat, rainbow and steelhead trout as well as kokanee salmon, while sea fishermen will find coho and chinook salmon, and a variety of bottom fish along the scenic coastline. Wildlife watchers will see waterfowl and diving birds, including eagles hunting for salmon. Hiking trails have been developed along ocean shorelines and old logging roads into an otherwise inaccessible wilderness. The Powell Forest Canoe route connects 12 lakes by portage trails, providing excellent opportunities for kayaking or canoeing and camping.

Powell River's economy is based largely on forest products. The original settlement was a pulp and paper-milling centre, and now the local paper mill is the world's largest. (The smell can hit you long before you reach the town.) The community (population 13,000) is restoring some of its older homes as well as the turn-of-the-century hotel, theatre and courthouse. Powell River is one of the province's main diving centres. Fishing charters are available, as are houseboat, bicycles, kayak and canoe rentals.

There is a choice of accommodation and RV facilities, some of which we have listed. And since this is vacation land as well as 'cottage country' to many city families, you are assured of a good selection of restaurants. Oyster and clam digging is a favourite way of acquiring dinner for a beach barbecue.

North of Powell River, the tiny, secluded fishing village of **Lund** is gateway to **Desolation Sound Marine Park**. Desolation Sound may have seemed appropriate to the explorer who named it, but now it is far from desolate to thousands of divers, canoeists, sea-kayakers and adventurers from around the world. The park's waters, with surface temperatures up to 21.7°C (71°F), are warmer than in any Pacific coast area north of Mexico and invite year-round diving. Because the shoreline shelves at different levels, divers of any proficiency can enjoy the experience. (Among inhabitants is the giant Pacific octopus, with arms 2m (6ft) long and a head larger than a football. Fortunately they are totally friendly.) Lund accommodation is listed, and we have included two local adventure organizations.

Driving south, **Saltery Bay** is about 30km (19 miles) from Powell River. This is terminus of the ferry to **Earl's Cove** on the Sechelt Peninsula; the peninsula's most popular area is **Pender Harbour**, 22km (14 miles) south. Visitor accommodation is available and good fishing is to be had out of local communities. This is also a great place to observe the orcas (killer whales) who travel offshore in pods of up to a hundred or more. **Sechelt** is a pleasing little town which, for good reason, attracts cottagers and retirees. Its long gravel beach is littered with decades of driftwood. Lovely views from shore are of the Strait of Georgia and Vancouver Island's snow capped mountains. Close to the town centre, the Sechelt National Reserve became the first self-governing native community in Canada back in 1988. A cluster of commemorative totems here makes your visit worthwhile for the photo opportunities alone. A crafts store adjoining the information centre has excellent but fairly expensive traditional carved wooden masks, pottery, woven cedar bark baskets as well as jade and shell jewellery, all created in various coastal native centres.

Gibsons is a quaint fishing village with a picturesque harbour. It was the location of a long-running television series, *The Beachcombers* and in consequence receives lots of visitors. This in turn has brought antique and crafts shops. Charter operators offer some of the best fishing on this coast. Accommodation is listed for Gibsons. A further 5km (3 miles) brings you to **Langdale**, and the ferry to Horseshoe Bay, just north of Vancouver.

Additional Information
— Pacific Islands & The Sunshine Coast —

Places to Visit

Duncan

Native Heritage Centre
200 Cowichan Way
Open: daily May to September
☎ (604) 746-8119

British Columbia Forest Museum
Trans-Canada Hwy
Open: daily May to September
☎ (604) 746-1251

Nanaimo

Nanaimo Centennial Museum
100 Cameron St
Open: daily, closed Monday September to May
☎ (604) 753-1821

Quadra Island

Kwagiulth Museum and Cultural Centre
Cape Mudge
Open: daily May 15 to September 15, Sunday afternoons
☎ (604) 285-3733

Victoria

Royal British Columbia Museum
675 Belleville St
Open: daily
☎ (604) 387-3701

Parks

Pacific Rim National Park
PO Box 280
Ucluelet
BC V0R 3A0
☎ (604) 726-7721
Open all year but interpretive centre from mid-March to mid-October

Cape Scott Provincial Park
67km (42 miles) west of Port Hardy
☎ (604) 248-3931

Strathcona Provincial Park
via Hwy 28
☎ (604) 248-3931

Ferry Services

BC Ferries
☎ Vancouver (604)669-1211
Victoria (604) 386-3431

Tsawwassen (Vancouver) to Swartz Bay (Victoria)
Summer sailings hourly on the hour, starting at 7am, crossing time 95 minutes. There can be queues in peak periods

Horseshoe Bay (West Vancouver) to Nanaimo
Sailings every two hours from 7am, crossing time 95 mins

Comox to Powell River
Four sailings daily, crossing time 4 hours

Saltery Bay to Earls Cove
Nine sailings daily in summer, eight in winter, sailing time 50 minutes

Langdale to Horseshoe Bay (West Vancouver)
Eight sailings daily, crossing time 40 minutes

Tsawwassen (Vancouver) to Nanaimo
Eight sailings daily, starting at 8am
Crossing time 2 hours

Port Hardy to Prince Rupert
Sailings every other day late May to 30 September , twice weekly in May, once weekly the rest of year. Sailing time 15 hours. One way passenger fare in peak season, approximately $100; for car, driver and passenger approximately $400. Fares are lower between September and May.

Prince Rupert to Skidegate (Queen Charlotte Islands)
Four to five sailings weeky from each port in summer, three weekly rest of year, crossing time 8 hours

Tourist Information Offices

Queen Charlotte Islands
Queen Charlotte InfoCentre
Box 337
Queen Charlotte BC
V0T 1S0
☎ (604) 559-4742

Sunshine Coast
Tourism Association of Southwestern BC
Suite 304
828 West 8th Avenue
Vancouver BC
V5Z 1E2
☎ (604) 876-3088

Vancouver Island
Tourism Association of Vancouver Island
Suite 302-45 Bastion Square
Victoria BC
V8W 1J1
☎ (604) 382-3551

Victoria
Travel Victoria
812 Wharf St
Victoria BC
V8W 1T3
☎ (604) 382-2127

3 • By Gold Rush Trails To The Yellowhead

Describing a circular drive from Vancouver into the centre of the province, Chapter 3 is presented in two parts. The first can easily be driven in two or three days. The second expands on this drive to take in some country that deserves at least another week. Almost all of the itinerary can be travelled by train using both Via Rail and BC Rail services. Rail passenger traffic is very heavy in summer, so bookings, (especially if sleeper accommodation is required) should be made up to six months in advance.

Via Sea & Sky

This journey covers approximately 400km (250 miles) on a circular route from Vancouver through the Southern Coast Mountains. It provides plenty of scope to explore on foot or horseback, by canoe, and sometimes all-terrain vehicles. For so short a distance the countryside is unusually varied. Leaving Vancouver along the picturesque shoreline of Howe Sound, you will enter a region of lush coastal rainforest. Later, passing through the mountains, the climate changes and you are into a hot, dry ranching region. Turning south, the route continues down the Fraser Valley, with its memories of gold miners and road and railway builders, before reaching Hope and connecting with the routes described in Chapter 1. Detours and diversions will add distance to this itinerary. BC Rail will take you along the route as far as Lillooet, after which it goes on to Quesnel and Prince George (see page 69).

Leaving Vancouver via Hwy 99 (the Sea-to-Sky Hwy) it is 65km (40 miles) to **Squamish**. In a scenic alpine setting, overshadowed by snow-capped peaks, this is a lumbering centre where huge log booms are assembled for towing to Vancouver-area mills. Regular vacationers to the region know it as the gateway, via paved road, to **Garibaldi Provincial Park**, a 1,958 sq km (756 sq mile) wilderness park which takes its name from 2,678m (8,786ft) Mt Garibaldi and the 3,000m (9,800ft) deep lake created when a long-ago lava flow formed a dam. This beautiful park embraces mountain peaks, meadows smothered in alpine flowers, streams and lakes, all dominated by a series of unusual volcanic rock formations of which the most prominent is called Black Tusk. Black bears and grizzlies, mountain goats, deer, wolverines and martins, along with golden eagles and plenty of other birdlife to please the watchers, all inhabit this park. You'll have to take a hike to see them though, because vehicles are not allowed inside its boundaries and access is limited to five trail heads encompassing various segments of the park.

A further 75km (47 miles) along Hwy 99, on the northwestern side of Garibaldi Provincial Park, **Whistler** is not considered *Off the Beaten Track* by the hoards of winter visitors who come for some of Canada's best skiing on Whistler and Blackcomb Mountains. Between them they have a total of 117 ski runs, up to 11km (7 miles) long. Helicopters take experienced skiers to snowfields atop nearby glaciers. Resort facilities include lodges, condominiums and pensions, as well as a full-service campground for RVs. The complex's hub has swimming pools and health clubs, shops, restaurants, bars and night clubs.

Late spring through early fall visitors to Whistler find a quieter scene. It is not every day you can go from Cloud Nine to Seventh Heaven in a few hours, but that is the invitation here in summer when ski lifts are practically empty and mountains (including the above named) are so sparsely populated that you can walk for miles in alpine meadows without meeting another person. Local hotels and restaurants will pack a picnic lunch for hikers. Helicopters will take you further afield for a picnic and walk around an alpine lake, then collect you again at a designated time. River rafting, horseback riding, golf and tennis, mountain biking down the ski trails, windsurfing, kayaking and fishing are just some summer pursuits designed to make Whistler a year-round resort. Music festivals and mountain top concerts, a jazz festival and street performers provide lighthearted entertainment. Walking trails start in the village, day excursions are easily arranged, and rail transportation is available daily from North Vancouver. There is actually little need for a car during your stay at Whistler.

While the road from Vancouver to Whistler is heavily travelled, the continuation is definitely *Off the Beaten Track*. It is about 32km (20 miles) via Hwy 99 from Whistler to ***Pemberton***, an agricultural community and a mecca for hikers, campers and fishermen. From here it is about 100km (62 miles) to Lillooet. Along the way **Mount Currie** is a Salish Indian reservation where traditional woven baskets are sought-after souvenirs. This community springs to life each

May when it holds its rodeo. Leaving Mount Currie, continue on Hwy 99, which is the Duffey Lake road skirting the Joffre Lakes Recreation Area and then Duffey Lake's southern shore. Here you have beautiful picture-postcard views of the Joffre Glacier, alpine meadows and lakes. Without a doubt it is some of the most majestic scenery in western Canada. A side trip could be to D'Arcy, part of which is open only in summer and is best suited to four-wheel-drive vehicles. This is the old Douglas Trail between Langley and Lillooet used by gold miners until the Cariboo Road was constructed. Just west of Lillooet, Seton Lake has heady views of mountains reflected in the deep blue-green waters which are especially unforgettable at sunset.

At the foot of the Cascade Mountains on the west bank of the Fraser River, **Lillooet** is a village (population 1,800) in an area with a large aboriginal population. During the 1850s gold rush, it was a major staging post for miners who came this far by river on their way to the interior. It was also terminus of the Cariboo Road until the section through the Fraser Canyon was built. The main street here is one reminder of its past, in that it was made wide enough for a twenty-oxen wagon team to turn around without backing up. Another is the Bridge of 23 Camels, named after a prospector who imported camels to carry his mining equipment. Although a great success as beasts of burden, their smell was so over-powering that they were set loose to fend for themselves. Modern Lillooet is a 'pull out' point for rafting trips down the Fraser River. The area has the largest collection of Indian rock paintings in western Canada. Directions to these can be had from the Lillooet Travel InfoCentre.

The route to Lytton down the Fraser River Valley follows the original section of the Cariboo Road (now Hwy 12) southeast to Lytton, a distance of 64km (40 miles). While this narrow, twisting road makes driving a little difficult, the views are worth the effort. This is sagebrush country where ranchers still ride horseback to tend their cattle. Since irrigation brought cultivation to the valley, you will see parts of the countryside covered with arbours shading ginseng, a Canadian plant which sells well in the Orient. It takes three or four years to mature, but when harvested brings up to $80,000 per hectare ($200,000 per acre.)

Lytton, another staging post and supply centre for the gold fields, stands at the forks where the clear glacier-fed waters of the Thompson River are swallowed by the muddy Fraser. Named after Sir Edward Bulwer-Lytton, the nineteenth-century British politician and novelist (he wrote *The Last Days of Pompeii*), it is a village (population 430) of pleasant tree-lined streets, recognized as one of the warmest and driest spots in Canada. Fishing here is excellent, especially for steelhead trout. With eighteen major rapids on the Thompson River to the north of town, it is one of the country's major white-water rafting centres. River rafting trips can last anywhere from a few hours to several days. (One company is listed in the Accommodation & Eating Out section.) The area has several resorts. It is a further 105km (65 miles) to Hope, where our route joins the Trans-Canada Hwy and the previous itinerary.

The stretch between Lytton and Hope is packed with memories of the Gold Rush era. Jackass Mountain used to be called 'Hill of Despair' by the prospectors having to climb it. Its Jackass name is from all the mules employed in hauling loads up this steep incline. Now it simply affords some very fine river views. In this region the road and railways are cut into a series of tunnels, driven through bluffs that once forced travellers to cling to perilous ledges and platforms overhanging the river below. Nobody seems to know why the two railway lines cross the canyon via massive bridges to exchange sides.

At **Hell's Gate** the Fraser River pushes twice Niagara Falls' volume through a canyon only 36m (118ft) wide, but 180m (590ft) deep. The name was given by early pioneers to the swirling waters at this point. When the gap was narrowed even more by rock slides during railway construction, hundreds of thousands of migrating salmon who pass this way each year found it an impossible challenge. Now, concrete 'ladders' slow down the flow to give the salmon a fighting chance. An airtram takes visitors 153m (500ft) into the canyon where a footbridge spans the rushing waters. A restaurant is located at the base, as well as a visitor centre in which the salmon's life cycle is explained.

Spuzzum, where the Alexandra Bridge takes you across the river, is the site of a cairn commemorating the Royal Engineers who built the Cariboo Road (see page 65) and who named the original bridge here in honour of the Princess of Wales, later King Edward VII's Queen.

Yale was the site of a fur-trading post built in 1848. Ten years later when gold was found in the river-bed gravel it became a boom town of 2,000, with stern-wheelers coming and going, outfitters, boarding houses and gambling halls. Later it was southern terminus of the Cariboo Road, and then an important railway construction link. When the line was completed in 1885, Yale was left to become a virtual ghost town. Plaques now record its colourful past.

Summer skiers on Blackcomb (Chapter 3)

A glacier in Garibaldi Park (Chapter 3)

Trail riders setting off near Pemberton (Chapter 3)

For something more tangible, visit the 1859 Anglican church of St John the Divine, the oldest church in British Columbia to remain on its original site. A further 32km (20 miles) brings you to Hope, (described on pages 41-2) from where you can return to Vancouver.

The Gold Rush Trail

This itinerary extends the route described above, taking you further north into the centre of British Columbia. It starts at Lytton or Lillooet, goes northward to Williams Lake, Quesnel, (with side trips to the restored gold rush town of Barkerville, and for outdoors lovers to Bowron Lake Park), on to Prince George, then east to Tête Jaune Cache between the Cariboo and Rocky Mountain Ranges. If you include a side trip to Mt Robson, you can connect with a tour of Alberta's Rocky Mountains described in Chapter 9. Returning south, it follows the Thompson River to Clearwater and Wells Gray Park, then to Kamloops to connect with the itineraries described in Chapters 1 and 5.

The first section of this itinerary follows the path of the original Cariboo Road, built between Lillooet and later Yale to the gold fields at Barkerville. The 'rush' started when Indians went into the Hudson's Bay Company's posts to trade the gold flakes and nuggets that they had found in the Cariboo's streams and river beds. By 1858 the news was out. Miners and adventurers rushed in from California, eventually coming from as far away as Europe, Australia and China.

The government, wanting fast yet reliable access from the head of navigation on the Fraser River to the interior, decided to put a wagon road through the Fraser River Canyon. A contingent of British Royal Engineers under Colonel R. C. Moodie surveyed the 650km (400 mile) route, then built the most difficult sections themselves and left the rest to private contractors. Construction, which took two years, was completed in 1864. Anyone driving this section of what is now the Trans-Canada Hwy cannot fail to be impressed by the work of those military engineers.

The journey from Lytton takes you through hilly semi-arid ranching country where cowboys tend their cattle on horseback. **Spences Bridge** is 37km (23 miles) north at the point where the Nicola River flows into the fast-flowing Thompson. Fishing is excellent in the Nicola, and some of the region's large cattle ranches accept guests. At Spences Bridge, the Steelhead Inn has comfortable lodgings and an attractive indoor/outdoor restaurant. It is said to be British Columbia's oldest inn.

Continuing north through the granite slopes of the Thompson River valley with the Canadian National Railway on one bank and the Canadian Pacific's main line on the other, you come to **Ashcroft**, site of some of the world's largest open-pit copper mines. Tours are available. Brothers Henry and Clement Cornwall established a ranch, provision store and roadhouse here in 1863 and named it Ashcroft after their home in England. They introduced many English traditions, including fox hunting for which they substituted coyotes for foxes, and were well known for their hospitality. Clement later became Lieutenant Governor of British Columbia. A fire in 1943 destroyed the original Ashcroft Manor; a replica now contains regional displays and a tearoom. The Ashcroft Museum portrays southern Cariboo history, its aboriginal peoples, and the settlers who came here in the 1880s.

It is 50km (31 miles) in all from Spences Bridge to **Cache Creek**, a trading centre long before Europeans arrived in the 1860s. This was a stagecoach stop on the Cariboo Road, as were **100 Mile House** and **150 Mile House** to the north. If you are travelling by train, you will stop at **Williams Lake** a further 14km (9 miles) north. This is a logging and mining centre, and ranchers bring their cattle here to the province's largest cattle stockyard. The Williams Lake Stampede, which attracts 5,000 visitors over the first weekend in July, is acknowledged as one of Canada's best rodeo events.

Off the Beaten Track motorists will savour the 457km (284 mile) drive from Williams Lake via Hwy 20 (the Chilcotin Hwy) across the Chilcotin Plateau, through **Tweedsmuir Park** and down the valley to **Bella Coola** at the head of the North Bentinck Arm of the Pacific Ocean. Alexander Mackenzie arrived here in 1793 and a fur-trading post was established in 1828, but it is still a sparsely populated region, where ranching, mining and logging are the main occupations. You will find a vast panorama of boulder-strewn plains and cattle spreads, including the huge Saudi-owned Gang Ranch. Great forests of jack pines, and lakes and rivers teaming with fish are back-dropped by snow-capped mountains. Residents of the area (more than half are from various native reserves) are rugged individualists who delight in their isolation.

Spread over 9,942 sq km (3,840 sq miles) Tweedsmuir is British Columbia's largest provincial park. It was named after Lord Tweedsmuir, who was Canada's Governor General between 1935 and 1940, and perhaps better known as John Buchan, author of *The Thirty-Nine Steps*. The park offers plenty of camping, canoeing, and horseback riding. Also limited accommodation, with more at Bella

Coola and nearby Hagensborg. There is not a single traffic light on the Chilcotin Hwy. Large sections are gravelled and drivers will encounter huge logging and supply trucks, so be prepared to drive defensively. Remember too that it is a prudent driver who fills his vehicle's fuel tank when given the opportunity.

Returning to the main itinerary, 120km (75 miles) north from Williams Lake brings you to **Quesnel**, named by Simon Fraser after a companion in his famous 1808 expedition. In 1860 Quesnel became a river port en route to the Cariboo goldfields and the town became so important it was a candidate in the bid to become capital of British Columbia. For this, and more historical data, follow the river walk past a series of exhibits which explain all. Today Quesnel (population 8,000) is a centre for forest products, mining, ranching and tourism. Hunting and fishing are terrific here and if you want to play cowboy, do contact one of the area's several ranches that take paying guests. (The Cariboo Tourist Association can supply names of local dude ranches.) Quesnel is a major BC Rail stop with plenty of accommodation. Two hotels are listed in the Accommodation & Eating Out section of this book, and Ten Mile Lake Provincial Park on Hwy 97 has a campground suitable for RVs.

A little north of Quesnel turn east on the Barkerville Hwy (Hwy 26) for the scenic 80km (50 mile) drive into the Cariboo Mountains and two of interior British Columbia's biggest attractions, namely Barkerville and Bowron Lakes Park.

A short distance along Hwy 26, **Cottonwood House** was built in 1864 as a roadhouse to accommodate travellers on the Cariboo Road. Considered one of the best on the road, and operated until the early 1950s, it is now restored and furnished as a museum to the gold-rush period. **Wells**, named after a prospector who discovered gold here in the 1930s, grew to a population of 3,000, but since the mine closed in 1967 it has dwindled to less than 300. Still, Wells is worth your time, and film, since the false-fronted buildings reflect its earlier life as a prosperous mining town.

Barkerville Historic Park is one of western Canada's finest recreated communities designed to bring history to life. Approximately seventy-five buildings are restored or reconstructed to resemble the originals that were here in the 1870s, when Barkerville became the largest of three goldfield towns on Williams Creek. It is named after Billy Barker, the Cornish canal worker turned sailor who joined the California gold rush and then came to try his luck in the Cariboo. Barker and his companions staked an already discarded claim. As fellow prospectors derided their folly, Barker and his pals dug down 16m (52ft) where they struck pay dirt. As one would expect, other miners rushed in to stake their claims nearby, and soon a settlement had grown. Over four years, Barker's shaft yielded $600,000, at a time when gold brought $16 per ounce. In all the Cariboo produced $50 million in gold.

During its boom years, Barkerville had close to 3,000 inhabitants. As well as miners there were resident builders, merchants, bankers, saloon keepers, entertainers, gamblers and preachers — in essence all the characters that the movies have led us to expect of a wild frontier town. Hotels and bunk houses accommodated them, saloons, dance halls, and a theatre (often with acts imported from Europe) entertained them. There was even a race course. A church took care of spiritual needs, and cemetery headstones now tell of many who never returned to their family homes. The Chinese had their own community within the town. The province's Chief Justice, Baillie Begbie, enforced a fair but swift form of law and order, assisted by John Bowron, one of the original Overlanders (see page 70) who first became constable here, then gold commissioner.

After close to twenty years the gold was exhausted, and most of the miners drifted away from the Cariboo. Some stayed to become ranchers, farmers and lumbermen. Barker married a widow who left him once his money was spent, and he died a pauper in Victoria thirty years later. The legendary Begbie, who enjoyed a long and distinguished legal career in British Columbia, received a knighthood from Queen Victoria. Bowron gave his name to our next destination.

At Barkerville's reception centre you can learn about mining techniques, community life in the Cariboo and the impact of the gold discoveries on British Columbia generally. Among the restored or reconstructed buildings are hotels, stores, the assay office, restaurants and cafes, a schoolhouse and church. Actors play their roles admirably portraying the town's prominent — though not always entirely respectable — citizens. Regular services are conducted in St Saviour's Anglican Church, while its minister conducts interesting tours of the cemetery. Restaurant menus include typical miner's fare as well as Chinese dishes. You can try your hand at panning for gold, and may even find a few grains. Incidentally, if you have a sense of *déjà vu* it could be that you have seen Barkerville in a movie or television show, since it is used often as an authentic locale for filming.

While Barkerville Provincial Park has some tenting and RV facilities, the larger **Bowron Lakes Park**, about 25km (15 miles) to the east has more. Among outdoors enthusiasts, this is one of British Columbia's best loved parks. Canoeists come from all over the world to follow the 116km (72 miles) of water and portage trails through stunning wilderness which takes in a chain of ten lakes. These long, fjord-like lakes, so perfect for canoeing, provide an undisturbed habitat for moose, black and grizzly bears and bald eagles. There are campsites and cabins along the seven to ten day circuit. Portages require that those who attempt it be physically fit and well prepared. The Canadian Recreational Canoeing Association (address in Canada Fact File) conducts safaris with experienced guides. Their base camp is at Kruger Lake just outside the park's northern boundary. At an elevation of 975m (3,200ft) in a very picturesque setting, the camp has dormitory-style accommodation reminiscent of that used by trappers, traders and prospectors who once came this way. Canoeists travelling independently can set up their own camp along the route. In winter cross-country ski and snowshoe enthusiasts follow the same route. Because access to the trail is limited, it is best to make advance reservations (especially in July and August.) The park address is given in the Additional Information.

After Barkerville and Bowron Lakes Park, return to Hwy 97 and continue north through the gentle hills of British Columbia's vast central plateau, scattered with ranches and small settlements. A further 102km (63 miles) brings you to **Prince George** (population 73,000), capital of northern British Columbia and a major transportation centre. Simon Fraser established a fur-trading post here in 1807 and the Overlanders (see page 70) passed through on their way to the goldfields in 1862. However it was the arrival of the railways in the early 1900s that led to the forest products industries on which Prince George thrives today. The city has urban attractions and hotels in various price ranges, as well as campgrounds with facilities for RVs. Airlines, rail and bus services connect here. It is also a convenient centre for outdoors activities, with fishing, hunting and wildlife safaris in particular.

The route east of Prince George follows the Yellowhead Hwy along the Fraser River 266km (165 miles) to Tête Jaune Cache. This route is one long scenic drive, passing through prosperous ranching country, forests and brilliant green meadows towards the jagged peaks of the Rockies. Should you decide to stay for a bit, you will see signs indicating B & B accommodation in local homes. At the tiny community of Tête Jaune Cache, you turn south along Hwy 5.

However, by continuing on a short distance from Tête Jaune Cache you will come to **Mount Robson Park**. Towering Mount Robson, at 3,954m (12,972ft), is the highest peak in the Canadian Rockies. This glorious 2,170 sq km (838 sq mile) park has mountain peaks permanently draped in snow, vast forests and deep canyons, icy lakes and rushing rivers. The Yellowhead Pass which leads to Jasper (see pages 137-40) is on the park's border with Jasper National Park. Tête Jaune, or Yellowhead, is named after a light-haired Iroquois guide and trapper who stored his furs in this area. The pass through the Rockies is lower than those to the south and was used by the Overlanders, a party of eastern Canadians who took this overland route to the Cariboo gold fields. They arrived there after unbelievable hardship. Another group took the route described in this itinerary, finally arriving at Fort Kamloops.

Driving Hwy 5 south to follow the North Thompson River Valley, you will arrive at **Valemount**, gateway to a four-season recreational area with cross-country skiing, heli-skiing, river rafting, wildlife safaris and water sports on nearby Lake Kinbasket as seasonal options. From here the 215km (133 mile) drive south to Clearwater takes you away from the mountains through areas of forested hills and open meadowlands, as colourful as an artist's palette in spring when the wild flowers bloom.

Clearwater is gateway to **Wells Grey Provincial Park**, a 5,153 sq km (2,000 sq mile) preserve of enormous scenic variety. It is a region of high mountain peaks, glaciers and waterfalls of which Helmcken Falls (135m, 443ft) is its most awesome. Climbing the cinder slopes of Pyramid Mountain is an unusual experience, rewarded by awe-inspiring views from the peak. In summer, the Trophy Mountains' alpine meadows are ablaze with wild flowers. Wildlife watching can bag you a grizzly bear or moose, and some of the 220 species of birds living within the park. Although this park is mostly wilderness, accessible only by hiking trails and canoe routes, RV facilities are available beside the Clearwater River. There is some accommodation inside the park, and in Clearwater and neighbouring communities. White-water rafting, canoeing and horseback expeditions are organized within the park. Certified guides are available. (One organization providing such services is listed in the Accommodation & Eating Out section. Names of others can be obtained from the High Country Tourism Association.)

Continue south for 125km (77 miles) through more meadows and hay fields in the broad North Thompson River Valley and you will reach **Kamloops** (population 75,000) at the confluence of the

FOREST FIRES

Every summer, Canada's news media brings audiences face-to-face with that awesomely destructive and sometimes fatal phenomenon: the forest fire. To Off the Beaten Track travellers, such fires may mean a hasty change of plans.

When it is hot and dry, hundreds of fires can be burning across the country at any one time. Communities are evacuated. Fire fighters use water bombers and chemicals to contain the conflagrations as they wait for rain or at least a wind shift. Inevitably someone adds up the tremendous cost.

Fire caused by lightning strikes has been a fact of life in the forest since time began. The effect was good and bad, in an essential part of the life cycle. As charred land recovered, fast-growing plants sprang up to attract forest creatures (including deer and moose) to feed on the abundant greenery. Slower-growing trees, including some with seeds that can only regenerate after a fire, gradually took over. Eventually their shade again reduced the undergrowth, causing larger animals to move out. Squirrels and their small friends remained — until the next fire.

Now humans have changed all that. Their carelessness causes about two thirds of all forest fires. Because these fires threaten fields and commercial forests, communities and recreational areas for hundreds of miles, they have to be controlled. Fire prevention is a constant preoccupation of forest staff. Hill-top towers and forestry planes, even satellites keep watch. Residents keep anxious vigil. Roadside warnings tell motorists the current degree of fire hazard.

If the danger is high, campfires may be prohibited. You may even find the way to your planned campground barred, so it is a good idea to have an alternative in mind. Pack a gas-fired stove in your gear. Even when the fire danger is minimal, try to build your fire in a pit if one is provided, on sand or an exposed rock, but never on moss. Make absolutely sure any camp-fire you light is thoroughly dowsed before you leave.

North and South Thompson Rivers. The name Kamloops, meaning 'meeting of the waters', was given by the Shuswap people who had lived here for 7,000 years when American traders established Fort Kamloops in 1812. When employees of both the Hudson's Bay

Company and the North West Company arrived, their presence led to at least one bloody skirmish. Area grasslands provided good fodder for pack horses, making the fort an important way-station on routes used by fur traders and later by gold prospectors. With increased traffic, it became a river port served by stern-wheeled steamers. As the Canadian Pacific Railway pushed through this region in 1880 it brought in countless Chinese labourers who worked and lived under terrible conditions. Many are buried here in their own cemetery, which because of its traditional layout is unique in Canada and has become a heritage site.

The lively yet informative Kamloops Museum features area history dating back to this region's first inhabitants. It also has a reconstruction of the original Hudson's Bay Company fort. Kamloops has scheduled airline services and bus connections and is a stop on Via Rail's trans-continental passenger service. There is a good selection of hotels and campgrounds, some of which we have listed.

From Kamloops, you may choose to drive east along the Trans-Canada Hwy (Hwy 1) to **Salmon Arm** and **Sicamous** and join up with the Okanagan Valley route described in Chapter 5. Or, you can return to Vancouver via the fast Coquihalla Highway (Hwy 5), a 250km (152 mile) toll-road which joins the Trans-Canada Hwy at **Hope**.

Additional Information

— By Gold Rush Trails To The Yellowhead —

Places to Visit

Ashcroft
Ashcroft Museum
4th and Brink St
Open: daily July-August, Monday to Friday rest of year
☎ (604) 453-9232

Barkerville
Barkerville Historic Town
Open: daily
☎ (604) 994-3332

Hell's Gate Canyon
Hell's Gate Airtram
Boston Bar
Trans-Canada Hwy at Hell's Gate
Open: daily April to mid-October
☎ (604) 867-9277

Kamloops
Kamloops Museum and Archives
207 Seymour St
Open: daily
☎ (604) 828-3576

Parks

Barkerville Provincial Park
Barkerville
☎ (604) 565-6270

Bowron Lakes Provincial Park,
100km east of Hwy 97 at Quesnel
c/o 540 Borland St
Williams Lake BC
V2G 1R8
☎ (604) 398-4414

Mount Robson Park
Hwy 16, west of Jasper National Park
c/o Box 579
Valemount BC
V0E 2Z0
☎ (604) 566-4325

Tweedsmuir Provincial Park
440km west of Williams Lake via Hwy 20
mailing address and telephone as Bowron Lakes Park

Wells Grey Provincial Park
40km north of Clearwater
c/o 1210 McGill Rd
Kamloops BC
V2C 6N6
☎ (604) 828-4494

Tourist Information Offices
Section of itinerary west of Bowron Lakes
Cariboo Tourist Association
Box 4900
Williams Lake BC
V2G 2V8
☎ (604) 392-2226

Eastern section of itinerary
High Country Tourist Association
Box 962
Kamloops BC
V2C 6H1
☎ (604) 372-7770

Lillooet
Lillooet Infocentre
790 Main St
Lillooet BC
V0K 1V0
☎ (604) 256-4308

4 • The Fabulous North

This itinerary starts in Prince Rupert as a continuation of the drive up Vancouver Island and ferry trip north described in Chapter 2. It takes you inland to Prince George, across the northern section of British Columbia where it connects with the itinerary described in Chapter 3. An alternative after leaving Prince George is to travel by air or bus to Whitehorse for a tour of the Yukon Territory described in Chapter 7. In northern BC filling stations are not necessarily there when you need one, so it is prudent to get fuel when the opportunity presents itself. Also, if you plan any off-the-road adventures, be sure to include a good repellant among your supplies. Biting insects can be by far the most prevalent form of wildlife encountered.

Although **Prince Rupert** was named after the Hudson's Bay Company's first Governor, it was established only in the early 1900s when it became the terminus of the predecessor to the Canadian National Railway. It was intended to rival Vancouver as a major Trans-Pacific port, but although the railway arrived the expected boom never materialized (and the town's founder perished on the *Titanic*). However Prince Rupert did become an important base for construction of the Alaska Hwy and a World War II shipbuilding centre.

Now the city (population 16,000) has pulp and paper mills, and calling itself the 'Halibut Capital of the World', it is a major fishing centre with a fleet of around 2,000 boats. The modern, efficient port exports coal, lumber and grain brought by rail from the interior. Kaien Island, on which Prince Rupert is located, has been home to native peoples for 5,000 years and was once the meeting place for Tsimshian and Haida bands. Now city parks preserve totem poles and other relics of this heritage. The Museum of Northern British Columbia contains displays on native culture as well as developments since arrival of the first fur traders and pioneers. And about 15km (9 miles) south of the city, the North Pacific Cannery Village Fishing Museum at **Port Edward** is a restoration of one of 200 remote cannery complexes which dotted this coast around the turn of the century. Visitor accommodation here matches all budgets. Be warned, though, Prince Rupert also describes itself as the 'City of Rainbows', which is a way of saying you can expect rain.

Leaving via Hwy 16 (the Yellowhead Hwy), our route takes you along the super-scenic Skeena River Valley called by local aboriginals 'The River of Mists'. Although the first section is in a broad valley, you will never lose sight of 2,000m (6,000ft) high snow-topped mountains in the distance on either side of the highway.

Terrace is 160km (100 miles) from Prince Rupert and has accommodation, restaurants and other facilities, including the first filling station you will encounter on this road. Named after the natural terraces which form nearby river banks, this community (population 11,000) is a large recreational centre. Snowfall in the mountains to the north is the greatest in North America, providing excellent skiing in magical scenery. For an interesting diversion, take Hwy 37 south to **Lakelse Lake Provincial Park** about 16km (10 miles) from Terrace. The park has a range of recreational facilities, forested campsites suitable for RVs and a broad sandy beach around the lake. Further along, **Mount Layton Hot Springs** has a resort where guests can luxuriate in the mineral hot springs. **Kitimat** (population 11,500), a further 20km (12 miles), is the site of one of the world's largest aluminum smelters, using the area's abundant hydro-electric power to convert alumina from Australia into the silvery metal. Tours of the plant are available.

Returning to the Yellowhead Hwy and continuing east, the valley narrows as you enter a region where the Skeena surges through steep-sided rocky canyons. Particularly impressive are the Seven Sisters, a series of snow-covered peaks to the east.

At **Kitwanga** Hwy 37 (The Cassair Hwy) leads 730km (453 miles) north to Upper Laird, YT, on the Alaska Highway. Much of this road travels through wilderness country, punctuated with the occasional small settlement or ghost town, and includes some of Canada's most magnificent scenery. Fishing and wildlife viewing opportunities up here are sensational. The road is a combination of gravel and paved surfaces, conditions vary with the weather, and vehicles should be specially shielded against flying stones.

If you have the time and want to take in some indescribably beautiful scenery, consider a 440km (273 mile) excursion along a paved section of the highway as far as **Meziadin Junction** and then, past the foot of the majestic robin-egg blue Bear Glacier to **Stewart**. This town is at the head of the 150km (93 mile) long Portland Canal,

DRIVING IN THE FAR NORTH

When driving a rented vehicle, make sure that the rental agreement and insurance cover include driving on highways in the far north. Advise the rental company of your itinerary and, if possible, have headlights, radiators and gas tanks suitably shielded against flying gravel. Have at least five good tires, as well as spare fan belts and cooling system hoses.

Canada's northern highways are exceptional pieces of engineering, designed to connect communities year-round, but while long stretches have paved surfaces, there are gravelled sections as well. The steeply sloping sides of berms — sometimes over 2m (6ft) high, they carry roads over permafrost to prevent melting — call for extra vigilance. In early winter and spring, river ferry services are disrupted by melting ice.

Before setting off along a highway in the far north, check at available information booths for up-to-date advice on road conditions.

If your vehicle is not equipped with daytime running lights, use your headlights at all times.

You will be sharing the road with very large truck-trains, so be prepared to drive defensively, slowing down when meeting oncoming traffic and overtaking with care.

Driving on gravel calls for special attention. Be prepared for reduced visibility caused by dust, and for flying stones which can damage windshields and headlights. When driving through dust, close windows, open vents and turn the fan to defrost.

Refuel when you can, and heed highway signs telling you the distance to the next filling station (frustratingly, the sign is usually placed just past the last station). Book overnight en-route accommodation in advance.

Because of the enormously long distances to be covered, drivers must guard against fatigue and boredom. Stopping for a rest and refreshment every two hours or so is a good idea. Since radio reception is limited, take along audio tapes of favourite music and perhaps a talking book or two.

a fjord forming part of the border between British Columbia and Alaska. Stewart has a boom-and-bust history based on gold, silver and copper mining, but lumbering and mining are major industries here now. It has been the location for a number of Hollywood movies. Tourists come for the scenery and the wildlife. Surrounded by towering mountains which rise directly from the ocean, the fjord offers scenery so very majestic it appears unreal. Approaching Stewart, some twenty glaciers are visible at one time along the mountain peaks. You will see lots of mountain goats here, as well as porcupines sauntering along the roadside behind their protective quills. During the summer at Fish Creek, bald eagles and families of bears compete for the salmon catch (remember to keep out of their way.) The fishing, needless to say, is superb, for Dolly Varden and steelhead trout in freshwater streams; cod, halibut and chinook salmon in salt water.

It is 43km (27 miles) from Kitwanga to **New Hazleton**, a town dominated by the snow-capped peaks of the Rocher Déboulé Mountains. This was originally a Gitksan Indian dwelling-place, occupied 8,000 years ago and known as *Git-an-maks* or 'the place where people fish by torchlight.' European settlers who arrived in 1872 named it after the hazelnut trees growing in the rich soil. In the 1870s it became a river-port serving the nearby Omineca gold-diggings. When railway construction started in this area, two other Hazletons were established by speculators who gambled that their community would be selected for a station. New Hazelton was the winner and became a communications centre. The original (now Old) Hazelton, at the junction of the Bulkley and Skeena Rivers about 8km (5 miles) to the north, has retained its 1890s pioneer architecture. There is a South Hazleton too.

The Hazeltons' main attraction is **'Ksan Village**, an authentic reconstructed Gitksan village which is best understood by joining one of the guided tours. Here, you will learn how the people used to live by hunting and fishing, leaving themselves plenty of time to develop a rich culture which included colourful ceremonies with song and dance. Contact with Europeans had already eroded this culture when well-meaning missionaries and government officials banned their 'pagan' ceremonies and dances, destroyed their buildings and carefully carved totems. The village now recalls native life during those earlier times. Traditional cedar plank methods were used to build tribal long-houses, a carving school and workshop, museum, crafts shop and reception centre. Native carvers produce totems and other artifacts here now. On Friday evenings in summer the villagers present a program of traditional song and dance and perform the ancient ceremonies of their ancestors.

Accommodation is fairly limited in New Hazelton, so reservations should be made in advance if you plan on staying overnight.

Camping, including RV facilities are available at 'Ksan Village. An alternative is the campground at **Seely Lake Provincial Park**, where vertical snow-capped mountains are reflected in the lake.

Driving eastward from the Hazeltons, the highway follows the Bulkley River, continuing on Hwy 16 across the interior of British Columbia. The **Moricetown Indian Reserve** has been inhabited for 5,000 years, for reasons which become obvious to passing motorists. Visible from the highway here, a 500m (1,640ft) wide river narrows into a canyon before plunging over a 60m (200ft) drop into a pool renowned for its fishing. During the summer and autumn salmon runs, teams of residents can be seen gaffing these very large fish as they fight their way upstream. You can join them in the fishing for a small fee, or buy some ready caught fish, cleaned and ready to cook, or smoked for consumption later.

Smithers (population 5,000) was a stop on early fur trade routes. In 1865 it became a construction centre of the Collins Overland Telegraph, a line intended to connect the United States to Europe largely overland through Siberia, Alaska and the Northwest Territories. The Atlantic cable rendered it obsolete immediately but manager Colonel C. S. Bulkley gave his name to the river. In 1913 the Grand Trunk Railway established a switching point here, and named the town after one of its directors. Surrounded by the Babine Mountains, this town has developed an Alpine theme. It offers year-round skiing and is a centre for mountain climbing, trail riding, rockhounding and fishing for salmon and steelhead. **Hudson Bay Mountain Recreation Area** has summertime hiking in the flower-splashed alpine meadows as well as superb skiing during winter. **Driftwood Canyon Provincial Park**, 17km (11 miles) northeast of the town, preserves beds of insect and plant fossils. **Tyhee Provincial Park**, beside Tyhee Lake has a beach, camping and boating facilities and float-planes can be chartered for those who wish to participate in some remote fly-in fishing.

About 65km (40 miles) east of Smithers, **Houston** is nestled between the snow-wrapped Babine and Telkwa Mountains where the Bulkley and Morice Rivers meet. In consequence the town can rightfully claim to have one of British Columbia's most beautiful settings. Fishing is excellent here, especially for the fabled fighting steelheads. Canoeing is popular. Hiking, too, but hikers should keep an eye out for bears and wolverines. At **Topley**, 30km (19 miles) to the east, a side road leads north to the 177km (110 mile) long **Babine Lake**, British Columbia's largest freshwater lake, known for its trophy-sized trout, salmon and Rocky Mountain whitefish.

Topley and **Red Bluff Provincial Parks** provide access to the lake, while Red Bluff Park has camping facilities suitable for RVs. **Burns Lake** and **Fraser Lake** are among the communities along this stretch of highway which offer fishing, hiking and more camping opportunities.

Approximately 65km (40 miles) north of **Vanderhoof** via Hwy 27, **Fort St James** dates from 1806 when Simon Fraser established a trading post near a Carrier Indian village. In 1821 the fort became the capital of New Caledonia, a vast trading district in the interior of present-day British Columbia. A mission was built in 1843 and its church, Our Lady of Good Hope built in 1870, is one of the province's oldest churches. **Fort St James National Historic Park** has a mix of original 1880s buildings, and reconstructions of others to represent the late 1890s when the fur trade had started to decline. Enthusiastic costumed animators demonstrate day-to-day life in those times while audio-visual presentations and exhibits reflect the fort's long history. Simon Fraser's canoe route between the fort and Prince George is well travelled by modern adventurers, in part for the ample wildlife seen along the way.

Fort St James, considered the longest inhabited European settlement west of the Rocky Mountains, today has a population of 2,000. It is an air transportation centre, linking isolated lumbering and mining communities with roads and rail lines to the south. Fly-in fishing charters are a local speciality. There is some accommodation and campers and RV travellers will find sites in **Paarens Beach Provincial Park**.

It is 97km (60 miles) from Vanderhoof to **Prince George**, described on page 69. At this crossroads of northern British Columbia, the travel options are many. You can join up with the itineraries described in Chapters 3, 5 and 9 to the south or east travelling either by road or rail.

Alternatively, you can drive north on Hwy 97 to Fort St John on the Alaska Hwy, then continue through northern British Columbia to Whitehorse in the Yukon (see Chapter 7). It is 1,640km (1,020 miles) from Prince George to Whitehorse through some astonishingly varied country, which includes snowy mountains, vast forests and meadows, and innumerable lakes and rivers. You may decide to leave the driving to Greyhound Bus Lines while you sit back and enjoy the scenery. The bus journey to Whitehorse takes about 30 hours and there are at least three trips a week.

Additional Information

— The Fabulous North —

Places to Visit

Fort St James
Fort St James National Historic Park
Open: daily May to October
☎ (604) 996-7191

New Hazleton
'Ksan Indian Village
6km (4 miles) north of Hwy 16 at New Hazelton
Open: daily mid-May to mid-October, closed Tuesday and Wednesday rest of year
☎ (604) 842-5544

Port Edward
North Pacific Cannery Village Fishing Museum
1889 Skeena Dr
Open: daily mid-May to mid-September
☎ (604) 628-3538

Prince Rupert
Museum of Northern British Columbia
1st Ave and McBride St
Open: daily mid-May to Labour Day, closed Sunday rest of year
☎ (604) 624-3207

Parks

Lakelse Lake Provincial Park
c/o Bag 5000
Smithers BC
V0J 2NO
☎ (604) 847-7320

Paarens Beach Provincial Park
Near Fort St James
c/o Box 2045
4051 18 Ave
Prince George BC
V2N 2J6
☎ (604) 565-6340

Seeley Lake Provincial Park
Hwy 16, south of South Hazelton
☎ (604) 847-7322

Tourist Information Offices

For the entire region:
North by Northwest Tourism Association
Box 1030
Smithers BC
V0J 2N0
☎ (604) 847-5227

Prince Rupert
Prince Rupert Travel Infocentre
1st Ave and McBride St
Box 669
Prince Rupert BC
V8J 3S1
☎ (604) 624-5637

Seton Lake (Chapter 3)

Airtram over Hell's Gate in Fraser Canyon (Chapter 3)

Actors portraying everyday life in Barkerville (Chapter 3)

Driving the Dempster Highway (Chapter 4)

North-western Canada is ideal 'Off the Beaten Track' country (Chapter 4)

5 • Through Okanagan Orchards To The Rockies

This trip takes you from Hope in the Lower Fraser Valley (see page 41-2), through the Okanagan Valley and the interior mountain ranges of British Columbia to the Continental Divide which forms the border with Alberta. Although this is one of the favourite routes for travellers from Vancouver to the mountains, it nevertheless provides many opportunities for *Off the Beaten Track* diversions.

Leaving Vancouver, drive eastwards along the Trans-Canada Hwy (Hwy 1) following one of the routings described in Chapter 1. Approaching Hope, where there are a series of intersections, select Hwy 3, the Crowsnest Hwy. It is 26km (16 miles) along this highway to the west entrance of **Manning Provincial Park**, the first place of interest.

The drive within this 665 sq km (255 sq mile) park takes you from lush coastal rain forest to the interior's dry forest land, the abrupt change occurring about halfway along at Allison Pass (1,342m, 4,400ft). Manning is a park for all tastes and all seasons. Mountain climbers, hikers, nature lovers, birders, picnicking families — even gold-panners — will enjoy this park. During May and June the display of wild Pacific rhododendrons at Rhododendron Flats close to the park's west entrance is a delightful and unusual spectacle. This is one of only five locations in Canada where rhododendrons grow wild. Thriving in their native rain-forest, they are much more delicate and attractive than the cultivated varieties we have come to expect in public parks and gardens. With the rhododendrons finished, in July and August the park's sub-alpine meadows are ablaze with other wild flowers.

Travelling deeper into the park, you will come across more of its amenities. There is a resort and four campgrounds which include RV facilities as well as opportunities for wilderness camping. Cascade Lookout, accessible by road, gives majestic views of the Cascade Mountains with the Similkameen Valley below. You may want to spend a day hiking around the lakes, or a week following fur-traders' trails. And since this is the northern trailhead for the Pacific Crest Trail, truly ambitious hikers can set off on a 4,000km (2,486 mile) trek through the United States and down into Mexico. Wildlife — deer, bears and coyotes mostly — are often seen from the road. At least 160 species of birds from tiny hummingbirds to owls, hawks and falcons have been reliably reported. Grey-crowned rosy finches nest in rock crevices within the snowfields and glaciers, as do sky-blue mountain bluebirds. After leaving the park, the highway continues through countryside which is largely semi-arid but was originally rich in minerals. Mines were opened during the late nineteenth and early twentieth centuries, and communities established. When families drifted away following closure of the mines, they left some interesting ghost towns for *Off the Beaten Track* explorers. One example is **Coalmount**, on the road to **Otter Lake Provincial Park**. This used to be a railway junction for the nearby coal mines, but now there is a mere handful of homes, a general store and hotel. **Granite Creek** is so small it comes as a surprise to learn it was a community of 2,000 people during an 1890s gold-rush. **Princeton** is situated at the confluence of the Tulameen and Similkameen Rivers. It used to be called Vermilion or Red Earth Forks for the mineral ores so apparent, and long before Europeans arrived native peoples were mining red ochre here to trade with other tribes. Renamed after the Prince of Wales who visited here in 1860, this has been a mining centre for gold, copper, silver, arsenic and coal. The open pit Similco copper mine, 12km (7 miles) west of the town is a major employer still. Leaving Princeton, the road passes through 70km (43 miles) of grasslands and mountainous slopes to **Keremeos**.

This town (the name is pronounced 'care-ee-mee-oos') is surrounded by mountains, even though numerous fruitstands indicate a productive fruit-farming area. There are some vegetable and flower farms here as well as vineyards. Fur trader Alexander Ross came this way in 1811 and it became a stop on the traders' route. Later, its lush grasslands prompted the Hudson's Bay Company to erect a fort where the draft horses and oxen used on the wagon roads were pastured.

The first settlers arrived in 1860, the first commercial orchard established in the 1890s. A small provincial park nearby contains some unusual basalt columns and lava beds, while the 330 sq km (127 sq mile) **Cathedral Lakes Provincial Park** in the Cascade Mountains to the south features some truly grand alpine scenery. Here mountain lakes and meadows are brightly coloured by flowers in spring. Wildlife includes bighorn sheep and mule deer. Bird watchers come to study the golden eagles and smaller bird-life. The park has campsites as well as a commercial resort.

Turning eastwards, follow Hwy 3 for 46km (29 miles) through the Similkameen Valley to **Osoyoos**, very close to the border with the United States. (Hwy 3a is a short-cut that will take you on a 45km (28 miles) direct route to Penticton.)

The Hudson's Bay Company's supply trains passed through the Osoyoos region between 1812 and 1848. Gold prospectors who later helped open the area were followed by ranchers. In 1919 an irrigation canal brought water for agriculture and now the town, (population 3,000), is the centre of flourishing orchards and vineyards. With a climate and terrain similar to some parts of Spain, the inhabitants have selected an Iberian theme for their buildings. Despite the arid surroundings, its lake-side location gives access to 19km (12 miles) of sandy beach and one of the country's warmest lakes.

Leaving Osoyoos, the itinerary continues northward along Hwy 97 through the entire Okanagan Valley. An option is to continue eastwards along Hwy 3 to follow the Kootenays routing described in Chapter 6.

Following the present itinerary, you will drive 20km (13 miles) north on Hwy 97 to **Oliver**, situated in the so-called 'vest pocket desert' at the northern tip of the Great American Basin Desert stretching down the continent into Mexico. Except where irrigation has changed the landscape, this is a region of gentle hills covered with sage-bush and cactus, where small groups of thoroughbred cattle browse on the scant vegetation. The town was named after a premier of British Columbia who played an important role in bringing irrigation to the valley. Now, there are fruit farms and wineries here, but the still barren hillsides show what the environment was like prior to irrigation. For a closer look, follow the road leading east from the town to **Inkaneep Provincial Park**, one of many small parks and reserves which preserve the natural environment, plant and animal life. There are only seven campsites here, but lots of cacti, sage-bush and greasewood. Further north, and also just east of the road, **Vaseux Lake Provincial Park** is a wildlife sanctuary and a chosen nesting ground for Canada geese and other wildfowl. California bighorn sheep can often be seen on the bluffs above the highway.

Close to this point the road enters the southern end of the Okanagan Valley. This 200km (125 miles) long by 20km (12 miles) wide valley is one of Canada's most favoured regions, because of its beautiful scenery and mild climate, with 2,000 hours of sunlight and only 30-40cm (12-15in) of rainfall a year.

The Okanagan people were already living here when the first European fur traders came through in the early 1800s. Missionaries arrived at the northern end in about 1840. When American miners began using the valley as a route to the Fraser and Cariboo goldfields in the late 1850s, some entrepreneurs decided to stay and set up ranches here. More miners arrived from the east, the United States and even from China following a small gold-find near Vernon in 1857.

Father Charles Pandosy planted the valley's first apple trees in 1860, but it was Lord and Lady Aberdeen who brought the first commercial fruit crops into production in the 1890s and so precipitated a land boom. Lord Aberdeen was Canada's Governor General from 1893 to 1898. The Aberdeens were social crusaders who, while in Canada, devoted much of their time to good works which sometimes led to clashes with the Conservative governments of both Britain and Canada. Lady Aberdeen was a dynamic woman, who was an active suffragette in Britain. In Canada she created the Victorian Order of Nurses and the Canadian branch of the National Council of Women. The community of Armstrong near the head of the valley was originally named Aberdeen in their honour, but later changed in favour of a London banker who helped to finance a local railway.

Penticton, Kelowna, Vernon and other towns were founded, and the introduction of large-scale irrigation transformed the valley into Canada's fruit basket and vineyard. Population growth here is one of the fastest in the country, but you will not be aware of it because recreational areas and amenities have also increased.

The valley has plenty of visitor accommodation as well as campgrounds. There are two large provincial parks and a number of smaller ones, splendid public beaches and picnic grounds. In summer, when vacationers double the population, festivals are held throughout the valley. Winter brings good conditions for skiing, while in spring you can actually ski the mountains in the morning and golf in the valley that same afternoon. Lakes are excellent for fishing and watersports. *Off the Beaten Track* travellers will find many opportunities for alternative routes and side excursions.

Penticton, 40km (25 miles) north of Oliver, lies between the lower end of Lake Okanagan and Lake Skaha. Natives who had lived here for centuries called it *Pen-tak-Tin*, meaning 'a place to live forever' — a sentiment that most visitors agree with wholeheartedly. Early European history goes back to a North West Company expedition which came here in 1813 to establish a route along the lake between the Columbia and Fraser Rivers. Cattle ranching started in 1866. The first orchards in 1890 were followed by irrigation systems in 1905, but it was not until 1912, when plans for the Kettle Valley Railway were announced, that settlement took root in earnest. By 1915 the railway brought widespread access, connecting the town with Vancouver in the west and eastwards to central Canada through the Crowsnest Pass. Today the city (population 26,000) has a mixed economy based on agriculture, mining, manufacturing and tourism. An excursion trip northwards along the east side of the lake to **Okanagan Mountain Park** (see page 86) will give you an interesting *Off the Beaten Track* experience. On the way, **Naramata** is a small community with accommodation and some private wineries which welcome visitors. The roadbed of the now defunct railway with its long-abandoned station sites provides added interest for hikers.

Summerland, 16km (10 miles) north of Penticton is a prosperous community of 7,500 surrounded by orchards and vineyards. The valley's first commercial orchards were established in this town and it still depends on fruit cultivation as the main industry. Here, as elsewhere along the highway, stands offer local fruit fresh from the trees. There are two worthwhile stops: **Sun-Oka Beach Provincial Park**, with good swimming and picnic sites, and the Agricultural Research Station opposite. The station, which specializes in fruit-growing technology offers tours, but generally visitors are more attracted by its ornamental gardens and picnic sites. Further north, Peachland (population 3,500) is a fruit-growing, mining and logging community. The area has small provincial parks which offer a range of swimming, hiking and camping opportunities. Here, Château St Clair Winery is one of the region's several wineries open daily in summer to visitors. There is the usual wine tasting here and fabulous views from its hilltop site. Just north of Peachland, Hwy 97c, also known as the Okanagan Connector, leads to the Coquihalla Hwy, and the fastest route to Vancouver or Kamloops.

The highway enters **Kelowna**, 23km (14 miles) to the north, via a unique floating bridge. In 1859, Oblate priests built a mission in what is now Kelowna (an Indian word meaning grizzly bear) and planted the valley's first fruit trees. Today this is the valley's largest community, with a population of 60,000. Farmers from the Kelowna area ship one third of all the apples harvested in Canada, as well as peaches, pears, plums, apricots, cherries and many vegetable crops. Local wineries, which include some of Canada's largest, welcome visitors. There is a good beach and excellent harbour. Regattas and festivals are featured throughout the summer, a wine festival at harvest time, and there are a number of winter sporting events. Visitors should also know about Kelowna's well-known theatre company, its symphony orchestra, art gallery, and excellent museum.

Although it is *Off the Beaten Track* to many Canadians, Kelowna is connected by direct airline services with Calgary and Vancouver. Vacation accommodation is plentiful in all price ranges. Lake Okanagan Resort, beautifully sited above the lake, has its own golf course, tennis courts, horseback riding and marina.

If local history interests you then visit the reconstructed Father Pandosy Mission, where fruit and vine crops were introduced to the region. Also, the Gray Monk Cellars north of Kelowna, or one of the other neighbouring estate wineries are worth a visit. Many are operated by migrants who brought their own vines and wine-making skills from Europe. While there are lots of opportunities in and around Kelowna to leave the beaten track, one of the most interesting is the drive south along Hwy 33 to Rock Creek on Hwy 3, described in Chapter 6. For outdoors enthusiasts, a suggested excursion from Kelowna is to **Okanagan Mountain Provincial Park** 20km (12 miles) to the south, on the eastern side of the lake. This is an undeveloped park, with semi-arid terrain covered with sage-bush and cacti. The only way in is along an access road which ends at the park gates, or you can take a boat from Peachland (see above). There are 24km (15 miles) of trails, but no facilities so your campsite is where you choose to pitch your tent. Be sure to take some warm clothes; it can get quite cold up here, even when it is warm in the valley. The park's Squally Point is one of several places where Ogopogo has been sighted. Ogopogo is Okanagan's answer to the Loch Ness monster and is equally elusive. Native legend has this creature living in a cave near Kelowna. It is said to be between 9 and 22m (30-72ft) long, with the head of a horse, or perhaps a sheep, or even one at each end of its body. Recent sightings of Ogopogo were claimed to be of a two-headed creature rising from Lake Okanagan.

It is 46km (28 miles) from Kelowna to Vernon along the eastern side of Lake Okanagan. Two provincial parks along this route are particularly interesting. An underwater marine park, **Ellison Pro-**

vincial Park on Lake Okanagan is a mecca for scuba divers, but anyone will enjoy the beautiful lake views and some of the Okanagan's finest beaches. Further north, **Kalamalka Lake Provincial Park** is an 890ha (2,200 acre) preserve of virgin grassland which gives some impression of how this region was before ranchers, fruit farmers and property developers took over. The park displays four area ecosystems and access is restricted in some sections to protect the fragile environment. In spring the wild flowers are a special delight, while the beaches attract visitors all summer.

Vernon (population 20,000) is situated between Okanagan, Kalamalka and Swan Lakes. This was a camp on the fur-trade route and site of a mission settlement in the 1840s. Some prospectors who were first attracted by the 1860s mini-goldrush decided that agriculture was preferable to mining. By the 1890s several large cattle ranches were well established when Lord Aberdeen bought the huge Coldstream Ranch from its owner Forbes Vernon. He resold the land in small lots and encouraged fruit farming. Most of today's fruit farms are further south, but Vernon is still a centre for vegetable crops. The farmers' market held on Mondays and Thursdays in summer is western Canada's largest.

Cattle ranching continues to be an important industry here, and for a glimpse at how it used to be, the O'Keefe Historic Ranch is a living museum just north of Vernon on Hwy 97. In 1867 Cornelius O'Keefe and his partner Thomas Greenhow decided there was more money to be made from feeding miners than digging for the gold. They drove their first herd overland from Oregon and in the next forty years their property grew from an initial 65ha (160 acres) to an empire of 6,000ha (15,000 acres). Their spread included a village complete with post office and the area's oldest Roman Catholic church.

Vernon has good motels and resorts in town, and a campground very close by. The Greater Vernon Museum and Archives is a good source of local history. An enjoyable excursion is to the mountaintop **Silver Star Provincial Park**, which offers year-round recreational activities as well as a variety of resort accommodation. Skiing here is among the best in Canada and mountain biking is a summer speciality. Cedar Springs, on the road leading to the park, has a public pool fed by hot mineral springs.

It is 75km (45 miles) from Vernon to Sicamous. Around **Armstrong** and **Enderby** the cooler, slightly damper section of the valley is now devoted largely to dairy farming and mixed agriculture, although logging is still important.

Sicamous is a small resort town between Shuswap and Mara Lakes, self-described as the 'Houseboat Capital of Canada'. With approximately 350 of these floating cottages available for rent and 1,000km (620 miles) of warm navigable waterways, Sicamous offers a safe and enjoyable vacation requiring no special skill or previous experience. This region has some twenty provincial and marine parks and is well-known for its watersports, trout and salmon fishing. Every October the nearby Adams River is the scene of hundreds of thousands of sockeye salmon returning to their birth-place to spawn and die, after a journey of 500km (310 miles) from the Pacific Ocean.

At Sicamous, on the Trans-Canada Hwy (Hwy 1) this itinerary turns eastward through various mountain ranges towards the Rockies. (An alternative would be to travel westward to Kamloops and the itinerary described in Chapter 3.) The highway runs parallel with the Eagle River to reach **Craigellachie**, named after a high rock in Scotland. One of Canada's most famous photographs was taken here, showing the symbolic 'last spike' being driven on 7 November 1885 to mark the completion of the Canadian Pacific Railway. Beyond this point, the road crosses the Eagle Pass and continues on to **Revelstoke**, situated on the Columbia River between the Selkirk and Monashee Mountain Ranges. The town (population 5,500) was founded as a Canadian Pacific Railway construction settlement, and named in honour of Lord Revelstoke, whose Bowrings Bank funded completion of the line. Although it is still an important railway town, mining, lumbering and hydro-electric power also contribute to its economy now. North of town, the 175m (575ft) high Revelstoke Dam has a visitor centre which describes how electrical power is generated. East of town is **Mount Revelstoke National Park**, 260 sq km (100 sq miles) of mountains, meadows and valleys on the western edge of the Selkirk Range. A side trip takes you along Summit Road, rising for 26km (16 miles) to the top of Mount Revelstoke (1,938m, 6,358ft) and passing through various vegetation zones as the elevation rises. There are no campgrounds in this park. Hiking trails from the road provide access to forests and wild flower-strewn meadows for walkers of even the most limited endurance.

Fifteen kilometres (9 miles) of highway separates this park and **Glacier National Park** to the east. This 1,350 sq km (521 sq mile) park, named after its glaciers — more than 400 of them — straddles a section of the ancient Selkirk Mountains formed millions of years before the Rockies. Steep slopes, heavy snowfalls and mild temperatures often combine to produce avalanches which leave light green streaks where vegetation is regenerating. You will also see long snow sheds protecting the most vulnerable sections of road, as well as places where military howitzers are used to dislodge snow before accumulations become dangerous. In the middle of the park **Rogers Pass** (1,320m, 4,330ft) is one of Canada's most scenic stretches of mountain road, where shades of forest and meadow greens contrast with bare rock and the white of snowfields. Early railroad builders would have had different sentiments, as the steep valleys, avalanches and rock slides made this one of the most difficult sections to contend with. An information centre near Rogers Pass elaborates on this history; descriptive displays on local environment tell about the glaciers and avalanches. The park has camping facilities. (Bears can be a particular nuisance here, so be sure to follow the park rangers' instructions.) There are hiking trails into the interior, some of which lead to ice fields and glaciers, as well as plenty of opportunities for mountaineering. Illecillewaet Campground is a centre for one-day guided hikes in summer and for ski-touring in winter.

Leaving Glacier National Park, the road descends into the Rocky Mountain Trench and the Columbia River valley. At the confluence of the Columbia and Kicking Horse Rivers, the town of **Golden** (population 3,600) is an outfitting centre for hiking, horseback and rafting expeditions into the region's national parks. (For information on local accommodation and outfitters, contact the Travel Infocentre — address is in the Additional Information.)

Yoho National Park, which embraces 1,313 sq km (50 sq miles) of the Rocky Mountains' western slopes, provides scenic hiking and horseback riding, canoeing and camping. For more *Off the Beaten Track* opportunities, drive up the Yoho Valley, a scenic 13km (8 mile) switchback road leading to the Takakkaw Falls, where the river jets over a sheer cliff to fall 384m (1,260ft) into the valley. You can view the falls in the distance from the road, or hike along the trail for a closer look. (*Takakkaw* means 'Wow!' in the local native dialect and *Yoho* expresses astonishment). There is a lookout to the Cathedral Mountain spiral tunnel from this road — see below.

Park headquarters in the village of **Field**, 16km (10 miles) from the pass, has an information centre. Close by is the Burgess Shale Deposit, one of the world's most important fossil grounds, deemed a UNESCO World Heritage Site. Fossils of some 120 species of marine animals found here date from the Cambrian period 530 million years ago. West of Field, a road leads to the lovely Emerald

Lake with an idyllic walking trail of 5km (3 miles) around its perimeter. Just off the highway, you will see a natural bridge where the rushing waters of the Kicking Horse River have undercut the limestone.

It is 15km (9 miles) from Field to the **Kicking Horse Pass** on the Alberta/British Columbia border, (see page 136). This pass (elevation 1,627m, 5,338ft) was selected in 1884 as the route of the Canadian Pacific Railway through the Rocky Mountains despite its difficult steep grades. In 1909 railway engineers solved the gradient problem by blasting the two famous spiral tunnels which together form a figure eight inside Mt Ogden and Cathedral Mountain. It is worthwhile stopping at the usually busy roadside lookout above the lower spiral tunnel just west of the pass. Twenty to thirty trains come through here each day and when a long train is on the line, you can see its locomotives emerge before the tail disappears at the other end.

It is 55km (34 miles) from the Kicking Horse Pass to Banff, described on pages 131-7 and the starting point for the itinerary described in Chapter 6.

Additional Information
— Through Okanagan Orchards To The Rockies —

Places to Visit

Kelowna

Father Pandosy Mission
Benvoulen Rd, off Hwy 97
Open: daily in summer
☎ (604) 860-8369

Gray Monk Cellars
Camp Road
23km north via Hwy 97, west of Winfield
Open: daily May to November
☎ (604) 766-3168

Vernon

O'Keefe Historic Ranch
Hwy 97 12km (7½ miles) north of Vernon
Open: daily mid-May to mid-October
☎ (604) 542-7868

Parks

Glacier and Mt Revelstoke National Parks
PO Box 350
Revelstoke BC
V0E 2S0
☎ (604) 837-5155

Manning Provincial Park
Hwy 3, east of Hope
c/o Box 10
Cultus Lake BC
V0X 1H0
☎ (604) 858-7161

Yoho National Park
Box 99
Field BC
V0A 1G0
☎ (604) 343-6324

Local Tourist Information Offices

For section of itinerary south of Sicamous
Okanagan Similkameen Tourist Association
104-515 Hwy 97 S
Kelowna BC
V1Z 3J2
☎ (604) 861-7493

(For the Rocky Mountain section of the itinerary see the Rocky Mountain Visitors Association, page 102.)

For the section between Okanagan and the Rockies, see the High Country Tourist Association, page 73.)

Golden

Travel Infocentre
Box 1320
Golden BC
V0A 1H0
☎ (604) 344-7125

Sicamous

Travel Infocentre
Box 346
Sicamous BC
V0E 2V0
☎ (604) 836-3313

6 • Discovering The Kootenays

This itinerary starts where the previous chapter ends at Banff in Alberta's Rocky Mountains, and returns westward to con nect with those areas closer to the Pacific coast covered in Chapters 1 and 5. After leaving the Rockies, it crosses a number of valleys in the often unbelievably beautiful Kootenay region. These valleys present great opportunities for Off the Beaten Track touring and travellers with limited time have difficult choices to make. Whatever you do here, wherever you go, you are in for some of the continent's most spectacular country.

The first segment of the drive, from Banff to Radium Hot Springs is a distance of 132km (82 miles). Leave Banff driving westward along the Trans-Canada Hwy (Hwy 1) for about 20km (12 miles), then take Hwy 93, which leads southward over the Vermilion Pass (1,651m, 5417ft) and into **Kootenay National Park** (1,406 sq km, 543 sq miles). This is a UNESCO World Heritage Site, representative of Rocky Mountain landscape, and the only Canadian national park with both glaciers and cacti and a whole spectrum in between. Within the preserve you are likely to see mountain goats, bighorn sheep, elk and deer. They may actually be looking for you in the crags above the hot springs pools near the park's west entrance. Hot and cool pools are open daily, all year round, surrounded by a wide range of accommodation and campgrounds.

For all their natural assets, compared to Banff and Jasper both **Radium Hot Springs** and Kootenay National Park are far more *Off the Beaten Track*. Radium is a nice little community with pleasant if basic accommodation and restaurants, and few of the gift shops that are expected in such towns. The Radium Hot Springs Resort, a short distance from town, is a first-class facility with a very scenic golf course, a large swimming pool and excellent spa facilities. High above town, Alte Liebe Motel and Restaurant serves good food in a homey Bavarian ambience. Owner Ahmed Purchwitz is an accomplished photographer whose wildlife pictures cover the restaurant walls. Guest rooms and an outdoor terrace have a tremendous view of the valley spread out below.

While in this area, an interesting excursion for outdoors adventurers is to the **Bugaboo Glacier Provincial Park and Alpine Recreation Area** in the Purcell Mountains. Reached by gravel road from Brisco, 35km (22 miles) north on Hwy 95, this area has glaciers and mountain peaks over 3,000m (10,000ft) high that attract mountain climbers and hikers from all over British Columbia and Alberta. Resident wildlife includes porcupines with a taste for rubber. To protect your car tires, you are advised to use the wire mesh and logs provided by park rangers.

The main itinerary, however, continues south down the majestic Columbia-Windermere Valley through **Invermere**, a well-known year-round recreational area beside Lake Windermere to Fairmont Hot Springs. The four hot mineral springs had been attracting Kutenai Indians for centuries before the first Europeans arrived here in 1840. As settlement advanced, the springs became a rest-stop for weary stagecoach travellers, and a resort was established in 1922. Today, the springs attract visitors from all over and recreational opportunities include watersports, golf as well as cross-country and alpine skiing. Fairmont Hot Springs is near the northern end of Columbia Lake, the source of the 2,000km (1,240 mile) long Columbia River which flows into the Pacific near Portland, Oregon. The river (named after his ship by an American trader) gives its name to British Columbia.

About 70km (43 miles) south of Fairmont Hot Springs, the road forks, providing two alternative destinations.

The eastern branch (Hwy 93) leads to **Fort Steele**. This community, first known as Galbraith's Ferry, traces its beginnings to the 1860s when miners were attracted by gold finds at Wild Horse Creek, and then to a second gold rush in 1884, which brought friction between the miners, ranchers and local aboriginals. Such altercations led to the establishment of the first North West Mounted Police post west of the Rocky Mountains. The settlement was renamed after the NWMP's commander, Superintendent Sam Steele., who gained a reputation for always being where the action was hottest. Starting as a militia private, he was commissioned soon after being appointed sergeant-major in the newly-founded police force. Later, he fought in the Boer War and World War I, finally retiring as a knighted major general.

More mineral discoveries transformed it into a town of 4,000 and a busy port for stern-wheelers plying the river with ore and supplies. When railway builders bypassed Fort Steele in favour of Cranbrook, decline set in: buildings were abandoned and the police post closed. Now those boom town days are recalled with sixty restored buildings which include police barracks, the courthouse and jail, stores, hotel and a museum. During the summer season, a staff of appropriately dressed animators re-enact and describe their life during the late nineteenth century, in this and other southeastern British Columbia communities.

If, instead of going to Fort Steele, you take the western branch (Hwy 95a) via **Ta Ta Creek** you will arrive at **Kimberley**. Ever since the discovery in the 1890s of deposits of zinc-lead-silver, iron and tin this has been a mining and smelting town. Now its last mine is expected to close in the year 2,000. This community (population 7,400) has an elevation of 1,120m (3,675ft) and a very scenic location, nestled as it is between the Purcell and Rocky Mountains and overlooking the Valley of a Thousand Peaks. In developing a tourism industry, it is adopting a Bavarian theme. Its pedestrian mall is the Platzel. The Bauernhaus Restaurant is a 400-year-old building dismantled in Bavaria in 1987 and rebuilt here. The Bavarian City Mining Railway offers 20-minute train rides on a narrow-gauge mine track, with fine valley views and an on-board commentary. In July and August an alpine slide (1,233m, 4,045ft) is reached via a chairlift.

From Kimberley, it is 28km (17 miles) to Cranbrook. *Note*: Just north of this city Hwy 3 leads eastwards to the **Crowsnest Pass** and then to **Medicine Hat** in Alberta. On this road **Fernie** is a coal mining and forestry town nestling in a basin surrounded by steep mountains. The coal is mined with jets of water and extremely long trains take it to Vancouver for export. The town is a year-round recreation centre with lakes and rivers close by. There is some impressive skiing in the **Snow Valley Ski Area**.

Cranbrook has a similarly beautiful location. This busy city (population 16,000) is the major distribution centre for southeastern British Columbia, an area which is expanding with forest products and coal mining. A must for railway enthusiasts is the city's Canadian Museum of Rail Travel, where pride of place is occupied by the *Trans-Canada Limited*.

For a little extra Off the Beaten Track before leaving Cranbrook, take the Old Airport Road for about 6km (4 miles) north of the city to the St Eugene Mission. Founded in 1874 by Oblate missionaries this was an outpost of civilization before Cranbrook was even surveyed. By 1890 there was a residential school and hospital and,

CANADA BY RAIL, AS IT USED TO BE

For vintage railway fans, the Canadian Museum of Rail Travel in Cranbrook is a fascinating stop. The centrepiece of its rolling stock in various stages of preservation is the *Trans-Canada Limited*, a luxury train built in the late 1920s with dining, sleeping and observation cars. Similar to Pullmans in the United States, this all-Canadian train carried passengers prepared to pay handsomely for its civilizing comforts. Quality reflects pride of workmanship in the individual seats, Axminster carpets and rich mahogany panelling. Superbly prepared meals were served on crested china with silver-plated table accessories. Bedrooms were as luxurious as any world-class train anywhere. Service, too, was first-class, supervised by an elaborately uniformed conductor.

Even more luxurious were the ornate business cars used by railway executives to inspect their empire of land, tracks, tunnels and bridges. CPR President Thomas (later Baron) Shaughnessy used a private car with his own valet and personal chef. Leaving his own dining room, he could sip brandy in an observation car where he would often check on the train's progress with his own set of gauges. The museum's *Strathcona* was among the last of these luxury cars. Exceptionally heavy and well sprung, it was used as a car-of-state by the Prince of Wales during his visit in 1927, by Winston Churchill during the Quebec conference of 1943 and eight years later by the then Princess Elizabeth.

Among the collection of less prestigious cars are some with original furnishings and mahogany panelling. Others appearing as they were when last used, are refurbished in the 'railway art deco' style of the 1960s when railway companies believed passengers preferred grey paint and vinyl. As an extra bonus, the museum has a working scale model of trains operating in the Kootenays during those golden days of railroading.

because the mission had to be self sufficient, a farm and a flour mill. The Gothic-style mission church, built in 1897 and restored in 1983 is one of the oldest in British Columbia. An interesting story here tells of the priest who staked a claim and sold it to a miner for $22,000 to finance construction of the church.

Leaving Cranbrook, continue for 107km (66 miles) west along Hwy 3 to **Creston**. This small town is situated in a pocket of fertile agricultural land, reclaimed from the delta where the river flows into Kootenay Lake. The flat landscape with broad fields gives it a unique appearance in that only its mountain backdrop distinguishes this from a Prairie town. The Creston Valley Wildlife Management Area Centre, 10km (6 miles) west of town on Hwy 3, is a 70 sq km (27 sq mile) wetland reserve for migrating wildfowl. It is visited by 250 different species, which include wild swans, ospreys and hummingbirds.

A further attraction for visitors is the centre's broad range of wetlands plants, reptiles and mammals. Picnicking, hiking, canoeing and camping amenities are provided; guided walking and canoe tours are offered by the staff. The Creston Valley Museum relates the region's history. Among its artifacts is an example of the Kutenai Indian canoe, a unique design which appears to have been brought to this continent by migrants from the Amur River region of Russia 10,000 years ago. (*Kutenai* is a native word meaning 'water people'.)

Driving west towards Vancouver from Creston presents two alternatives. Hwy 3, the most direct route, rises continually to the Kootenay Pass (1,774m, 5,820ft), which is Canada's highest stretch of paved highway. It is a spectacular drive in good weather, but even in June large patches of snow will be seen among forests below the roadside. In winter it is frequently closed by snow, avalanches and poor visibility.

If you have the time, take a diversion north on Hwy 3a along the east side of Kootenay Lake for the ferry from **Kootenay Bay**, across to **Balfour** and on to Nelson. This delightful trip across the lake, flanked by the Selkirk and Purcell Mountains, is described as the world's longest free ferry ride. With an hourly summer service, and fairly small ships, you can expect delays. (If so, Tasty Treats restaurant serves homemade snacks, and the tranquil lake view is free.) Fishermen are often detained in Balfour, lured by prospects of catching the huge trout inhabiting the lake.

Nelson (population 9,000) originated in the late 1880s as a mining town, and when the gold and silver ran out its citizens turned to logging. In the surrounding countryside Russian Doukhobor settlers developed farms, and Englishmen planted orchards. By 1910 this progressive town was served by two railways and had its own streetcar service. Among its elegant new buildings was a courthouse designed by Francis Rattenbury the young British architect

'Ksan Village, Hazelton (Chapter 4)

Natives spearing salmon in Moricetown Canyon (Chapter 4)

Lake Okanagan Resort, near Kelowna (Chapter 5)

Farmers' Market, Vernon (Chapter 5)

O'Keefe Ranch, Vernon (Chapter 5)

A cowboy at Fort Steele (Chapter 6)

Railway Museum, Cranbrook (Chapter 6)

who gained international renown for Victoria's Legislature Building and Empress Hotel (see page 48). A communication centre still, Nelson has diversified in the past decade, and has in fact become a very attractive place in which to live. Two people who think so are the owners of Inn the Garden Bed and Breakfast, a handy block or two from Nelson's main street. In search of a more rewarding lifestyle they left secure professions in Toronto to locate in Nelson. Eight months of living with carpenters and plumbers, combined with the couple's creative ingenuity, have transformed this Victorian house into a showplace. Now all but two rooms have private baths. Steep flower gardens out front are wonderful in summer, while more plants prosper all year indoors. Guests have use of the lounge, and an alcove equipped with tea and coffee supplies. Ceiling fans and thick walls keep the home cool in summer, and its location could not be better for exploring the town on foot.

As part of Nelson's rebirth, some 350 buildings are now designated heritage sites. The town has a thriving theatre. Educational institutions include a resident school for Japanese university students. With the influx of new residents from other parts of Canada, Nelson has interesting restaurants, hotels and guesthouses. It is the type of town where art galleries, craft, antique and other speciality stores have friendly owners who are happy to chat. And at the tourist information office, they are keen to tell you about local walking and driving tours.

Hwy 6, 21km (13 miles) west of Nelson, offers opportunities for more *Off the Beaten Track* travel because it takes you into the Slocan region which is one of the most isolated areas of southern British Columbia. Once this was prosperous mining country; now the former boom towns are deteriorating in their splendid mountain landscape.

These communities were the scene of a less-than-proud period in Canadian history. They became, in effect, internment camps for about 5,000 of the 22,000 people (many of them Canadian citizens) of Japanese descent who were forcibly relocated from the Pacific coast following Japan's 1941 attack on Pearl Harbor. The internees lived under unnecessarily harsh conditions, and did not recover their homes or businesses after the war.

New Denver, which is at the junction of Hwy 31a, is a small lakeside town with a population of less than 600, so beautifully sited among mountains reminiscent of Switzerland it was originally called Lucerne. When gold was discovered, its name was changed to Eldorado, then to New Denver when the mother lode turned out to be silver. The town is situated directly across the lake from **Valhalla Provincial Park**, 500 sq km (193 sq miles) of lake and mountain wilderness which has hiking trails on former mining railway tracks. From here a side trip along Hwy 31a takes you to **Sandon**, one of the best known of the ghost towns.

Nakusp, once a logging and agricultural community and an important lake transportation centre, was transformed when the Columbia River was dammed to provide water storage and hydro-electric power to customers in Canada and the United States. A further 12km (7 miles) brings you to **Nakusp Hot Springs**, in a provincial park which has both skiing and hiking trails. There are two pools here (open year round) as well as resorts, motels and campgrounds.

While there are several alternative routes from Nelson (or Nakusp), our itinerary returns south to Hwy 3a and to **Castlegar**. Situated at the confluence of the Columbia and Kootenay Rivers, junction of regional highways and with the regional airport, this is considered to be the 'Crossroads of the Kootenays'.

The town is an important trade centre for the surrounding area, and many people who work in Trail to the south choose to live in Castlegar. There are surprisingly good visitor facilities here for such a small community. The Mountain Retreat Guest House, for example, is an unbelievable sight on an 8ha (20 acre) plateau high above the town. On this verdent plateau, reached by a steep zig-zagging road, the remarkable Gwen Mesley and her family built a palatial home with their own hands. (Her husband dug that road, Gwen did most of the carpentry. She and her father installed plumbing for all seven bathrooms.) Three elegantly comfortable guest rooms each have ensuite baths. From beyond the back garden, ripe with berries in summer, a herd of resident elk come visiting. A waterfall nearby ends in a natural pool where you can swim *au naturel* and swing Tarzan-like on vines. Gwen is a local teacher, and only recently opened her very private hideaway to paying guests year round.

There are several first-rate restaurants in Castlegar. Gabriels, in the centre of town, is worth a visit for its antiquities and stained glass alone. But there is an interesting menu too, offering well cooked and presented meals which make this a busy place.

In 1908 a group of Doukhobours immigrated to Canada from Russia. Peter Verigin, their charismatic leader who was assassinated in 1924, is buried here. Some of their abandoned farms and orchards can be seen from the highway, while the Doukhobour

BRITISH COLUMBIA'S DOUKHOBOURS

The original Doukhobours were a group of 7,400 pacifists who migrated to Canada from Russia in 1898-9, with help from Leo Tolstoy and British and American Quakers. They first settled near Yorkton, Saskatchewan, but difficulties arose for a number of reasons, including their wish to own land as communal property rather than as individuals. Unfortunately for them, these troubles occurred at a time when the government became less welcoming to settlers from Eastern Europe. In 1908 under their leader Peter Veregin, they bought land in the Kootenays, and by 1912, had established a community of 6,000.

Here in British Columbia, internal divisions continued, as did conflicts with authorities over land ownership and citizenship. A powerful Sons of Freedom group within the community would parade nude (as a sect member wrote 'in the manner of the first man, Adam and Eve, to show nature to humanity') in protest against government intervention. Some were imprisoned.

Basically, the already besieged Kootenay community disintegrated in the 1930s, largely under economic and social pressures. Now there are about 30,000 descendants living quietly and prospering in various parts of Canada, with many of them still adhering to some of the old traditions. Today, the Doukhobours are much respected in Castlegar and surrounding communities for their work ethic and lifestyle generally. In local schools, students are taught Russian instead of French as a second language.

Historic Village opposite the airport replicates one of their communal settlements.

Trail, 27km (17 miles) south via Hwy 22 is an industrial town which uses hydro-electric power to convert the minerals that are mined nearby. It is site of the Cominco lead-zinc smelter, one of the largest of its kind, employing 2,400 people.

From Castlegar, a further 214km (133 miles) along Hwy 3 brings you to Osoyoos, passing through several small communities on the way. Gold discoveries in 1859 led to the Dewdney Trail being driven between Hope and **Rock Creek**. The gold had petered out by the time it was finished, but the little town still has a frontierland flavour. Edgar Dewdney, the 24-year-old English engineer who built the Dewdney Trail, is one of western Canada's folk heroes. He went on to become a Member of Parliament and successively Lieutenant Governor of the Northwest Territories and British Columbia.

Osoyoos (see Chapter 5, page 83) is on the itinerary which leads west to the Pacific Ocean. However, the following is a very worthwhile *Off the Beaten Track* diversion along Hwy 33 from Rock Creek to Kelowna, which could form a loop with the lower Okanagan Valley. This 129km (80 mile) drive follows the West Kettle River, and a word of warning is in order: you will enjoy the scenery, but the road is fairly mountainous. Also, there is only one refuelling point, about half-way along.

The name Kettle may come from the shape of baskets woven by local natives or possibly from rock formations on the river further to the south. The valley gave its name to the railway which was part of a system operating from 1916 to 1964 between the Pacific Ocean and the Kootenays to the east. The railway and its history fascinate Canadian railway fans for the physical obstacles its engineers had to overcome. Also for the right-of-way conflicts between railway tycoons J. J. Hill (who controlled the United States' Great Northern Railroad) and William Van Horne of the Canadian Pacific Railway. At times these conflicts turned into fist-fights among competing railway labourers in the field. Although the railway is long gone, sections of the right-of-way provide hiking trails and abandoned stations, bridges and other facilities have acquired the status of industrial artifacts. A little museum, with a very enthusiastic young curator, in **Midway** about 20km (12 miles) east of Rock Creek along Hwy 3 has details of the railway's history.

About 6km (4 miles) along Hwy 33 north of your starting point, **Kettle River Recreation Area**, beside the river, has picnic tables and areas for swimming and fishing as well as campsites and RV facilities. A further 15km (9 miles) along this highway, a gravel road leads to **Conkle Lake Provincial Park**. Its 21km (13 miles) of rough road requires heavy duty tires and all your attention, so is not for trailers and RVs. Persevere with the road and you will be rewarded with some well-designed, semi-private campsites, a lovely lake with good beach and interesting hiking trails.

The small community of **Beaverdell**, about 60km (37 miles) from the start on Hwy 3, was once an important silver-mining centre but now caters for hikers and back-packers. The Beaverdell Hotel has modest accommodation. Its pub, with a turn-of-the-century decor, displays artifacts from the town's boom period. Between 1910 and 1936, **Carmi** was a gold-mining and railway town with school and hospital, stores, hotels and even a courthouse and jail. Closure of the gold mine in 1936 was a severe enough blow, but it was the subsequent elimination of railway services that resulted in the ghost town that is seen today.

About 45km (28 miles) north of Beaverdell, you will arrive at a side road leading eastward into **Big White Mountain Recreation Area**, which is one of the Okanagan Valley's finest ski areas, blessed with an average 12m (39ft) annual snowfall, ski lifts and many downhill and cross-country ski runs. There is a European-style mountain-top ski village with condominiums, stores and restaurants.

It is approximately 25km (15 miles) from this side road to Kelowna (see page 85).

Additional Information
— Discovering The Kootenays —

Places to Visit

Castlegar
Doukhobour Historic Village
Hwy 3a, near airport
Open: daily in summer
☎ (604) 365-6622

Cranbrook
Cranbrook Museum of Rail Travel
Hwy 3 downtown
Open: daily
☎ (604) 489-3918

Creston
Creston Valley Museum
219 Devon St
Open: daily in summer, otherwise by appointment
☎ (604) 428-9262

Creston Valley Wildlife Management Area Centre
10km (6 miles) west on Hwy 3
Open: daily in summer
☎ (604) 428-3260

Fort Steele
Fort Steele Heritage Town
Open: daily from mid-June to Labour Day, grounds open all year.
☎ (604) 489-3351

Nakusp
Nakusp Hot Springs
Open: daily
☎ (604) 265-4528

Parks

Kootenay National Park
Box 220
Radium Hot Springs BC
V0A 1M0
☎ (604) 347-9615

Conkle Lake Provincial Park
c/o RR3, Site 8, Comp 5
Nelson BC
V1L 5P6
☎ (604) 825-4421

Kettle River Recreation Area
(Address and ☎ as Conkle Lake Provincial Park)

Big White Mountain Recreation Area
Resort Reservations c/o Box 2039
Station R
Kelowna BC
V1X 4K5
☎ (604) 765-8888

Ferry Service

Between Balfour and Kootenay Bay. Hourly from 6am to midnight from Victoria Day to Thanksgiving, 90 minute intervals rest of year. Anticipate delays in vacation periods between 9am and 6pm.

Local Tourist Information Offices

For Rocky Mountain west of Creston
Rocky Mountain Visitors Association
Box 10
Kimberley BC
V1A 2Y5
☎ (604) 427-3344

For eastern section
Kootenay Country Tourist Association
610 Railway St
Nelson BC
V1L 1H4
☎ (604) 352-1656

Nelson
Nelson and District Travel Infocentre
225 Hall St
Nelson BC
V1L 5X4
☎ (604) 352-3433

7 • The Legendary Yukon

In Canada's northwest corner, Yukon Territory occupies 482,515 sq km (186,316 sq miles) or nearly five percent of the country's surface, and yet its residents number only 32,000. This area's first inhabitants were Asian migrants who crossed the Bering land-bridge about 10,000 years ago and it was their descendants who called it *Diuke-on* meaning 'pristine water'. The first Europeans to arrive were Russians led by the Dane, Vitus Bering, who explored the Arctic coast in 1741. Sir John Franklin's Arctic expedition of 1825 came this way too, but the first permanent contact was made in the 1840s by fur traders from the east.

However, it was gold prospecting, culminating in the Klondike Rush of 1897-8 that formed the basis of present-day Yukon. This turned out to be the greatest gold rush the world had known. Within two years, its population reached 40,000 and the Yukon was separated from the Northwest Territories. Once the easily mined gold deposits gave out people drifted away, and by 1918 the population had shrunk to a tenth of its former size. When the Japanese occupation of the United States' Aleutian Islands in World War II brought the enemy a little too close for comfort, 30,000 American and Canadian soldiers rammed a road from northern British Columbia through to Fairbanks, Alaska in just eight months. The Alaska Highway changed the Yukon's economy immeasurably. It also had a profound effect on the native population, who at first struggled to retain their traditional ways. Now, land and cash grants in settlement of land claims have introduced greater economic stability in their lives.

Copper, silver, tin, zinc and lead are all mined here, along with a little gold, and the tourism authorities work hard to promote growth in their industry. Visitors to this sparsely populated land have merely to define what a vacation *Off the Beaten Track* means to them, and their needs will likely be met. There is a good transportation network, and a wide range of visitor accommodation. Wilderness outfitters and wildlife guides are true experts. Museums and evening entertainment are part of the tourist package. All these choices and more are described in tourism brochures free for the asking. Travel agencies have information on cruise lines and tour companies offering all-inclusive packages.

Just being in the Yukon is exciting. If you have already seen the world's great cities, you will delight in the frontier-style history so carefully preserved in Whitehorse, the Yukon capital since 1953. The romance is still there, as well as the energy, the magic and the humour captured in literature that came out of the Gold Rush era. This is one of the world's last great wilderness regions where you can be overwhelmed by the magnitude and wild beauty of its vistas. Here you can hike and camp far from human habitation, fish in your own private lake, or climb one of the continent's highest mountains.

Often visitors arrive in the Yukon as part of a group travelling on an all-inclusive fly/cruise package to Alaska, then continue their touring independently. Alternatively, air or bus services from Vancouver or Edmonton will get you here. So will the Alaska Marine Highways car ferry from northern British Columbia. The road from British Columbia and Alberta to the Yukon used to be rough, but through constant upgrading, the highway is now almost fully surfaced. Still, this is a long and difficult drive (2,600km, 1,600 miles, to Whitehorse from Vancouver or 1,950km, 1,210 miles, from Edmonton) and it calls for careful planning. Once you arrive in the Yukon, you will find good roads and rental vehicles to drive on them. Also an excellent network of commercial and government-operated campgrounds suitable for both tents and RVs.

Information from the tourist office will show you the many options available, for either guided tours or independent travel. In this guide we give one itinerary by car. If that is too tame, you could canoe the early prospectors' route down the Yukon River, from the head of the Chilkoot Pass on Bennett Lake, (see below) to the Klondike, a total distance of 980km (609 miles), with numerous camping opportunities on riverbanks and sandbars along the way. Bicycle tours are becoming increasingly popular. So are ski and dogsled expeditions.

If you plan to strike out into the wilderness you will need help. Guides, some fluent in German, French and other languages, can lead you to remote lakes and rivers where fish have been allowed to mature. Regulations require hunters to be accompanied by a licensed guide, who will be just as happy to escort you on a photographic safari. Wildlife photographers will be greatly rewarded, since the Yukon is home to the world's largest concentration of grizzly bears and Dall sheep. Black bears, wolves, wolverine, moose, caribou, and mountain goats, ducks, geese and grouse are also easily seen. So are the fish, which in these pristine waters include Dolly Varden, lake trout, grayling and pike. Whatever your chosen expedition, an outfitter can provide everything from transportation, guides and gear to accommodation and the necessary licences.

This then is the magical Yukon, a land of contrasts where you can wallow in hot springs and explore Ice Age glaciers, camp under canvas or lodge in good hotels. You can ride the railway built on gold, and relive that era through Robert Service readings and the legends of characters who in memory remain larger than life.

When You Arrive Via Alaska

Often in summer Yukon visitors arrive in Whitehorse from Skagway, Alaska, a 180km (112 mile) journey that allows them to relive part of the gold rush experience. In 1900, three years after the Klondike discoveries, Skagway had grown from a single cabin to a turbulent town of 20,000 inhabitants. This is where the stampeders landed after sailing north from San Francisco, and prepared themselves for their arduous trek over the Coast Mountains and down the raging Yukon River.

Nowadays, Skagway is a pleasant tourist town of 700, which can get rather crowded when two or three cruise ships are in port. As part of the Klondike Gold Rush National Historic Park, operated by the US Parks Service, it recalls gold rush times with an interpretive centre, restored buildings and guided walks. Here is where you can pick up information on hiking the prospectors' route which follows an old Indian traders' path from Skagway along the Chilkoot Trail. A difficult trip still, it takes three to five days and is recommended only for experienced and well-equipped hikers. The first two days' hike up to the tree line is fairly easy, then things get rough as you enter boulder-strewn slopes and snowfields, finishing with the final steep ascent to the pass summit and the international border. You may prefer to do it in comfort, by helicopter.

During the gold rush era this 53km (33 mile) trail over the (1,062m, 3,484ft) Chilkoot Pass was strictly controlled by the North West Mounted Police. They admitted only those miners who brought their own equipment and enough supplies to keep them going for a year. This came to about 800kg (1,760lb) per man, a load that had to be broken down into thirty or forty individual packs. They were carried, one at a time, up steps hacked out of the ice and rock to the pass summit, then down the other side. There they were deposited for safe-keeping while the owner went back for his next load. Obviously, this was a place for only the very hardy, and yet 20,000 made the crossing in one year alone.

It is simpler to drive the present-day Klondike Highway. Leaving town, you follow the beautiful Skagway Valley, through rich rainforest, beside rushing streams and tumbling waterfalls.

As the elevation increases, terrain gives way to a landscape increasingly desolate and forbidding. Among the lichen-covered rocks and swamps of the Chilkoot Pass, you will see clumps of snow even in mid-summer. The reward is the view of fabulous mountain scenery. To the east, the rail line (see page 108) crosses the White Pass, closed by the Mounties after some 3,000 horses died of exhaustion before they even reached the summit.

Now well inside the Yukon, the highway skirts Tutshi Lake, Windy Arm and Tagish Lake, taking you past uncommonly varied vistas, even awe-inspiring as mountain sides plunge down into brilliant blue lakes. In summer, the meadows become a carpet of wildflowers. West of the highway, Bennett Lake was the next stop for miners humping their loads through the Coast Mountain passes. Thousands of men congregated here to prepare for the next step in their adventure, which was to cut down trees and build boats or rafts that would transport them with their goods down the Yukon River. A few with sufficient means could purchase these from entrepreneurs who had set up a tent town, sawmills and rough boat-building yards. Today's Chilkoot Trail travellers will come across remnants of this settlement, where even now large second-growth trees are fairly sparse.

Prospectors used to float past **Carcross** where the highway meets the old trail. Once a traditional hunting spot for the Yukon First Nations people, its name is an abbreviation of Caribou Crossing. This is the settlement from which prospector George Carmack set off on the trip which ended in his gold discoveries at Bonanza Creek. The Caribou Hotel, opened in 1898, is claimed as the Yukon's oldest hostelry. The Carcross Visitor Reception Centre in the former railway station has displays illustrating the transportation methods used in the Yukon's early days, when they included sternwheelers, stagecoaches and steam locomotives.

Miles Canyon and the White Horse rapids were the miners' final challenge before reaching the Yukon River's navigable stretch at Whitehorse, a few miles to the north. A power dam has tamed the river now, and a cruise boat retraces this stretch where miners had to transport their gear and supplies around a narrow canyon of rushing water and dangerous whirlpools.

Whitehorse

Tourists who begin their Yukon tour in Whitehorse and follow the conventional routes (including the itinerary in this guide) will find a city steeped in lively history. A self-guided walking tour as mapped out by the Yukon Historical and Museums Association is a fine way to start. The MacBride Museum captures the essence of this region through its presentations of wildlife, Indian culture, and the gold rush era immortalized in Jack London's stories and Robert Service poems such as *The Cremation of Sam McGee.*

Known as the Poet of the Yukon, Service was a teller in the Whitehorse branch of the Canadian Bank of Commerce in the early 1900s. There was a real Sam McGee, but he was not cremated, even temporarily, as the poem suggests

> The Northern Lights have seen queer sights,
> but the queerest they ever did see,
> was the night on the marge
> of Lake Lebarge
> I cremated Sam McGee … .

In truth the real McGee was a businessman who was buried in Winnipeg in 1941. In any event, the legendary McGee's log cabin is at the MacBride Museum. Other log buildings from earlier times are multi-storied rooming houses, which made good use of smallish plots. The old log church, now a museum, recalls the history of the Anglican Church in the Yukon. Here you will learn about Isaac Stringer, intrepid Bishop of the Yukon from 1906 to 1931. He travelled to outlying communities on foot and by canoe and dog-sled. On one of his trips he became totally lost, and when his food ran out resorted to eating his boots. 'Breakfast of sealskin boot, soles and tops boiled and toasted. Soles better than uppers', he wrote in his dairy. This story inspired the classic 1920s Charlie Chaplin film *The Gold Rush.*

SS Klondike II, now a National Historic Site beached on the Yukon riverbank, was one of the largest stern-wheeled riverboats carrying supplies and mineral ores between Whitehorse and Dawson. We suggest you allow time for the audio-visual presentation explaining the stern-wheelers' role in Yukon history. Yukon Gardens (at the junction of South Access Road and Hwy 1) has 9ha (22 acres) planted with flowers, fruit and vegetables. Experiments here have resulted in new strains of vegetables which grow in this climate.

In Whitehorse, you will doubtless see the White Pass and Yukon Route terminus. This narrow-gauge railway, built in record time by unsuccessful miners eager to gain a new stake, opened in 1900 to connect Whitehorse with the port of Skagway. In doing so it replaced the heart-breaking pack-trails over mountain passes between the ocean and the Yukon River. The railway has operated intermittently ever since, carrying valuable metal ores shipped from the interior by stern-wheeler, or more recently by truck. It operates passenger rail and connecting bus services between Skagway, Whitehorse and points in between. The scenery viewed from this section of the tracks past granite gulches and cascading waterfalls, is even more compelling than what you would see from the road.

Locals seem to keep going throughout the daylight hours in this Land of the Midnight Sun. Translate this into evening entertainment lasting long into the night and you have *The Frantic Follies*, a traditional gay-'90s style vaudeville featuring can-can dancers, humorous historic sketches, bawdy humour and lots of audience participation. Also the Gold Rush Inn's *The 1940s Canteen Show*, commemorating the days when the US army 'invaded' the Yukon to build the famous highway. Panning for gold is fun here and elsewhere in the Yukon, since you could actually find a gold flake or two in the gravel you buy. If you do not strike it rich, try a local crafts store. It will have ready-mounted local nuggets for sale.

A Suggested Yukon Itinerary

This is a self-driving tour of 1,480km (920 mile) which can be comfortably achieved in four days.

The first leg of the trip from Whitehorse takes you along the Klondike Hwy (Hwy 2) which in places parallels the Yukon River. Campers may want to use one of the ten Yukon Government parks along this highway. At **Montague** you will see the remains of a roadhouse, one of many built at 32km (20 mile) intervals for travellers to the gold fields.

It is 175km (109 miles) to **Carmacks**, named after a fur trader who found coal here and was one of the three prospectors who discovered gold at Bonanza Creek. This used to be a major stop on the Overland Trail between Whitehorse and Dawson, while the nearby coal deposits made it a refuelling point for riverboats. There is a small park at **Five Finger Rapids**, 22km (14 miles) to the north, where the river is broken into five streams. Today this is little more than a pleasant scene, with the river rushing and tumbling between small islands. Stampeders doubtless missed its beauty. Many lost their lives in the rapids after struggling this far over mountain passes and then down the river in overloaded, ramshackle boats. Riverboats at that time had to be winched upstream through the narrow northern passage.

Anyone interested in the early days of silver mining will enjoy an excursion from **Stewart Crossing**, about 165km (103 miles) further north. Here, the Silver Trail (Hwy 11) follows the Stewart River 53km (33 miles) through one of Canada's richest mining regions to **Mayo**. In the early 1900s, gold, silver and other mineral ores mined in nearby Elsa were taken by stern-wheeler to Whitehorse and on to the coast by rail.

Some 40km (25 miles) southeast of Dawson, you will come to the beginning of the Dempster Highway. This is Canada's most northerly road, running 740km (460 miles) through the Richardson and Ogilvy mountain ranges and across the Arctic Circle, before descending to sea level and **Inuvik** in the Northwest Territory, on the Mackenzie River delta. Camper vehicles suitable for this road can be rented in Whitehorse, where rental companies will advise on supplies to take with you and also on current road conditions. The very latest information on driving conditions is available at the Dawson City Visitors Centre. The road is built on a gravel berm that insulates the permafrost below, and calls for careful driving. It crosses the Peel and Mackenzie rivers by ferry. When ice conditions render the ferries inoperable, the road closes and access is by air only. There are roadside campgrounds and excellent hiking opportunities in the tundra. Inuvik, (see page 125) is a base for boat and plane tours to outlying communities and wildlife reserves in the more remote northern regions.

Our more prosaic itinerary continues on to **Dawson City**, located on the Yukon's east bank at the mouth of the Klondike River. On 17 August 1896, prospector George Washington Carmack and two Indian companions, Skookum Jim and Tagish Charlie, discovered gold in Rabbit Creek which runs into the Klondike River, a tributary of the Yukon. As the news spread, thousands of gold-seekers from southern Canada and the United States headed north. Rabbit Creek was promptly renamed Bonanza. Dawson, which had already been staked out by a farsighted prospector, grew quickly as the transhipment centre for men and equipment heading to the goldfields. By 1899, it was a rough and tumble town of 30,000 where tents and log cabins vied for space with government buildings and stately homes equipped with running water, electricity and telephones.

The town's decline was swift when the easily mined gold gave out and prospectors packed up, leaving a few high-technology mining companies in the hinterland. Two decades later, the Alaska Highway enabled Whitehorse to overtake Dawson as the territory's commercial centre. The capital was moved there in 1953 and the last gold mining operation on the Klondike closed down in 1966. But Dawson lives on, with restored buildings of white-trimmed brown-painted boards, and a year-round population of 2,000 to welcome visitors for a taste of the far north's gold rush era.

Tourism Yukon's visitor centre at Front and King Streets has interpretive programs and audio-visual presentations, as well as conducted tours. It also features its own radio station (96.1MHz) so you can hear what is going on before you arrive. In addition, Parks Canada operates a number of facilities collectively known as the Klondike National Historic Sites. The old post office, the sternwheeler *Keno*, and Harrington's Store Exhibit offer a further peek into the past.

The Dawson City Museum tells about regional history. In Robert Service's refurbished cabin, a ghost reads his verses, and there is also an exhibit on Jack London, whose *White Fang* and *Call of the Wild* are based on his Yukon experiences. The Grand Palace Theatre, a reconstructed turn-of-the-century theatre is open for touring during the day, while presenting the *Gaslight Follies*, a Klondike-style musical comedy review at night. The story of frontier showman Arizona Charlie Meadows, and how he came to build this theatre from lumber salvaged from an old riverboat, is one of the local legends. In Diamond Tooth Gertie's Gambling Hall, roulette and black-jack tables recall an era when fortunes in gold-dust were won or lost with a spin of the wheel or a turn of a card. Gertie leads her can-can dancers and entertainers through less bawdy performances than were given by her 1890s peers, as the sweating honky-tonk piano player thumps out the music.

You will want to see the site of Claim 33, 10km (7 miles) south on Bonanza Creek Road, which started the rush; also there are signs telling the story of gold mining along the creek. Dredge #4, a mammoth wooden mining machine which operated on the creek for years, is open to visitors. Then, just in case you feel some of George Carmack's luck has rubbed off on you, here is a chance to pan for gold.

The four-day Discovery Days weekend commemorating Carmack's gold find on 17 August 1896 is a great event in Dawson, with parades (it is said half the town parades, while the other half cheers), dances, gold-panning contests and canoe races. The years 1996 and 1998 which mark the discovery and gold-rush centennials promise to be special.

The town has a nice assortment of tourist accommodation, for which advance reservations are recommended in summer. There are also commercial RV campgrounds, and government highway campgrounds either side of town.

The next segment of this circular itinerary loops across the United States border, open daily between 9am and 9pm. Non-Canadians will require a passport and US visa. Leaving Dawson, and heading west, follow the gravelled Top of the World Highway for 108km (67 miles) to **Boundary**, Alaska, then south 120km (75 miles) to Tetlin Junction, on the Alaska Highway. It is about 180km (112 miles) to the Canadian border.

Beaver Creek (population 125) is Canada's most westerly community. A visitor reception centre here has its own broadcasting radio station and there is some visitor accommodation. The area's Russian names for geographic features, including the Nutzotin Mountains and Alaska's Wrangell St Elias National Park, are reminders that this was once Russian territory. An interpretive panel at Mile 1202 on the Alaska Hwy recalls completion of the highway in August 1942.

Approximately 40km (25 miles) south of Beaver Creek, the highway skirts the eastern edge of the Kluane Game Sanctuary and **Kluane National Park**. Established in 1972, this 22,000 sq km (8,500 sq mile) park includes wildlife preserves set aside during construction of the Alaska Highway. It's very grand Mt Logan, at 6,050m (19,850ft), is Canada's highest and the continent's second highest peak. The world's largest collection of non-polar glaciers and icefields dominate this park, but there are also boreal forests, tundra, alpine meadows, and verdant valleys. Unusually high concentrations of grizzly bears, many black bears and the extremely rare blue variant (black bears with a distinct bluish tinge) live in the park. As do 5,000 Dall sheep, wild goats, enormous numbers of caribou and moose, wolves and many smaller animal species. Golden eagles, horned owls, and ravens are among the 175 species of birds in residence. Rivers and streams yield trout, grayling, pike and kokanee salmon. Not surprisingly, Kluane has been declared a UNESCO World Heritage Site. At **Burwash Landing** the acclaimed Kluane Museum of Natural History has a huge topographical map of the area, plus displays of the region's wildlife, geology, native artifacts and crafts.

Back-packing, cross-country skiing and fishing are popular pursuits in this largely wilderness park. You can organize your own expedition along the 250km (155 miles) of hiking trails or join a trek organized by an adventure tour company. If you want to reach the park's deep interior, flying is the best option. The mountains, some of which have never been scaled, lure climbers from all over the world. For motorists, the highway's lookout at km 1,810 (formerly mile 1,128.5) has marvelous views of the Donjek River Valley, surrounding Icefield Ranges and the St Elias Mountains. Families travelling by car or camper will enjoy Kathleen Lake, south of Haines Junction, for its well-organized camping and picnic facilities.

Haines Junction (population 600) stands at the foot of the Kluane Range. Park headquarters are located here and a visitor centre features award-winning interpretive programmes. (More are presented at the Kathleen Lake campground.) This community has accommodation, gas stations, stores, banking and other services. It is 160km (100 miles) from Haines Junction to Whitehorse via the Alaska Hwy, or 256km (159mi) via Hwy 3 to the port of Haines, Alaska.

About 16km (10 miles) from Whitehorse, a soak in the modern pools fed by **Takhini Hot Springs** will bring this trip to a satisfactorily warm conclusion. A picnic and camping park here serves as base for hikes and horse-back rides into the surrounding mountains.

Restored buildings in Nelson (Chapter 6)

Northern wildlife: the Daal Ram (Chapter 6)

The Dempster Highway, crossing the Arctic Circle (Chapter 7)

Mid-summer in the Yukon (Chapter 7)

Additional Information
— The Legendary Yukon —

Places to Visit

Carcross

Carcross Visitor Reception Centre
km 106, Klondike Hwy
Open: daily mid-May to mid-September.
☎ (403) 821-4431

Dawson City

Dawson City Visitor Reception Centre
Front and King Sts
☎ (403) 993-5566

Dawson City Museum
5th Ave
Open: daily May to September
☎ (403) 993-5291

Klondike National Historic Sites
Various locations
Write c/o Box 390
Dawson YT
Y0B 1G0
Open: daily June 1st to mid-September
☎ (403) 993-5462

Palace Grand Theatre
3rd Ave and King St
Open: mid-May to mid-September
☎ (403) 993-5575

Whitehorse

MacBride Museum
1st Ave & Wood St
Open: daily mid-May to mid-September
☎ (403) 667-2709

Klondike II National Historic Site
2nd Ave and Alaska Hwy south access road
Open: daily mid-May to mid-September
☎ (403) 667-4511

Takhini Hot Springs
Takhini Hot Springs Road
10 km (6 miles) from km 198, Klondike Hwy
Open: daily
☎ (403) 633-2706

Yukon Gardens
Junction South Access Rd and Hwy 1
Open: daily mid-May to mid-September
☎ (403) 668-7972

Yukon Historical and Museums Association
3126 3rd Ave
Open: daily mid-May to mid-September
☎ (403) 667-4704

Park

Kluane National Park
Box 5495
Haines Junction YT
Y0B 1L0
☎ (403) 634-2251

Local Tourist Information Offices

Contact Tourism Yukon (see Canada Fact File).

8 • Adventuring In The Northwest

This is the one place left in Canada where mountains remain unnamed, lakes uncounted and caribou herds still thunder across the plains. For modern adventurers who come this way, it is an exciting new frontier with challenges enough for even the fittest individuals. For naturalists the Northwest Territories are a realized dream. Some of the world's largest lakes are up here, also four national parks and four heritage rivers, four time zones and a population of only 64,000 people in a space nearly half the size of the United States of America.

But modern times are catching up with this vast land. For years boat or dog-sled provided transportation. Then came small aircraft and later snowmobiles. Now in Yellowknife, the Territories' capital, modern government buildings and shopping malls, community centres and even fast-food outlets can have you momentarily thinking you are in the south.

Natives who used to be known as Eskimos and Indians are now described as Inuit and Dene (pronounced Denay, this name includes a number of different peoples including Dogrib, Chipewyan and Slavey.) You will see large numbers of Dene in the western territories and around Great Slave Lake. Métis (of native and European heritage) are likely to be teachers and technicians, whereas their forefathers in the fur-trade era earned recognition as guides and river pilots. The Inuit live mainly in the Arctic Islands north of the tree line. But wherever they live, their ancient traditions are kept alive. Fathers teach their sons to live off the land, and survive the rigours of an Arctic climate without use of modern technology. Trapping lines are still passed on from father to son, who in turn must use or lose them.

The northern natives are immensely creative. Some communities have more artists per capita than most places in the world. Their distinctive paintings, weaving and appliqué work are readily sold in tourist areas. Made only from natural products, everything is representative of their aboriginal cultures.

It has taken until now for the far north to be so organized that visitors can easily reach it, and really enjoy what they have come for. Of course, it is expensive to fly into a fishing camp or hire the services of private guides for a hunting party. Supplies too have to be flown in. But it can be done. Tour groups come here from other parts of the world, or you can join a group once you are here.

Nowhere is too far for northerners, and trips can be arranged for all seasons. For example, outfitters and travel experts will fly you to Resolute Bay in the High Arctic, then fit you out for a visit to the Magnetic North Pole. They will escort you on hiking trails and bird-watching safaris, and to native-run camps that put you in touch with Dene and Inuit ways. You can hunt for polar bear using sleds and dogteams, or picnic on caribou steaks and bannock and smoked char, on a summer's night when the sun is still high though it is way past bedtime.

Obviously the northern experience is not for everyone. But, if the sub-Arctic or Arctic regions are on your dream vacation list we urge you to come now, ahead of the crowds, while it is still as the promoters promise: *Within Reach, Yet Beyond Belief.*

Because there are so few highways in the Northwest Territories, this guide departs from the itinerary format used elsewhere in this book. True, Inuvik is accessible by road from Dawson City in the Yukon, and the Great Slave Lake region can be reached by road from Alberta and British Columbia. It is also possible to drive to Fort Smith, for access to Wood Buffalo National Park. However, these are long, arduous routes, and once you arrive there is little need for a car. It is far more practical to fly to the Territories, then hop around on commuter or charter planes as northerners do.

Scheduled air services to Yellowknife are from Calgary, Edmonton and Winnipeg. Once there you can arrange for day trips, or longer expeditions to outlying regions. Established on the northern arm of Great Slave Lake in 1934 following discovery of gold, Yellowknife is the hub of government, transportation and communication throughout the Northwest Territories.

The land around Yellowknife (named after the local natives who carried copper knives) had been a hunting ground for thousands of years, when a Hudson's Bay Company officer named Samuel Hearne arrived in 1772. A few years later his company built an outpost here, which was still in existence when Sir John Franklin made his journey to the Coppermine River in 1820. Gold was first noted at Yellowknife Bay in 1896 by miners on their way to the Klondike, but it took the 1930s gold rush to shape a permanent settlement.

THE INUKSHUK

You see them all over the place — slabs of grey rock piled to resemble the human form. Some look like rock scarecrows, there to ward off scavenging birds. Others appear to stake out claim to a piece of land. And, in towns they stand as silent greeters, welcoming you to a hotel or park. Any of these explanations may be given when you ask what the inukshuk is about.

In fact they are from Arctic cultures of the distant past, and had many uses. Large ones without arms were built on hill tops to show family territory. A single inukshuk (or two close together) on the banks of a river indicated a fording place. On barren lands they provided a marker to guide travellers; some even had one arm pointing the way. Others contained a peep hole in the centre, and anyone looking through it toward the horizon would see the tiny dot of another inukshuk far away. On a barren coastline they served as navigation tools for travellers at sea.

Inukshuks worked cleverly for hunters. Erected in two parallel lines, they provided a channel through which startled cariboo were directed. Behind the stone figures, hunters waited until they were close enough to be picked off with bows and arrows. Similarly, the inukshuk would be used to funnel caribou into the deep part of a river. Forced to swim for their lives, they became slow-moving targets for hunters waiting nearby in kayaks.

The Arctic is a vast, often lonely place. Travellers have said that the emotional effect of seeing another person, even one made of stone, after weeks or months without human contact is overwhelming. That simple stone person tells of someone else coming this way. Maybe it was a couple of thousand years ago, but they were here, travelling this very route. Apparently the urge to build a second inukshuk alongside it, or on another lonely stretch is irresistible.

Two large gold mines continue to operate within the city limits, and Yellowknife is a centre for mining exploration. Present hopes are for the realization of profitable diamond mining in the area.

Yellowknife is a busy community, population approximately 17,000, many of whom are government employees. It has several multi-storey buildings and an efficient airport nearby. Yet for all its modernity, visitors soon become aware they are in the extreme north. Restaurants serve caribou meat, local whitefish and Arctic char. Art galleries specialize in the work of native artists. And as a link with arctic cultures, rock figures known as inukshuks stand outside the city's largest hotel.

First-time visitors to Yellowknife will find the **Northern Frontier Visitor Centre** beside the airport road an excellent orientation, as well as an information source. Allow at least two hours for the nearby **Prince of Wales Northern Heritage Centre**, an ultra-modern territorial museum with archives and a library and galleries depicting the vast region's geology and wildlife. One gallery is dedicated to aviation, another to early trading posts. Others have fascinating exhibits on various aspects of the Dene and Inuit cultures, as well as the history of European settlement.

Prior to 1993, the Territory's twenty-four legislators met in various hotels, community centres and school gymnasiums. Then the splendid Legislative Building was opened. Designed to fit into the lakeside site with the minimum destruction of trees, it is constructed largely of native materials. During a tour you will learn how it accommodates the Territory's unique governing style, based on the aboriginal tradition of consensus government rather than the political party system. Facilities permit simultaneous translation between the region's eight official languages: English and French plus six native languages.

The museums, Legislative Building, City Hall and community swimming pool are within a pleasant walk of central Yellowknife via the Frame Lake Trail. Circling the lake, this 5.6km (3.5 mile) trail takes you through a wilderness area without leaving the city.

Yellowknife's courthouse building is worth a visit for its small collection of native art, and other objects which illustrate the often sympathetic administration of justice in the Territories.

The most fascinating 90 minutes you spend in Yellowknife will probably be a walking tour of the **Old Town**, that rough-and-ready frontier community where it all began. A clutch of original structures remains, assembled in the 1930s from whatever materials came to hand by fortune-seekers who had little to spend on accommodation. Its most famous street is Ragged Ass Road (named after a now-defunct gold mine), where houses continue to represent the individuality of early settlers, as well as present inhabitants. Some residents have actually moved their houses to barges moored offshore in order to avoid the municipal taxes. Among the original

FRONTIER JUSTICE

Between 1955 and 1966, Judge John Howard Sissons travelled by plane and dogsled to administer law in his 3.4 million sq km (1.3 million sq mile) judicial district. In outlying communities he would hold court in kitchens and igloos, and once did so in the cabin of a wrecked bush plane. Always fair, and sympathetic to the harsh life of people living off the land, he was known by them as The One Who Listens to Things.

During his decade in the north, Sissons was an avid collector of Inuit art. When a prisoner who was found 'Not Guilty' of killing his father presented the judge with a soapstone carving portraying his impressions of the proceedings, it was the start of a very special collection. From then on, following completion of a particularly interesting trial, the judge would commission a carving to represent it. On his death in 1969, the collection was given to the people of the Northwest Territories and is now displayed in the lobby of the Yellowknife courthouse.

Most depict violent crimes. One shows several people accused of murdering a woman they believed was possessed by evil spirits. Another has a man resting on a rifle in an igloo, while three onlookers stand by. (They were found guilty of aiding the fourth man to commit suicide, and were given suspended sentences.) A more joyful scene shows a baby girl, Katie, being handed over to adoptive parents in a way customary to the Inuit, but contrary to the Adoption and Child Welfare Ordinance. Judge Sissons upheld the traditional adoption as valid.

Several deal with natives killing big game at the wrong time or in the wrong place. One such trial, still talked about in Yellowknife today, saw a local man called Sikyea charged with shooting a female mallard duck out of season. He argued he had 'the ancient right to hunt, trap and fish for food at all seasons of the year ....' Judge Sissons ruled him 'Not Guilty'. There was an appeal against the decision, and for two years the government spent tremendous sums on legal expenses. Finally, Sikyea had to pay a small fine, and until the day he died he complained that he had lost the duck as well. The little stuffed mallard (now known as the 'Million Dollar Duck') is displayed in the courthouse, along with a carving showing Sikyea committing his dastardly deed.

Old Town dwellings newer buildings include private homes. Two of these are B & Bs listed in the accommodation section. At the end of the walk you will be in the traditional Dogrib community of N'Dilo.

Waterfront facilities in the Old Town include float plane docks and the original Canadian Pacific Airlines base, now the Bush Pilot's Brew Pub where the wing of a De Havilland Beaver serves as bar. Across the road is Yellowknife's most famous restaurant, the Wildcat Café, first opened in the 1930s. Reservations are not accepted, and in the friendly spirit of the north, you are encouraged to share your table with strangers. The atmosphere is great, the menu includes caribou and muskox meat. Nearby Trapper's Cabin is another favourite, for its locally caught fish, served with chips.

At the top of a rocky outcrop, the Bush Pilot's Monument affords panoramic views of the entire Old Town, with the buildings of the new town on the skyline. On the way back to the new town, you will want to call in at the North West Company Trading Post on Bryson Drive. It stocks a terrific selection of native crafts, furs and mounted trophies, while plaques and displays on the outside walls tell of the company's history and its relationship with the local peoples. Items for sale range from locally-made wall plaques and ornaments costing around $10 to $20 to a 2.75m (9ft) long polar bear skin rug for $5,000, mounted heads of muskox or bull moose for about $2,000, or a dressed Arctic fox fur with a price tag of $175.

Visitors who intend using Yellowknife as a jumping-off point for safaris further afield will find plenty to do here before leaving town. Close to the airport, **Fred Henne Territorial Park** has all the traditional picnicking, boating, camping and RV facilities of developed provincial parks to the south. Its Prospector's Trail is a 4km (2½ mile) loop which points out the area's very varied geological features.

More of the region's unique geological wonders are examined from the scenic **Ingraham Trail** (Hwy 4) which winds for 71km (44 miles) east through boreal forest, past lakes and rivers to Tibbett Lake. The trail has boat-launches and campgrounds as well as hiking trails and snowmobile routes. All but the most informed visitors will benefit from an escorted walk led by ecologist and author Jamie Bastedo of Cygnus Ecotours. Through his expertise you will have a real sense of northern wilderness, within minutes of leaving the city.

In summer, sightseeing and fishing excursions on the Ingraham Trail are organized out of Yellowknife. Again, these trips put you in

YELLOWKNIFE — THE AVIATION BUFF'S IDEA OF HEAVEN

Flying in from the south, you will probably arrive aboard a small passenger jet and cross the tarmac to Yellowknife's modern terminal. Glance around and you will see that the rest of the aircraft here sport old-fashioned propellers. Many planes date to the 1950s and 1960s. Others are Curtis C-46 Commandos and DC-3 Dakotas and similar relics from World War II. These are the workhorses that carry passengers and supplies to remote communities and mining camps, exchanging wheels for skis once the snow flies.

Down in the Old Town, float-plane docks show another side of the story. Some planes here are modern, some well into antiquedom. There are big turbo-engined de Havilland Beavers and Twin Otters, a vintage Norseman or two, and tiny Piper trainers which carry a single student. In all, seventeen aviation companies (employing 350 pilots) fly out of Yellowknife, the transportation hub of the Northwest Territories and for many communities they are the only link with the outside world.

The city has not forgotten its debt to its early aviation pioneers. The Bush Pilot's Memorial above the Old Town honours the pilots who opened up the north and the lives that were lost in the process. Below it is the base where Max Ward founded a flying service that grew into the highly respected Wardair charter airline, later absorbed by Canadian Airlines International.

On a pedestal above Airport Road, a Bristol Freighter which worked in the north is reminiscent of others used for 1950s flights from England to the Channel Islands. In the Prince of Wales Northern Heritage Centre, an entire gallery is devoted to aviation. Its exhibits include photographs and aviation artifacts, and a de Havilland Fox Moth reconstructed from the wreckage of three such planes which flew in the north. There iss also a mock-up of a cockpit for children to play in.

If you want to learn more about the pioneer days of aviation in the north, return to the Bush Pilot's Brew Pub. Here, pilots still swap tales of emergency flights from ice-strewn lakes, of hair-raising takeoffs in snowstorms and landings on soggy runways.

touch with nature, allowing you to experience the wilderness solitude and essence of the true north, within a short ride of the city. Lake ice has pretty well gone by the first week of June, and the fish will be biting soon after. Walleye, lake trout and northern pike reach record size in the lakes around Yellowknife. You need a licence: $15 for three days if you are a Canadian resident, $30 for non-residents, plus 7% tax. Local outfitters provide everything, even a bug jacket if you are out late at night when more than the fish are biting. A growing number of outfitters in the north have a 'Catch and Release' policy. This means you can examine your catch, measure the big ones and have yourself photographed with them, but you must then return the fish to the water. Such a policy is run by Yellowknife Outdoor Adventures' proprietor, conservationist, teacher and fishing guide Carlos Gonzalez. If your barbless hook catches something really nice, say an 11kg (25lb) northern pike, Carlos will record its details on film, weigh and measure it, and have it replicated for you. These imitations are even more lifelike than the real thing preserved by a taxidermist. As part of his fishing expeditions, Carlos cooks a gourmet lunch on shore, where you can sit and watch enormous beavers working on their lodge below.

This is one of several local organizations able to customize any sort of outdoors experience in the Northwest Territories: bear hunts, polar bear tracking, dog sledding and more. They will fly you to a wilderness lodge where you are catered to, or a wilderness camp where you are left to look after yourself.

Contrary to popular belief, tourism in the Northwest Territories does not shut down in winter. Winter visitors come mainly to view the Northern Lights and to participate in dogsled tours. Some even try their hand at building igloos. In late March/early April the Annual Canadian Championship Dog Derby, a three-day 240km (150 mile) race on Great Slave Lake attracts dog mushers from across North America.

Car rentals are available in Yellowknife, but with so few roads leading out of town, driving options are limited. One possibility is to drive west along Hwy 3, for 108km (67 miles) to the twin communities of **Rae-Edzo**. Fort Rae was originally a Hudson's Bay trading post established in the centuries-old hunting grounds of the Dogrib people. Although Rae gained road access in 1960, the government decided to relocate the people because of poor drainage. For this reason Edzo was built 24km (15 miles) away. Now in the two communities, you will find a fascinating mix of traditional and modern ways. Rae (population 1,600) is the largest Dene community in the Territories. Natives here continue to hunt, fish and run traplines, while making use of modern public facilities. Native crafts are on sale, and outfitters conduct hunting and fishing expeditions.

In neighbouring Edzo, a unique experience is provided at Sah Naji Kwe Camp. This holistic healing centre on the shores of Great Slave Lake is geared largely for small groups. (Its name translates as Bear Healing Rock.) Programs are designed to bring a sense of peace, rejuvenation and healing that comes from living in close communion with the natural world according to native traditions. Therapeutic clay from lake deposits feature in treatments, as do extracts of plants gathered along the shoreline. Accommodation is in well-furnished canvas lodges.

Most travel from Yellowknife is by air. These days residents use commuter and charter planes as the rest of the world uses buses and taxis. Now outlying communities are reached in hours where they used to be weeks, even months, away.

Fort Smith is less than an hour by air from Yellowknife (but 743km, 462 miles, by road) which means it is possible to visit for a day. This is hardly practical though, when Wood Buffalo National Park lies on its doorstep. If you decide to drive, the road will take you around the western arm of Great Slave Lake. About two thirds of the way, **Hay River** lies in an area inhabited for thousands of years by the Slavey or Slave people after whom the lake was named. This town (population 3,000) is the northern terminus of the main highway from Alberta, staging port in the Mackenzie River system and centre of the lake's commercial fishery. If you are driving between Alberta and Yellowknife, you will find it a good stopover.

From Hay River, a further 269km (167 miles) brings you to **Fort Smith**. This friendly little community was once a strategic link in the portage route which led from the Prairies to the Mackenzie River, and was the site of a Hudson's Bay Company fort built in 1874. Until 1967 it was the unofficial Territorial government headquarters. Now its 2,500 residents depend largely on subsistence fishing, trapping, tourism and government employment. A self guided one-hour walking tour of Fort Smith is mapped out in pamphlets from the Visitor Information Centre in Conibear Park. It includes the **Northern Life Museum**, started by the Oblate Fathers with their collection of Indian artifacts and handicrafts, wildlife specimens, ancient fossils and bones. Photographs are of the explorers, traders, missionaries and bush pilots. Among the town's few stores 'North of 60° Books' has one of the world's largest collections of maps, charts and books dealing with the north.

Australian tour companies use Fort Smith as an overnight stop for their flights from the South to North poles. Summer visitors find this an ideal base for canoeing, kayaking and hiking expeditions. Also for wildlife viewing, which starts right in town with the pelican rookeries on the islands of the Rapids of the Drowned (so named after a tragic accident in 1789). These are the northernmost nesting grounds of the North American white pelican. Coming from Mexico, the Caribbean and southern United States when the ice breaks up in April, the birds stay to breed and raise their young before returning south. During the long hours of sub-Arctic sunshine, each pelican eats over 3kg (7lb) of fish per day, but they still leave plenty for the rest of us.

The headquarters of the **Wood Buffalo National Park** are in the Government of Canada Building close to the Visitor Information Centre. A stop here is essential for anyone going into the park. It has an excellent slide presentation and brochures, as well as an obliging staff on hand to answer questions. Straddling the border between the Northwest Territories and Alberta, this is Canada's largest national park. At 44,800 sq km (17,300 sq miles), it is slightly larger than Switzerland. It was established in 1922 to protect the continent's last remaining herd of wood bison which, in spite of deadly diseases in recent years, numbers around 6,000. Moose, caribou, wolves and black bears all live in the park, while pelicans, hawks and eagles are visible without binoculars. The most astonishing of bird residents are the very rare whooping cranes which migrate from Texas each spring to this, their only northern nesting ground. The cranes, standing 150cm (5ft) tall, have well-established nesting sites, so a competent guide can easily locate them for you. Even newcomers unaware of the cranes' habitats will realize their presence from their unmistakeable bugle-call. Both the cranes' wetland habitat and the large freshwater Peace Athabasca delta are natural features which have earned the park its UNESCO World Heritage status.

There are no commercial services within the Wood Buffalo National Park, but you may hike, paddle and camp where you wish, subject to some restrictions. (One being that you need a permit for any of these activities.) The only campground accessible by road is at Pine Lake, about 60km (37 miles) south of Fort Smith. Spectacular when seen from a low-flying plane, this deep, crystal clear lake has a beautiful blue-green tint caused by suspended algae. The surrounding area is pocked with water-filled sink-holes in the limestone, giving it the appearance of one huge slice of green Swiss cheese.

The most astounding feature in the park, unless you are a bird watcher perhaps, is the accumulation of salt from springs emerging at the base of a low escarpment. These remarkable salt plains have in the past attracted native peoples, missionaries, traders and settlers who collected the salt, either for trade or for their own use. Now they attract wildlife, and an overlook reached within an hour by road from Fort Smith is a favourite viewing stop for day visitors. An alternative is to hike along the trails that range from 1km (⅔ mile) to 20km (12 miles) into the plains. Park rangers conduct some interpretive programs, including 'buffalo creeps' to view the herd. The irrepressible Jacques van Pelt of Subarctic Wildlife Adventures provides sightseeing and guiding services within the park for a day or longer. His treks to the salt plains, and overnight stops in tents here are very popular. On these overnight trips guests sleep facing their tent walls with cameras poised, and are awakened as the buffalo approach to lick on the salt.

Since accommodation is limited in Fort Smith the best advice is to book through Subarctic Wildlife Adventures. Jacques uses several first-rate Bed and Breakfast establishments for his tours. One is handily located across from his own remarkable home, and its owner is an excellent cook, who will by arrangement provide modestly priced meals for guests. Another is an interesting log hexagon structure. Both properties have ensuite guest rooms. (Addresses are listed in the Accommodation & Eating Out section.)

Even further *Off the Beaten Track* is **Nahanni National Park Reserve**. The nearest road access point is Nahanni Butte, roughly 700km (435 miles) west of Yellowknife via the Mackenzie and Laird Hwys, or 100km (62 miles) north of Fort Laird in British Columbia. River access is available from the west. Almost all visitors fly in from Fort Simpson in a small float plane loaded with gear, and their canoe strapped to a float strut. Within minutes of arriving at their starting point they can, if they wish, be left to their own devices.

Prospective visitors should contact the Northwest Territories' tourism office for listings of licensed outfitters and guides able to fulfil special requirements. If you plan to dispense with guide services, do understand that adventuring in this park is not for novices. The rivers, beautiful as they are, can be relentless. Many have stretches of dangerous white water, and thunderstorms can raise river levels by as much as 30cm (1ft) in an hour. Adventurers following the Nahanni from its headwaters west of the park will encounter forty-two sets of rapids in the first three days. Some of these rate 'grade 3 — difficult' on the international scale of 6. You are required to register when you enter and leave the park, and it is useful to contact park authorities in advance of your arrival.

Like Wood Buffalo National Park, the 4,700 sq km (1,815 sq mile) Nahanni is a UNESCO World Heritage Site. The South Nahanni is one of the world's most impressive rivers. All who tackle it are awed by its waters surging between vertical canyon walls up to 1,000m (3,200ft) high, the incredible waterfalls, ancient caves and natural hotspring pools. Hikers can expect to see moose and beaver as well as deer and Dall sheep, along with the occasional bear, and heart-wrenching wilderness scenery that has to be seen to be believed.

Inuvik, 200km (125 miles) above the Arctic Circle, is as far north as you can drive by public road. This 'planned' town, started in 1954 to replace neighbouring Aklavik, has scheduled air service to Edmonton, Yellowknife and Whitehorse. Inuvik is not a vacation destination, so much as jump-off point for Arctic explorations. For example, **Tuktoyaktuk**, a short flight away on the edge of the Beaufort Sea, has restored traditional buildings and boat trips to watch beluga and bowhead whales offshore. **Sachs Harbour** on Banks Island is the most northerly community in the western Arctic. In spring, dog teams take visitors on photographic hunts for polar bear and muskox. Summer brings the geese and seabirds, and the tundra takes on wonderful hues of the alpine plants growing in wild profusion. This is the time when visitors come to canoe or raft down the Thomsen, the most northerly navigable river in Canada.

Arctic travel is specialized, and must be well planned before your arrival. The address for Northwest Territories' tourism department is given in the Canada Fact File and it is suggested that readers contact this office for brochures listing activities and excursions. Addresses of outfitters are given so you can follow through with plans for a visit. The outfitters named are personally known to the authors.

Additional Information
— Adventuring In The Northwest —

Places to Visit

Fort Smith

Northern Life Museum
110 King Street
Open: daily June to Labour Day, Sunday and Tuesday to Friday rest of year
☎ (403) 872-2859

North of 60° Books
Box 1050
Fort Smith NT
X0E 0P0
☎ (403) 872-2606

Yellowknife

Northern Frontier Visitor Centre
Airport Rd
#4-4807 49th St
Yellowknife NT
X1A 3T5
☎ (403) 873-3131

Prince of Wales Northern Heritage Centre
Open: daily June to August, closed Mondays rest of year,
☎ (403) 873-7551

NWT Legislative Assembly
Tours: weekdays all year, but suspended when the House is in session, so telephone first
☎ (403) 669-2200

Parks

Fred Henne Territorial Park
c/o Economic Development and Tourism
Box 1320
Yellowknife NT
X1A 2L9
☎ (403) 920-2472

Nahanni National Park Reserve
Box 348
Fort Simpson NT
X0E 0N0
☎ (403) 695-3151

Wood Buffalo National Park
PO Box 750
Fort Smith NT
XOE 0P0
☎ (403) 872-2349

Local Tourist Information Offices

Yellowknife

Northern Frontier Visitor Centre
#4-4807 49th St
Yellowknife NT
X1A 3T5
☎ (403) 873-3131

Fort Smith

Fort Smith Chamber of Commerce
Box 121
Fort Smith NT
X0E 0P0
☎ (403) 872-5626

9 • Alberta's Fabled Rockies

For visitors, Alberta is Canada's fairytale province, home of the Canadian Rockies with their snow-capped peaks and mountain sheep. This is where you can hike along rock-strewn paths into vistas of story-book quality, dip your paddle into turquoise lakes, photograph black bears and prehistoric-looking moose beside the highways. The promotional posters and provincial guides do not exaggerate and the nine million tourists who come here each year are not disappointed. Such is the grandeur of this province it has five national parks, three of which are in the Rockies. East of the mountains, fertile soil makes central and southern Alberta rich in agriculture. North of Edmonton, dense forests stretch to the Northwest Territories border.

More than just another pretty face, Alberta is rich in natural deposits. Oil is a multi-billion dollar industry with more reserves here than in Saudi Arabia. Coal reserves exceed any in Canada. There is so much natural gas that it is piped into other provinces and to the United States. Tourism has been an important industry here for over 100 years, and much of the provincial wealth has been used to create world-class visitor facilities. Historical and cultural sites are recreated or restored with such zeal that they are truly exciting.

Completion of the Canadian Pacific Railway through the Rockies was responsible not only for the influx of settlers, but also for widespread tourism to Alberta. Company president William Van Horne's much repeated line 'If we can't export the scenery we must import the tourists', certainly rings true here where Canadian Pacific's castle-like resorts and hotels (all updated to meet modern demands) are filled to capacity most of the year.

Dinosaurs roamed this land millions of years ago. Their bones are still being recovered in the Badlands they inhabited, and are preserved now at the Royal Tyrrell Museum. The first humans were aboriginals, whose way of life was rudely dismissed by traders and settlers. Of all the museums portraying their culture, Alberta's Head-Smashed-In Buffalo Jump is one of the most remarkable and perhaps most disturbing. Regional museums tell of local heroes and characters. Like 'Kootenai' Brown, an adventurer from England who was one of the wildest, whereas Father Albert Lacombe who devoted his life to the Prairie Indians and Métis, was one of the most dedicated. At Rocky Mountain House, the area's trappers and traders are recalled. Fort Macleod is named after the first commissioner of the North West Mounted Police, who brought his men on a dreadful trek from Manitoba to stop the illegal whiskey trade here. And do not forget Twelve Foot Davis, a prospector who filed a 12ft claim between larger claims and removed $15,000 from it. These are just some of the larger-than-life westerners that you will learn about when travelling through Alberta.

Ranchers established frontier towns that grew into rough and tumble cities, refined today with corporate headquarters and shopping centres. The visual and performing arts prosper in modern theatres and galleries. Both Edmonton and Calgary have opera companies, symphony orchestras, and grand entertainment complexes.

When the frontier days are relived in rodeos and stampedes, nobody is a stranger. It is a time for the whole community to get involved. Local merchants wear costumes from the late 1800s, and everyone is invited to the street dances, cook-outs and casinos.

This then is Alberta, where practically everything is *Off the Beaten Track*. While summer crowds in downtown Banff can be daunting, much of the splendid scenery remains unspoiled. You can still canoe and walk wilderness paths, encounter wildlife and climb the mountains, explore the grasslands and ranching country, and travel for miles across glacial lakes. And sense what it was like for them — the traders, the settlers, the adventurers, the railway builders and the dreamers who came before you.

Alberta is one of Canada's most diverse regions, where enormous mountain areas have been set aside as natural preserves drawing visitors from around the world in all seasons. In these national parks visitors can stay at resorts, hotels and motels and campgrounds. Facilities are organized for all-year-round adventure, sports and leisure. In a book this size no more than a few highlights can be mentioned. For more detailed information the Alberta and local tourism information centres are excellent sources. They will supply material on all aspects of your proposed visit, from companies and outfitters specializing in this immediate region to hiking trails and canoe routes away from the crowds.

The Alaska Highway near Kluane National Park (Chapter 7)

Rafting in Kluane National Park (Chapter 7)

Kathleen Lake, Kluane National Park (Chapter 7)

Alberta's three mountain national parks, Waterton Lakes, Banff and Jasper are described in this chapter.

Waterton Lakes National Park

Approximately 230km (143 miles) south of Calgary, via Hwys 2 or 22 and then Hwy 6, Waterton Lakes National Park is not the most famous of these parks, nor is it the largest. And herein lies the appeal. Sparsely populated, it contains some of the most fabulous mountain scenery in the Rockies, and is reminiscent of Banff and Jasper National Parks as they were several decades ago. Located on the eastern slopes of the Rockies, Waterton's western boundary is the crest of the Rocky Mountain divide. Its eastern border is in the foothills of Alberta and in the south it joins Montana's Glacier National Park. Unlike Banff and Jasper National Parks, this was never served by rail, so received little publicity and fewer tourists in its early years. Even now there is no major highway slicing through it, which means it is strictly a destination park, unspoiled and undeveloped except for a small townsite, some roads and trails. Because of its location where mountains meet the prairies, abruptly and with no intervening foothills, the weather is unpredictable and enormously changeable. This can translate into heavy rain, literally out of the blue, but the sometimes inclement weather is more than outweighed by the solitude and the wildlife.

Created as a national park in 1911, Waterton encompasses 528 sq km (204 sq miles) of a region known to the natives as Land of Shining Mountains — and this it is. The first white men to come through were members of a trading party led by David Thompson in 1800. The first white inhabitant was the legendary Kootenai Brown.

The most prominent building in the park today is the seven-storied chalet-style Prince of Wales Hotel, erected on a knoll outside the townsite in 1927. Every window frames a lake view. Vintage buses bring in guests who arrive at the town dock by boat from the American side of the lake. Snuggled cosily between the mountains, the park's townsite resembles a Swiss alpine village. It has the usual visitor amenities: accommodation, restaurants, souvenir shops, launderette and sports and leisure facilities. But all this is incidental to the area's natural attributes; the mountains and lakes, wildflowers that proliferate in early July, the stillness disturbed only by birds and rushing waterfalls and deer wanting to lick your hand.

Waterton's high country, reached by hiking paths, is studded with ice-blue lakes and streams. In all there are twenty such trails.

KOOTENAI BROWN

Kootenai Brown was one of the many legendary characters who made the 'wild west' a little wilder, who grew to love its beauty and its challenges, and was eventually tamed by the little patch he chose as home. Kootenai lived in Waterton Lakes National Park. He once said this is the most beautiful spot in Canada. He should know as he saw most of western Canada before settling here.

George John Brown was educated at Eton and Oxford, and served in India as a military officer before striking it rich in the Cariboo goldfields. There he made and lost what he termed 'a little fortune'. A man of many trades, and many adventures, he next became a Pony Express rider, buffalo hunter, whiskey trader, and scout. His nickname 'Kootenai' came from his association with the Kootenai Indians.

It seems that Kootenai never had a dull moment. One time, on his way to Fort Edmonton, he was shot in the back by Sioux natives, and survived only after his friends removed the arrow and poured half a can of turpentine into the wound. Another time when carrying the mail he was captured by Chief Sitting Bull, and was probably destined for a very nasty death. He managed to escape by jumping into a lake, and arrived at his destination with no mail, no clothes and a lot of mosquito bites.

Kootenai Brown married twice, each time to a Cree woman. His second wife, called Blue Flash of Lightning, was so beautiful that he exchanged five horses for her on sight. It is said that he won all the horses back during the wedding festivities that followed.

An intrepid hunter of big game during his early years in Canada, he later became a keen conservationist. In 1889 he built a cabin at Waterton Lakes, supporting his family by hunting, trapping and fishing. He also became a well-known guide. When he and other settlers in the area suspected that Waterton was about to be uncontrollably developed, Kootenai was instrumental in its becoming first a forest reserve in 1895 and in 1911 a national park. At the age of 71 he became the park's first superintendent. John George 'Kootenai' Brown 1839-1916 is buried here alongside his two wives, on the shore of Lower Waterton Lake that he loved so well.

Conducted hikes in summer last from one hour to ten hours, so there is something for everyone. A two-hour walk around Cameron Lake at the foot of snow-covered Mount Custer is always popular. So is the fairly easy 3km (2 mile) trail to Bertha Falls. Majestic red-tailed hawks and golden eagles, often seen gliding over the mountains, are among the 228 bird species recorded in the park.

Two memorable drives are to Cameron Lake and Red Rock Canyon. The first, 16km (10 miles) from the townsite, is on a road bordered by flowers. Once there you can hire a boat, walk the trails, and use up rolls of film on the sensational view. En route you will pass a sign commemorating the site of Oil City. Incongruous as it seems, this is where the first oil well in western Canada was drilled. As the story goes, a prospector suffering an injured leg was treated by an Indian woman who used thick oil as a healing agent. He mentioned the incident to a Dominion land surveyor and together they traced what they thought to be the oil's source. Wells were drilled and houses built. Several attempts to pump the oil in quantity failed, and finally in 1929 the 'city' was abandoned. Geologists later explained that surface pools causing the excitement probably seeped from a reserve well beyond the park.

Red Rock Canyon, 18km (11 miles) from the townsite, is even more dramatic in appearance. Here, mountain slopes wear a verdant cloak patched with dark green pines, its hem embroidered with alpine flowers. Long thin waterfalls hang like silver ribbons on a bride's bouquet. The canyon's walls are brick red.

A favourite evening stroll is along a lakefront path from the centrally located Bayshore Inn to the outskirts of town. The view from this path is what the park is about, with snow-fringed mountains rising from shimmering moonlit water. A turnabout point is a little park frequented by deer. Sit here for a while and you will likely hear a loon's woeful cry across the lake.

Banff National Park

This most famous of the mountain parks is 128km (80 miles) west of Calgary via the Trans-Canada Hwy, or 128km (80 miles) from Radium Hot Springs in British Columbia, via Hwy 93. First-time visitors will want at least a brief stay in the town of Banff, set in a mountain-rimmed valley with the Bow River gurgling through it. The year-round population is approximately 7,000, but summer and winter see it bulging with tourists who flock here at the rate of three million a year. As more accommodation is built for them, more tour buses find their way here, and the public outcry gets louder. Sadly such popularity has turned Banff into an unpleasantly crowded tourist centre in summer, with queues for restaurants and facilities. In late spring or fall you will undoubtedly enjoy it more. While so many summer visitors amble along Banff Avenue looking for souvenirs and fast food, the town's museums remain fairly quiet. The Parks Canada Museum, Natural History Museum and Whyte Museum of the Canadian Rockies will give you a good understanding of the region's wildlife, history and art. The Banff Centre for the Arts is one of Canada's major centres for the arts and music, with frequent public performances and displays.

Banff is Canada's oldest national park, established back in 1885 as the first link in a necklace of natural preserves strung across the country. It all began here two years earlier, when three intrepid railway workers descended a tree-trunk ladder into a cave and came upon sulphurous hot springs. Realizing the commercial possibilities, they erected a cabin nearby in the hope of establishing squatters' rights. Within a year several small hotels were accommodating guests who came to test the waters' curative powers. Ironoically, thanks to unmade roads and raft trips to the springs, some went home with more aches and pains than they brought with them.

Squabbles over ownership became serious, and eventually the government stepped in by creating a national park around the springs to keep them for public use. Known at first as Rocky Mountain Park it covered little more than the immediate area. Over the years its boundaries were expanded to take in more scenic phenomena, and now known as Banff National Park it covers 6,641 sq km (2,564 sq miles) of incredible mountain scenery.

While the hot springs are no longer the area's biggest draw, they should not be missed. In 1914 a large outdoor pool was built at the Cave, fed by hot springs discovered by those railway workers. It fell into disrepair and was rebuilt in 1985 as part of a grand Centennial Centre commemorating the park's 100th birthday. While this new pool (a replica of the original) closes at the end of summer, the centre's other attractions remain open. They include the original foul-smelling cave with hot water still spurting through its rocky walls, and the basin, which has a second thermal spring with an average temperature of 34°C (93°F). Once a popular swimming hole, the basin has reverted to its nineteenth-century appearance now, and for safety reasons is off-limits to bathers. Exhibits, plaques explaining various events connected with the springs, and a slide show will give you an interesting couple of hours here. A boardwalk above the Centennial Centre leads past the opening in the cave's roof. Benches along the trail invite you to sit and enjoy the view. A restaurant with seating both indoors and out, serves appetizing meals and snacks.

Three kilometres (2 miles) from Banff townsite, Sulphur Mountain's outdoor pool, served by the hottest of the mountain's five springs, is open all year. A car park close by allows you to drive to the 1,585m (5,200ft) level for a soak and a massage. Then, if you are not too drowsy, you might ride in one of the glass-enclosed gondolas to the 2,286m (7,500ft) peak. At the top, full meals are offered in the Summit Restaurant; walking paths lead to quieter places.

Understandably, walking and hiking have always been popular here because the trails take you to beauty spots that are inaccessible by car. Something like 1,300km (800 miles) of trails criss-cross the park. Short, self-guiding, interpretive paths from the townsite appeal to anyone interested in nature. The Fenland trail, (2km, 1¼ miles) for instance, is only minutes from town but will take you through marsh and forest inhabited by beaver, muskrat and waterfowl. The Vermilion Lakes, immediately west of town, are famous for their poster views of Mount Rundle and as home to migrating wildfowl and beaver families. North of town, the Buffalo Paddock has a species of bison which once prospered in this area. Campers on Tunnel Mountain invariably follow the path leading to unusual rock formations known as hoodoos. Some legends say these are tipis housing 'bad Gods'. Others that the hoodoos are giants who sleep by day and come alive at night to terrorize travellers. Almost any of the trails cut around Tunnel Mountain are great for bird watching, at the same time opening up wonderful alpine vistas.

One of the most arduous trails within Banff's townsite is an access route used by climbers bound for Tunnel Mountain's summit. Through 2.5km (1½ miles) of dense forest, then switchbacking into open slopes, it gives tremendous views of the Spray Valley. If you intend going further, a permit from the warden service is necessary.

Longer hikes are detailed in maps from the townsite visitor centre. Here are some to whet the appetite, and have you looking for more: The 20km (12 mile) Mystic Lake trail from Mount Norquay takes around six hours. From here you can continue to Johnston Canyon (a further 17km, 11 miles), definitely more arduous than the first leg but well worth the effort. (An alternative for non-hikers is to drive to the Johnston Canyon Lodge complex and walk for 1.1km (¾ miles) to the Lower Falls, or 2.7km (1¾ miles) to the Upper

Falls. Street shoes are adequate for this one, and your photographs will have the neighbours believing that you hiked for days to get them.) Another short-haul favourite that brings great scenic rewards is Moraine Lake, 15km (9 miles) off the Trans-Canada Hwy north of Banff. Here you leave your car and walk 500m to the top of the rockpile to view both lake and mountain peaks. If it all looks familiar, this is a favourite picture postcard scene and used to be featured on Canada's $20 bills.

Eight kilometres (5 miles) northeast of Banff townsite, boat tours on Lake Minnewanka give you plenty of photo opportunities. But again, this can be a very busy place in summer. Hikers can better capture the mountain view. Trails start at the boat dock and picnic area on the lake's western tip, cross the Stewart Canyon and follow the northern shore of the lake for the next 20km (12 miles). The complete circuit around this, Banff's largest lake, is 48km (30 miles) with campsites along the shore, and opportunities to rest on beaches strewn with driftwood.

As in all national parks, Banff's campground sites are offered on a first-come basis. In summer the daily turnover is large, so you should not be put off by the long lines of vehicles waiting for sites. Late morning is best time for new arrivals, because anyone leaving has probably gone by then. Visitor accommodation runs the gamut from cottages and cabins on the mountains' lower slopes and motels in and around town to the fairytale Banff Springs Hotel built by the Canadian Pacific Railway in 1888. The original wooden structure has been replaced by this baronial castle of local stone which now accommodates approximately 1,600 guests. Latest excitement here is the opening in 1995 of the hotel's own luxurious spa, utilizing mineral waters from local springs. The management is so proud of it all that public tours are conducted on most afternoons.

Motorists can drive to the park's more famous scenic sites then locate footpaths fanning out from them. For a better chance of seeing wildlife, use the Bow Valley Parkway (Hwy 1a), rather than the Trans-Canada Hwy. Often wildlife is more visible from highways than walks and trails because creatures frequenting roadside areas have become blasé about humans. They find it far easier to raid the garbage dumps and beg from tourists than to forage for themselves. For good reason, visitors are asked not to feed them. The larger animals can present a danger in built-up communities, and then have to be evicted to wilderness regions. If they find their way back again, they may be destroyed.

What will you see? Black bears are traffic stoppers. Elks, and

BEARS

Canada's parks are Bear Country. Seen from the safety of a vehicle, roadside bears can be highly photogenic models, but always remember they are potentially dangerous and deserve your respect. If bears are surprised, or feel threatened, they will attack to defend themselves, their young and their territory. Bears are unpredictable, strong and agile and they can inflict very serious injuries.

Every year hundreds of thousands of hikers, campers and canoeists peacefully co-exist with bears in Off the Beaten Track Canada. This is largely due to education. Study the pamphlets handed out at park entrances and act on their advice. Ask park rangers about local conditions and areas to avoid. If you wear a bell or carry a few pebbles in a can, it warns of your approach and allows the bear to get out of your way. Do not wear perfume — it can give a bear the wrong idea! Cook and eat well away from your tent. Remove all signs of food afterwards, and disposing of garbage carefully, preferably in the bear-proof containers provided.

The pamphlets give you several options for escape in the rare event of your confronting a bear. Novice campers may glibly tell you to climb a tree. In truth few of us are this agile, and bears are good tree climbers anyway. So, follow the advice of the experts who wrote these pamphlets, and notices posted in the parks, and you and the bears will keep out of trouble.

coyotes are commonplace. One moose used to hang around Banff's railway station so much, rumour had it he was on the company payroll. Bighorn sheep are so brazen that they may nip at your sleeve or lunch on that map sticking out of your pocket. Deer usually trot off after gazing at you with huge liquid brown eyes. Industrious beavers go about their dam building regardless of their audience, while timber wolves are more often heard than seen.

Local companies organize outdoors adventures which allow you to enjoy the environment without harming it. Trail riders can equip you for a half day, a week or for longer safaris. Others lead mountaineering expeditions. Canoeing, kayaking and rafting are popular with visitors, and so is fishing. Alpine skiers have World Cup challenges, and a season stretching from early November to late May. Where there is no danger of avalanches, hiking trails accommodate cross-country skiers in winter, and conversely some ski areas revert to superb hiking country in summer. Winter months can be magical in the Rockies, with dog sledding and ice skating, unforgettable Christmas and New Year parties.

Lake Louise, 55km (34 miles) north of Banff townsite suffers from severe tourist overload in summer. On a July or August weekend, the area's walking trails are almost as busy as London's Oxford Street on a Saturday morning. Be here in June or September and you can have the same good weather, with less likelihood of bumping into fellow hikers.

Unlike Lake Minnewanka, Lake Louise does not tolerate motorboats. Instead you can follow a foot trail around its shore, view it from above, and canoe across the glacial water so perfectly framed by towering mountains and glistening icefields. Recreational hiking in the Rockies first took root in this region. One of the first high trails cut in the park was to Lake Agnes, named after Susan Agnes who travelled here with her husband, Prime Minster John A. Macdonald in 1886. As more scenic wonders were discovered, employees of the Canadian Pacific Railway created new trails from Lake Louise. Now a favourite is to Lake Agnes Teahouse, 367m (1,205ft) above Lake Agnes, from where the views of Mirror Lake, Lake Louise and the Bow Valley are exhilarating at the very least. Located right on the shore, the famous Château Lake Louise has recently come through a costly renovation program. If you are not staying here, you may want to visit it anyway, for the huge lounges where plump armchairs face picture windows framing that ever-so-perfect lake and mountain scene.

The community of Lake Louise is on the former site of Laggan railway station which housed 12,000 men during the construction of the line through the famed Kicking Horse Pass (1,624m, 5,238 ft). The name recalls a time in 1858 when the Palliser expedition's geologist, Dr James Hector, was kicked by a packhorse. Our itinerary continues northwards. A popular alternative is westward along the Trans-Canada Hwy at Lake Louise, then through the Kicking Horse Pass and into British Columbia as described in Chapters 5 and 6.

It is possible to travel the 286km (178 mile) Icefields Highway (Hwy 93) between Banff and Jasper in three or four hours, but that would be foolish, for this is acknowledged as one of the most beautiful drives in the world. Even in unfriendly weather you will want to stop often, for photographs or simply to stand and stare at the majesty of snow-draped mountains reflected in translucent lakes. Side roads and walking trails from the Parkway are bound to detain you further, leading as they do to canyons and waterfalls, secluded spots where mountain avens, wild larkspur and violets prosper, and to other very special places.

Some sixty years ago only the hardiest of tourists attempted this journey, and it took them at least two weeks. The first road connecting Banff to Jasper was undertaken as a relief work project during the Depression, while the current parkway was completed in the early 1960s.

Bow Lake is a favourite stop for its glorious setting and the still green waters fed by glacier meltwaters. Driving northward, you reach the Bow Pass at 2,069m (6,788ft) and a sideroad leading to the Bow Summit Trail. This interpretive trail will take you to a forest area just below the tree line, and to meadows where in July you will find glacier lilies and anenomes peeking through the remaining patches of snow. It is a short walk along the trail to the Peyto Lake overlook, for a fabulous view of Peyto Lake. This lake's remarkably strong colours result from fine rock flour particles held in suspension, which in summer change the water from blue to turquoise as surface ice melts.

After leaving Bow Summit, the road crosses the North Saskatchewan River, which carries the meltwaters from the Rockies across the Prairies to central Saskatchewan. This is a good place for wildlife viewing, because the area's warm, dry micro-climate makes it a favoured spot for deer, sheep and goats. Outfitters used to dread the fast-flowing river crossing here, where packhorses could be submerged and expedition supplies ruined. Now you can simply slip across the bridge. A walk down to the warden station still gives some appreciation of the difficulties encountered by those early outfitters, and it continues to be a fine place from which to watch for expeditions.

Jasper National Park

A further 50km (32 miles) brings you to the Columbia Icefield bordering Jasper National Park. Three of the icefield's glaciers — the Athabasca, Dome and Stutfield — are visible from the Parkway. Hemmed in by 3,700m (12,000ft) high mountains, this huge cap of ice with fingers dipping into the valleys covers 390 sq km (150 sq miles). A sideroad off the Parkway takes you almost to the foot of the Athabasca glacier. You can park here and walk to the tip where you will learn that the ice is receding at around 60m (200ft) a year. Or you can drive up the mountainside to the terminal for a specially designed bus to take you onto the glacier. The earliest glacier tours involved horses wearing non-slip shoes. Then came the tank-like 'snow cats'. The excitement they generated when poised over a chasm has been lost to progress, since full-sized buses now transport fifty-six passengers apiece on a road cut across the glacier. In summer you are given a number, and must wait for it to be called before boarding, so it is worth your while to be here early in the day.

At the height of the tourist season, this facility is so crowded it hardly qualifies as being *Off the Beaten Track*. At the same time it is the world's only glacier ride. Also it does provide an understanding of nature's huge mountain-top ice factories, giving birth to so many of North America's rivers which end up in the Pacific, Atlantic and Arctic Oceans.

Leaving the Icefield area, the highway now descends into the scenic Athabasca Valley, a fairly mild ecoregion which attracts deer, elk, and black and grizzly bears. At Athabasca Falls, 73km (45 miles) north of the Icefield, the river is funnelled into a narrow gorge before plunging 22m (72ft) over a ledge of quartzite. The interpretive walkway through a canyon carved by the river provides more highly photogenic views.

First-time visitors may be curious about the names that they encounter here. The area was surveyed around the time of World War I, and Mt Edith Cavell in the distance was named in honour of the British nurse executed by the Germans. Mt Fryatt honours a British captain who evacuated many Allied troops, but was captured and executed in 1916. His ship, *The Brussels* is remembered in the name of another mountain peak.

From Athabasca Falls on a clear day you will see the unmistakeable shape of Pyramid Mountain forming a backdrop to Jasper, and you can reach this by returning to the Icefield Parkway. Or, having already crossed the river to see the falls, you can continue along the less busy Athabasca Parkway (Hwy 93a) until it rejoins the main road. Anyone staying in Jasper will probably retrace this Parkway on day trips anyway, since it leads to a number of local attractions. One, the Cavell Glacier, at the base of Mt Edith Cavell, is reached by a secondary road unsuitable for RVs. The mountain is popular with climbers. Hikers will enjoy the 43km (27 mile) trail which leads along the Astoria river and down Portal Creek to the trailhead on the Marmot Basin Road. The Icefield Parkway ends at Jasper Townsite. **Jasper** is close to the spot where a North West Company post was established in the early 1800s and was named after their employee, Jasper Hawes. Modern development started in 1907 when the Jasper Park Reserve was established in anticipation of railway construction through the Yellowhead Pass. The first railway arrived in 1911, and the forerunner to the present Jasper Park Lodge was built in 1915 as a tent community for vacationers. A few years later, the all-season road from Edmonton increased the flow of visitors.

Today the town (population 3,300), which remains dependent on transportation and tourism, has avoided much of Banff's crowding and commercialism. There are restaurants in all price ranges, stores and gas stations as well as a variety of visitor accommodation. Jasper Park Lodge, the former Canadian National Railway resort now owned by Canadian Pacific Hotels and Resorts, is beautifully sited on the shore of Lac Beauvert. This village of chalets and log cabins has a unique room service provided by waiters perched on bicycles. Open your bedroom curtains to see the sunrise over Lac Beauvert, and you may well find a deer or elk gazing at you through the window. In town all the services are within walking distance. Several stores specialize in native crafts, including superb soapstone carvings with price tags reading from several hundreds to thousands of dollars.

Different in character from Banff, Jasper National Park (10,900 sq km, 4,200 sq miles) is the largest of Canada's mountain national parks. Resident elk, bighorn sheep, deer and other large animals make this one of the finest areas within the Rocky Mountains to view wildlife. All of the park's best known features can be reached by road, but there are still many opportunities to escape from the beaten track. Safaris from Jasper along the 1,000km (620 miles) of back-trails, through the valleys and into the mountains, can last a few hours, a day or even longer. Raft tours frequent the Athabasca River now, where trappers and traders travelled 150 years before. Fishing, river-rafting, mountaineering and trail riding expeditions are easily arranged through hotels and agents in town. Golfers complain about the distracting scenery. In good weather, a rented bicycle is one of the best ways to get around town. The campgrounds adjacent to Jasper are suitable for RVs.

Whistler Mountain, named after the sound made by the resident marmots, has rugged campgrounds such as you see in advertisements but seldom find in reality. Whether camping or not, you will want to ride Whistler's tramway to an observation station at the 2,285m (7,500ft) level. In clear weather it affords panoramic views of Jasper and surrounding mountains. Hiking trails at this level are all the more interesting for plantlife in the alpine meadows. Resident ptarmigan may well be the main reason for a visit by bird watchers.

Sixty km (37 miles) north of town, Miette Hot Springs has the Rockies' hottest springs, cooled to a comfortable 40°C (104°F) and fed into large, rather utilitarian, outdoor pools. If you bring a picnic be prepared for raggedy mountain goats, big-horned sheep and other uninvited guests that may join you.

Maligne Lake, 50km (31 miles) east of Jasper by road, is another favourite excursion. It was the lake's majestic beauty that led to the park's establishment. This emerald-green body of water stretching 22km (14 miles) into the snow-covered peaks of the Front Range is a scene used often on postcards and calendars. It is best appreciated by boat. Cruises leave the dock regularly in season. Of Maligne Canyon it has been said that 'any other canyon is like a crack in a teacup'. This huge limestone canyon should be near the top of your 'must see' list for its spectacular water drop-off. The cool, damp micro-climate produces magnificent floral displays within the forest all summer. And bird watchers will enjoy this spot, particularly for the rare black swifts which arrive here in mid-June.

Jasper is on Via Rail's trans-continental service. There are bus connections to the east and west, as well as to Banff and Calgary. Continuing on from Jasper by road, you can either drive east along Hwy 16 (the Yellowhead Hwy) to Edmonton, connecting with the western prairies itinerary in Chapter 10, or west along the same highway to drive through central British Columbia as described in Chapter 4.

Additional Information
— Alberta's Fabled Rockies —

Places to Visit

Banff & Banff National Park

Cave and Basin Centennial Centre
Cave Ave west
Open daily, pool mid-June to Labour Day
☎ (403) 762-1557

Natural History Museum
112 Banff Ave
Open: daily
☎ (403) 762-4747

Parks Canada Museum
93 Banff Ave
Open: daily
☎ (403) 762-1558

Sulphur Mountain Gondola Lift
Mountain Ave
adjacent to Upper Hot Springs Pool
Open: daily
☎ (403) 62-2523

Upper Hot Springs Pool
Mountain Ave, 3 km from town
Open: daily
☎ (403) 762-2966

Whyte Museum of the Canadian Rockies
111 Bear St
Open: daily in summer, closed Monday, October to May
☎ (403) 762-2291

Jasper & Jasper National Park

Columbia Icefield Tours
Open: daily late April to early October
☎ (403) 762-6735

Jasper Tramway
6km (3¾ miles) south of Jasper via Hwy 93 and Whistler Mountain Road
Open: mid-April to Thanksgiving
☎ (403) 852-3092

Miette Hot Springs
Hwy 16, 60km (37 miles) north of Jasper
Open: daily, late May to Labour Day
☎ (403) 866-3939

Parks

Banff National Park
Box 900
Banff AB
T0L 0C0
☎ (403) 762-1550

Jasper National Park
Box 10
Jasper AB
T0E 1E0
☎ (403) 852-6161

Waterton Lakes National Park
Waterton Park AB
T0K 2M0
☎ (403) 859-2224

Local Tourist Information Offices

Banff

Banff Information Centre
224 Banff Ave
Banff AB
T0L 0C0
☎ (403) 762-4256

Jasper

Jasper Information Centre
500 Connaught Dr
Jasper AB
T0E 1E0
☎ (403) 852-6176

10 • Cattle, Oil & Dinosaurs

You will discover in the Prairies — an area comprising Alberta east of the Rockies, southern Saskatchewan and southwestern Manitoba — that even a short jaunt off the Trans-Canada Highway defies the stereotypical view of the Prairies as one huge, flat wheatfield. In all three provinces you are guaranteed some of the most dramatic, sometimes stark, often achingly beautiful landscapes you could hope to see anywhere.

The Land of the Big Sky, a phrase that appears on Saskatchewan's car licence plates, proves itself time and again, throughout the Prairies. In summer, it is not uncommon to witness at least four different weather systems at the same time. With a clear blue sky overhead you can have rain pelting down on either side, while a rainbow arches gloriously through distant skies. The summer months are a great time to visit. The days are long and the humidity is low, a perfect combination for enjoyable explorations. And make no mistake, there is plenty to explore. But to minimize the frustrations when travelling on prairie back roads, acquire a Grid Map on which all the country roads are shown, from local tourist information offices or a Rural Municipality Office.

Edmonton, Alberta's capital city (population 620,000) is at the cross-roads of all of Canada's major transportation routes, so it could never be described as *Off the Beaten Track*. However, because of easy accessibility you will likely pay it a visit and enjoy some of its many attractions. This city has much in common with Calgary, and with 2,200 oil wells within a radius of 40km (25 miles) it is accepted as Canada's oil capital.

Reached via Hwy 2, 294km (183 miles) north of Calgary, Edmonton is the oldest of Alberta's cities. Its roots can be traced to 1795, when a fur-trading fort was built as the centre of a Hudson's Bay Company trading area encompassing all of what is now Alberta and Saskatchewan, plus parts of Montana, Idaho and Washington. The fort prospered and became one of the largest settlements in the west.

As the fur trade declined towards the end of the nineteenth century, settlers attracted by the unusually fertile soil flocked into the area. Incorporated as a town in 1892, it really took off six years later when miners travelling overland to the Klondike Gold Rush stopped by for supplies from local outfitters. This was the beginning of Edmonton's role as a major transportation centre and gateway to the north, and it is still celebrated by the Klondike Days Exposition held in late July every year. In 1905 Alberta became a province and Edmonton was chosen as its capital.

Edmonton was already prospering when oil was discovered in nearby Leduc in 1947, marking the beginning of a booming economy. Soon the affluence spread to all sectors and this became one of Canada's most vigorous and forward-looking cities.

If you are in Edmonton with a few hours to spare you will want to see the impressive Provincial Museum of Alberta and the Legislative Building. Curiosity alone will likely draw you to the West Edmonton Mall. Among other things, this gargantuan indoor mall features 800 stores, 110 eating establishments, and leisure facilities which include an amusement park, water park complete with giant slides and wave pool, nineteen cinemas, miniature golf course and casino. To see is to believe.

Edmonton has an abundance of scenic parkland along the banks of the North Saskatchewan River. Pamphlets describing walking tours are distributed at Visitor Information Centres. Try to end your walk at the Hotel Macdonald, one of the traditional railway hotels, beautifully sited on the river banks. 'The Mac', as it is affectionately known, has been carefully restored to the times when it was centre of Edmonton's lively social scene.

Before heading south on our western Prairies loop, consider a worthwhile detour eastward on Hwy 16 to **Elk Island National Park**. Only 45km (28 miles) from Edmonton, it is a relatively small park, about 195 sq km (75 sq miles) encompassing meadows and forested hills, surrounded by prairie pastures and grainfields. Humans co-exist comfortably with nature in this park, established in 1906 as a wildlife preserve for buffalo, elk and beaver. Now there are also moose, deer and some 200 bird species living here. Leisure facilities include a nine-hole golf course, children's play areas, picnic sites campgrounds and more than 100km (60 miles) of hiking, cross-country skiing and interpretive trails. The Ukrainian Cultural Heritage Village just outside the park's east gate depicts the lifestyle of Ukrainian settlers. People of Ukrainian origin represent the largest ethnic group in this part of Alberta. Actively sought by

FORT EDMONTON PARK CAPTURES THE CITY'S LIVELY PAST

History books and films tell their stories well, but for a livelier sampling of Canada's past the recreated forts, missions and trading posts put you right into the picture. Fort Edmonton Park is designed to capture this city's past in a series of streets representing different periods between 1885 and 1920, and the Hudson's Bay Company fort as it was in 1846.

A self-contained community on the banks of the North Saskatchewan River, it housed approximately 150 Hudson's Bay Company employees and their families. The men looked after the business; wives did just about everything else.

The fort's factor was the ambitious and flamboyant John Rowand, who not only made the outpost profitable, but also introduced refinements uncommon this far from civilization. His home, Rowand House, is very grand, all 745 sq m (8,000 sq ft) of it, with solid pine furnishings and glass windows brought from England packed in kegs of molasses to avoid breakage. Here you will learn how Rowand dined well on local produce, imported foods and wines. Visiting Indian chiefs, among others, were entertained in the Great Hall as a preliminary to trading.

Alongside the fort replicated streets start with the 1885 Jasper Avenue, representative of the pre-railway era. Wooden sidewalks are lined with shops selling the necessities of life in a farming settlement. There is a boarding house of sorts, advertising 'private bed and bath'. A bit of cheek really when this translates into a bed, tin footbath and chamber pot — all in the same room.

The 1905 street shows that life was so civilized by then that an artist had set up shop and doubled as a photographer specializing in family portraits. These days he will lend you period clothes, and snap you as if you had posed in the early 1900s. 1920 brought a little leisure time, and the Ukrainian Bookshop did well. Farms prospered by then, as you will see from one here with livestock and a windmill, and implements ranging from pitchforks to agricultural steam engines.

Visitors are brought to the historic streets aboard either a steam train or a streetcar, both of which look very much at home here.

A Dene girl from the Northwest Territories (Chapter 8)

Skidoos, the modern mode of transportation over ice and snow (Chapter 8)

The houses in Ragged Ass Road in Yellowknife's Old Town are much like those used by the original settlers (Chapter 8)

Inukshuk guarding the shoreline (Chapter 8)

settlement agencies for their hardy, industrious and self-reliant qualities, most arrived here between 1895 and 1910.

Off the Beaten Track travellers will enjoy exploring the Beaver Hills area south and east of the national park. It is a favourite with local hikers, canoeists and nature lovers generally. **Beaverhill Nature Centre**, south of the park via Hwy 834, has been designated an internationally significant wetland. Approximately 250 species of birds have been recorded here, including snow geese and even the rare peregrine falcons, which are bred nearby and then released into the wilds. **Miquelon Lakes Provincial Park** is another resting point for birds on the great north-south flyway. It is also a resting place for visitors, since it has camping and picnic areas, boating and watersports and a nice long sandy beach.

It is a 294km (183 mile) drive down Hwy 2 from Edmonton to Calgary, but a less travelled 241km (150 mile) route via Hwys 21, 53 and 56 will take you on a well-justified detour. **Drumheller** in the Red Deer River Badlands, 138km (86 miles) east of Calgary via Hwy 9, is in a region that should not be missed. The Badlands, found in various parts of North America, are intricately shaped channels and gulleys eroded by prehistoric rivers in soft rock beneath the plains. Probably so-named by French explorers, those in Alberta have turned out to be not so bad after all. To date they have produced coal, and now oil, while their huge deposits of dinosaur fossils are of enormous scientific interest.

Dinosaur buffs will be delighted with the Royal Tyrrell Museum about 6km (4 miles) northwest of Drumheller. It is a large complex with complete dinosaurs discovered locally, fossils (including eggs), videos and movies. These are the world's most comprehensive dinosaur exhibits, and if you rent an audio tour cassette, you can expect to spend a busy half day here. Not surprisingly, this museum attracts crowds. Fewer visitors drive the Dinosaur and East Coulee Trails along the banks of the Red Deer River out of Drumheller. On these routes you will see cliffs where some of the earliest fossils were excavated, and strange mushroom-shaped hoodoos fashioned by sandstone erosion. There is good but limited accommodation, as well as RV sites in Drumheller.

From Drumheller it is a 138km (86 mile) drive to **Calgary**. This city was blessed from the beginning with lush grasslands and clear glacier-fed rivers. Successive cycles of nomadic hunters had lived here for 10,000 years when the first fur traders arrived at the end of the eighteenth century, and it was the whiskey traders who led to the establishment in 1875 of a North West Mounted Police post at

Fort Calgary (named by Assistant Commissioner Macleod after his ancestral home in the Scottish Hebrides). Following the railway's arrival, open-range cattle breeding and cereal farming became the dominant industries. Calgary has not looked back since Alberta's major oil discoveries in the 1940s.

Although now a modern, upbeat and sophisticated city, Calgary has never forgotten its cow-town roots. Heritage Park and Fort Calgary are both important historic attractions, while the Glenbow Museum provides an insight into southern Alberta's history. The famous Calgary Exhibition and Stampede (held annually in July) is considered part of the city's heritage. In keeping with the horse-based culture, Spruce Meadows features events which attract the world's most prominent equestrians.

With its close proximity to the Rocky Mountains, popular excursions from Calgary include Banff National Park and Waterton Lakes National Park which have been described in Chapter 9. Other side trips from Calgary might include:

Fort Macleod, in rich farm and ranching country 146km (91 miles) south of Calgary via Hwy 2, on the main road to Waterton Lakes. This is where the North West Mounted Police established their first post. Fort Macleod Museum, a representation of that post, includes a series of historic buildings and exhibits recalling the area's natives and early pioneers.

Head-Smashed-In Buffalo Jump, 18km (11 miles) northwest of Fort Macleod, via Hwy 785, is an exciting UNESCO World Heritage exhibit. It commemorates a way of life among Plains Indians before the white man arrived with his enormous appetite for buffalo meat and hides, and his efficient methods of destruction. Prior to the introduction of horses and guns, herds of buffalo were stampeded over the cliff here to their deaths in an operation which required ingenious planning and military precision. Then, in a camp set up below, the carcases would be butchered to provide food, clothing and other necessities through the coming winter. The 'jump', which was used continuously for at least 5,500 years, has now been carefully preserved. And, in case you are wondering, the centre's expressive name comes from a young Blackfoot brave who, 150 years ago, hid under the cliff to watch the buffalo falling and was crushed to death under their weight.

From Calgary it is another 185km (115 miles) east on the Trans-Canada Hwy (Hwy 1) to **Brooks** where Dinosaur Provincial Park, 48km (30 miles) to the northeast, provides an interesting *Off the Beaten Track* experience. Because of its fossil remains, which include thirty-five distinct dinosaur species, this park has been designated a UNESCO World Heritage site. It also preserves rare Badlands plant and animal life. The Royal Tyrrell Museum (see page 145) maintains a field station here with some exhibits similar to those in its main collection at Drumheller. The field station near the park entrance provides a bus service to the excavation sites, or you can drive yourself on a self-conducted tour. Displays are of partly excavated fossils as well as complete skeletons at the sites where they were discovered. To protect the environment, there is limited access along hiking trails into the park's nature preserve. Tickets are available in the early morning and early afternoon. A nearby campground is suitable for tents and RVs, but for other accommodation you should go into Brooks.

A 110km (68 mile) drive further east along the Trans-Canada Hwy brings you to **Medicine Hat**. Here is an opportunity to take the fairly lightly travelled Crowsnest Hwy (Hwy 3) through Lethbridge and across the Rockies to join the route covered in Chapter 6. Folklore dictates that Medicine Hat (population 42,000) is named after an infamous incident during a battle between the Blackfoot and the Cree, when a Cree medicine man lost his headdress in the river. Considered to be a bad omen, it was felt that this led to his nation's defeat. In the early 1800s, fur traders established posts in the area to trade with Indian and Métis hunters, but by the early 1870s the fur trade had been largely replaced by illegal trading of whiskey. (The termination of the whiskey trade is described in the history of Fort Walsh National Historic Park on page 148-9.)

Medicine Hat's existence was formalized by the arrival of the railway in 1882. By the early 1900s much of the land around Medicine Hat was cultivated by homesteaders including numerous Hutterite colonies. It is now a thoroughly modern town; the discovery of subterranean natural gas fields has resulted in a thriving industrial economy. An underground river keeps the city's surrounding farmlands adequately watered, and provides enough sustenance for local greenhouses to supply flowers to the rest of western Canada.

Rodeos take centre stage in Medicine Hat from spring to fall. The major event on western Canada's rodeo circuit takes place the last weekend of July, at the annual Medicine Hat Exhibition and Stampede. This three day explosion of chuck wagon races and rodeo events easily doubles the town's population.

From Medicine Hat it is approximately 56km (35 miles) along the Trans-Canada Hwy to the Saskatchewan border, and a further

FORT WALSH NATIONAL HISTORIC SITE

Although Indians, and later Métis, had hunted in Cypress Hills for many years, the introduction of the gun and the horse in the late 1700s radically changed the tempo of life here. A hundred years later the buffalo were extinct, open spaces had been fenced in by white settlers, and whiskey had been introduced to the Indian culture by white traders.

Several trading posts were established in Cypress Hills by American traders from Montana and the friction between them and the Native Indians was considerable. These traders showed scant respect for the indigenous peoples. In the winter of 1872, American wolf hunters approached some Assiniboine Indians who were camping besides the Farwell trading post and accused them of stealing their horses. In what is now known as the Cypress Hills Massacre, twenty Assiniboines and one of the wolf hunter were killed.

This unnecessary slaughter spurred the government in Ottawa to establish the North West Mounted Police, in order to keep the peace and to rid the west of illegal whiskey trading. The force marched west in 1874 and in 1875 Fort Walsh became the local headquarters for the newly formed police force 3km (2 miles) from the Farwell trading post.

Over the next eight years, the police miraculously brought law and order to the region, dealing with illegal whiskey traders, local native tribes, and thousands of Sioux warriors who sought refuge in Canada after confrontations with the cavalry in the

40km (25 miles) to Hwy 21. Now head south on Hwy 21 for 10km (6 miles) to **Maple Creek**, on the northern edge of Cypress Hills Interprovincial Park. Ranching continues to reign supreme in this part of southwest Saskatchewan. Heritage storefronts on the main street emphasis Maple Creek's frontier beginnings, and two museums focus on the early days of pioneering. From May to September the cowboy lifestyle is celebrated at the Maple Creek Cowtown Rodeo, the Jasper Jamboree, the Light Horse Show and its unique Cowboy Poetry Gathering/Stock Dog Trials which offer three full days of pickin', singin' and recitin' in mid-September. Visitors are also welcome to attend the weekly (Tuesdays) cattle auctions, where the 'cattle bawling' rakes in an astounding $30 million annually.

Cypress Hills Interprovincial Park straddles the border be-

United States. In 1883 the NWMP transferred their headquarters to Regina.

Despite its isolated position, a town sprang up around Fort Walsh. With two hotels, pool halls, a dance hall, a photography studio, and — being a real frontier town — bootleggers and prostitutes, it was for a while the largest community between Winnipeg and Vancouver.

After the NWMP abandoned the fort, private ranchers moved in. Later, in 1942, the RCMP acquired the Fort Walsh land and operated a remount ranch to train their horses for ceremonial events and their famous Musical Ride. In 1968 Fort Walsh was taken over by Parks Canada as a national historic site.

The faithfully restored buildings include the commissioner's house, NCO's quarters, officers' mess and the barracks, which provided primitive housing for up to fifty constables. The men had little time to ponder on their lot. Besides their police duties they were occupied with countless drills, target practice, and a miscellany of housekeeping duties.

The national historic site includes both the fort and Farwell's trading post (a bus transports visitors between the two). Restored to interpret life in the fur trading era of 1873, it is similar to at least thirty other such posts that once dotted the Cypress Hills. As well as trading beads, cloth and other more common goods for furs, these posts frequently adulterated their whiskey (or 'fire water') with such interesting ingredients as pepper, tobacco, ginger, strychnine and gun powder.

tween Saskatchewan and Alberta. First-time visitors are always taken aback by the sudden appearance of the hills which at their highest point stand some 610m (2,000ft) above the surrounding plains. The first French-Canadian fur traders to the area in the early 1800s mistook their thick covering of lodgepole pine for the jack pine, or cypress, of eastern Canada, and the area has been known by this misnomer ever since.

This region of 18,400ha (45,448 acres) was a vast prehistoric upland millions of years ago. Although much of the plateau eroded away, somehow Cypress Hills escaped this fate. Within this geological oddity, cooler temperatures and higher rainfall ensure a flourishing vegetation that is home to 200 species of birds, pronghorn antelope, elk, moose, white-tailed deer, mule deer, bobcat, coyote and red fox. The hills earned rave reviews from John Palliser who described them as 'a perfect oasis in the desert we have travelled' after his expedition camped here back in 1859.

This is the first interprovincial park to be created in Canada, and the Saskatchewan portion is 27km (17 miles) south of Maple Creek. The west block of Cypress Hills can be reached via Hwy 271 from Maple Creek, or along a road called The Gap, which connects the west and centre blocks of the park across a 16km (10 mile) wide valley. (During wet weather this scenic road is often impassable, so check before setting off.)

Other than the historic park, the Western Block is maintained as a wilderness preserve, while the Centre Block offers more man-made activities and facilities. There are 400 camping sites cut from the forest, including some for RVs. Additionally, a resort offers all-year-round comfortable accommodation with facilities ranging from saunas and hot tubs to golf, tennis, a riding stable and bicycles for rent. If you're feeling energetic, you can climb 1,281m (4,200ft) to Bald Butte, the highest point of land in the Centre Block.

From Cypress Hills take Hwy 21 south 34km (21 miles) to Hwy 13, (known as the Red Coat Trail in commemoration of the famous 1874 journey of the North West Mounted Police) and drive east for 54km (34 miles) to **Eastend**. This small town (population 630) is in the heart of the rugged whitemud cliffs of the Frenchman River Valley, now frequently referred to as the Valley of Hidden Secrets. The town is most famous for its spectacular discoveries of dinosaur bones. Many are displayed in the Eastend Museum, while others are in museum collections across North America. Knowledgeable guides with Eastend Paleo Tours conduct two-hour tours to the Tyrannosaurs Site and field research station three times daily, seven days a week. It is the only way to see one of only twelve full tyrannosaurs skeletons existing in the world, as the T. Rex site cannot be toured independently. Accommodation in the area includes several campgrounds suitable for both tents and RVs, and a couple of small hotels.

North of Eastend is Chimney Coulee, site of a Métis winter camp, a Hudson Bay Company post, and later, an NWMP post. Nearby are numerous Sioux campsites, including one set up by Sitting Bull in the aftermath of General Custer's Last Stand. Also the Continental Divide, a watershed in the hills 24km (15 miles) north of town. From here, waters north of the line flow northeast to Hudson Bay, while those south of the line flow to the Gulf of Mexico.

SOME CAUTIONARY ADVICE

The Grasslands National Park Information Centre in Val Marie is open daily from late May to the Labour Day weekend in September. As the park is pure wilderness, there is no help immediately available should a problem arise, and no facilities whatsoever. So study carefully all the information you pick up at the Centre. Necessities for a visit include a sun hat and sun block cream, water (summer temperatures go up to 40°C (104°F), sturdy walking shoes, insect repellent, good maps, and binoculars. Field guides will help you to identify birds, wildflowers and tracks. Prairie rattlesnakes are poisonous, but normally do not strike unless surprised or cornered. Wilderness camping is permitted, with pre-registration at the park office in Val Marie.

From Eastend, continue 33km (20 miles) east along Hwy 13 to Shaunavon, then take Hwy 37 south 52km (32 miles) to Climax and continue east another 57km (35 miles) to **Val Marie**, which is gateway to **Grasslands National Park**.

Val Marie was established in 1924 by homesteaders (many originally from France) and currently its population numbers around 150. One illustrious resident was Will James (1892-1942), a famous author of cowboy stories during the 1930s. A cowboy, rancher, rodeo performer, artist, actor and even a movie stuntman, he wrote two dozen books on ranching and cowboy life.

Worth checking out is the Perrault Museum in Val Marie. Located in the basement of a private home, its accessibility depends on whether the owner, is in. Her private collection includes fossils, antiques, Indian artifacts and oil paintings.

Less than 10km (6 miles) south of Val Marie, on the western edge of Grasslands National Park is the Two Trees Interpretive Trail. The fairly easy 1.5km (1 mile) walk along the edge of the Frenchman River Valley offers a close-up look at the prairie, some tipi rings and a sensational view of 70 Mile Butte, the highest hill in the park.

To reach the West Block, take Hwy 18 east from Val Marie for 14.5km (9 miles), then turn south and follow the road for about 4km (2½ miles). Watch for the Park sign. A land of rolling hills, rugged coulees and steep ravines, the West Block of the 450 sq km (174 sq mile) park centres on the Frenchman River Valley, while the East Block centres on the Killdeer Badlands where Canada's first dinosaur remains were discovered in the 1800s. (Ultimately plans call for the park to be twice the current size.) The virgin mixed-grass prairie is the only park of its kind in North America and the only place in Canada where you may see black-tailed prairie dogs in their natural habitat. Native habitation within the grassland region goes back at least 5,000 years. In more recent history, the Assiniboine, Cree, Sioux and Blackfoot frequented the area on a seasonal basis, and their cultural legacies include campsites, tipi rings, medicine wheels and bison drive lanes. With the decline of the bison herd, the settlers moved in and replaced the remaining bison with cattle herds. Large ranches comprising thousands of acres of grazing lands became the norm, until the Canadian government began to purchase it back in order to create the park.

To explore the park, you can either hike on your own (with great caution) or join a park interpreter on the Sunday hikes held during July and August. Another alternative is to rent an audio-cassette from the Information Centre and by car follow the numbered beaver symbols for an ecotour within the West Block.

The East Block is accessed from Hwy 18 — which basically loops around the west, north and eastern boundaries of the park — near Wood Mountain. From the Wood Mountain Regional Park take Hwy 18 south for 22km (14 miles), then turn west for 6.4km (4 miles). At the speed curve here, turn south and proceed another 6.4km (4 miles), then turn west and the entrance/exit is 2.4km (1.5 miles) ahead.

With no structured trails, the Grasslands offer a wonderful opportunity to experience the nuances of the prairie landscape. If you decide to climb 70-Mile Butte, you may well see deer or hear coyotes. From the top, the vast panorama unfurls endlessly. To the east, the Frenchman River Valley and the park itself. To the south is the state of Montana, while the northwest reveals the rolling landscape typical of southwest Saskatchewan.

Over 300 species of grasses and shrubs carpet the park's flats, uplands, coulees and river valleys. As well, 2,503 archaeological sites related to pre-contact occupation have been discovered, the largest quantity of archaeological sites recorded for any national park in Canada.

Other than two vacation farms, one in Val Marie, another south of McCord, a small camp ground in Val Marie, and wilderness camping in the park, the nearest hotel to use as a base for your explorations is in Mankota, north of the park on Hwy 18 (see Accommodation & Eating Out section).

From Val Marie there are several options. Depending on time

and inclination, *Off The Beaten Track* travellers can either continue east towards St Victor's Petroglphys Provincial Historic Park and the Big Muddy, or detour north to some of the French-Canadian communities along Hwys 13 and 43. A significant number of French-Canadians ultimately settled in this part of the country. Along with European settlers, they were attracted by the Canadian government's offer of 65ha (160 acre) homesteads for only $10. The proviso was that every new landowner had to build a house and cultivate a certain number of acres within three years.

Anyone interested in the French connection should take Hwy 4 north from Val Marie for 86km (53 miles), then Hwy 13 east for 18km (11 miles) to **Ponteix** (population 650). Founded by a French Roman Catholic missionary, Father Albert Royer, the town was originally Notre Dame d'Auvergne, but it was renamed after Father Royer's home parish in France. Here, Notre Dame d'Auvergne church on 1st Avenue West, the largest column-free church in southwest Saskatchewan, has a magnificent statue of Our Lady of Auvergne, carved from a solid block of white oak in the late 1400s. The Notukeu Heritage Museum has one of the largest collections of Plains Indians artifacts in western Canada, some over 10,000 years old, and a recently discovered 70 million-year-old plesiosaur fossil.

The town of **Gravelbourg** is considered to be the heart of Saskatchewan's francophone culture. To reach it from Ponteix, continue east along Hwy 13 for 70km (44 miles) to Hwy 58, which you follow north for 20km (12 miles) to Gravelbourg, where there are a couple of small hotels. Founded in 1906 by the Gravel family and named after Father Pierre Gravel, a missionary priest, the community's history is told in the Musée de Gravelbourg Museum. Town treasures include a remarkable collection of reproductions of Renaissance European masters in the Elementary School Art Gallery (formerly a chapel of the Convent of Jesus and Mary) and some dazzling stained glass windows in Our Lady of Assumption Cathedral.

Southeast of Gravelbourg is big-time ranching country. Enormous ranches flourished in the western prairies from the 1880s to the early 1900s, and nowhere more than in the open ranges from the Big Muddy Badlands to Wood Mountain. Close to 40,000 head of cattle grazed here by 1906. Ranching is still the main occupation and trail riding here is as natural as it gets. The cowboys you see here are for real.

From Gravelbourg retrace your route for 56km (35 miles) south down Hwy 58 to Hwy 18, and drive east 16km (10 miles) to **Wood**

Mountain. (For those coming directly from Val Marie, it is a 126km (78 mile) drive east along Hwy 18.) Considering its population of only fifty-seven inhabitants, Wood Mountain is almost overloaded with attractions. Although there are no motels, there is an excellent vacation farm, Bar F Country Vacations, almost 13km (8 miles) east of Wood Mountain on Grid Road 705, and a campground (tents and RVs) in Wood Mountain Regional Park, 7 km (4 miles) south of town. Despite appearances to the contrary, the Wood Mountain Café at the town's ice rink serves some of the best home-cooking on the Prairies.

Wood Mountain Stampede, held in Wood Mountain Regional Park every July since 1890, is the oldest continuous rodeo in Canada. Also in July the Wood Mountain Cowboy Poetry Gathering features authentic cowboy poetry and country-and-western music. Within the park the Wood Mountain Rodeo and Ranch Museum is dedicated to ranchers and rodeo cowboys. There is also an information booth for Grasslands National Park.

A small memorial atop of the hill behind the museum commemorates Sitting Bull, who camped in Wood Mountain for four years after the Custer Massacre in 1877. When he and most of his Sioux band returned to the US in 1881, fifty families of Dakota Sioux remained in Canada, and in 1911 were granted a reserve of land in Wood Mountain.

Nearby, Wood Mountain Post Provincial Historic Park is a reconstruction of the first Mountie post in southwest Saskatchewan, established in 1874. The small detachment faced a major challenge when Sitting Bull and about 5,000 Sioux arrived in the area in 1877, a year after the Battle of the Little Bighorn. The story of the special relationship that developed between Sitting Bull and Major James Walsh of the North West Mounted Police is well explained through interpretive panels and displays of NWMP and Sioux artifacts.

Another highlight of the area is **St Victor's Petroglyphs Provincial Historic Park**. If you do not mind driving along a gravel road, the quickest way from Wood Mountain is about 20km (12 miles) along Grid Road 705 to **St Victor**. A route that is kinder to your automobile takes you up Hwy 18 for 43km (27 miles) to Hwy 13. Head east for 20km (12 miles) to **Assiniboia**, one of the largest towns in the area, with a population of 2,900. A greatly anticipated event here is the three-day South Country Round-up and Rodeo mid-June, with chuckwagon and chariot races.

From Assiniboia continue east along Hwy 13 for 28km (17 miles) to Hwy 36 and head south for 15km (9 miles) to **Willow Bunch** (population 480). St Victor's Petroglphys Provincial Historic Park is 15km (9 miles) west of Willow Bunch along the aforementioned Grid Road 705. St Victor, a small hamlet with a population of just over 100, was first settled by French Canadians in 1908, and until the 1970s, the French language and culture were predominant here.

Best time to visit the petroglphys is early evening when the light casts shadows that seem to highlight the ancient grooves. Wooden steps lead up the hillside to a boardwalk over the rock, allowing a clear view of the carvings. Chiselled into the horizontal caprock of the sandstone cliff, they are one of the largest collections of carvings by prehistoric man, with over 300 individual drawings on the rock face. Believed to have been carved by ancestors of modern-day Sioux and Assiniboine peoples, their origins are not definitively known. You will easily identify a man's hand, faces (some happy, some gruesome), bison and antelope footprints, bird tracks and a turtle. This site is one of only five such sites in Canada, east of British Columbia's northwest coast. Flashlight tours are occasionally organized during the summer, around 11pm, led by a local archaeologist. Call ahead if you are interested.

Nestling in an attractive valley, Willow Bunch was founded in 1870 by Jean Louis Legaré, a Métis fur trader and scout. Sympathetic to Sitting Bull's predicament, he helped Major Walsh keep peace with the Sioux. When the natives' food ran out, he gave them supplies from his own store, and when they finally left for their homelands, he provisioned them for that arduous trek.

Another famous resident of Willow Bunch was the tragic Edouard Beaupré. Born in 1881 and believed to be the fifth tallest man in the world, this gentle giant was 8 feet 3 inches (251cm) tall and weighed in at 375lb (170kg) at age 23 when he died while working for the Ringling Brothers Circus at the St Louis World Fair in 1904. His ashes were eventually returned to be buried in the grounds of the Willow Bunch Museum. Erected in 1914 by the Sisters of the Cross, this heritage building contains some of Giant Beaupré's personal effects, a room dedicated to the Riel Rebellion and presentations on how the early settlers lived.

The **Big Muddy** is one of the most intriguing regions of Saskatchewan, if not the whole of Canada. This vast valley, sometimes more than 1.6km (1 mile) wide at the bottom and up to 152m (500ft) deep, meanders southeast from Saskatchewan down to the Missouri Valley. The Big Muddy River used to flow through it, but although oldtimers can remember a trickle of water as recently as the early 1900s it has long since dried up.

THE OUTLAWS OF THE BIG MUDDY

Valley County, in northern Montana was considered to be one of the most lawless counties of the state in the late 1800s. The American economy was so depressed that hundreds of men joined gangs — such as Butch Cassidy's — to rustle cattle, steal horses and rob trains. Big Muddy's terrain combined with its proximity to the US border attracted a significant number of outlaws like Sam Kelly, Dutch Henry and the Pigeon-Toed Kid, and the Nelson-Jones Gang. Caves in the hills provided well-sheltered protection and they soon became the northern-most station on Butch Cassidy's infamous Outlaw Trail, which stretched from Big Beaver, Saskatchewan down to Mexico. Along the way, every 24km (15 mile) or so, a way station provided fresh horses and supplies.

Tours of the Big Muddy include Sam Kelly's Caves. From these enlarged wolf dens, the outlaws had a clear view to Peak's Butte on the Canada/US border where a gang member was always posted to keep an eye out for law enforcers. The nationality of the approaching authorities determined which way the bandits would escape. A nearby cave held up to twenty-five horses, and from it there was an escape route to the other side of the hill. The cave is more peacefully occupied now by orange-breasted swallows.

The landscape is a memorable mix of weathered buttes, cone-shaped hills, perpendicular cliffs and large sandstone monuments that look like petrified tree trunks. Much of the land is still leased out by the government to ranchers, while wild gooseberries, raspberries, chokeberries and saskatoon berries flourish in the coulees.

The best way to appreciate the Big Muddy is to sign up for a guided tour (book ahead), with Coronach and District Tours. **Coronach**, 36km (22 miles) south of Willow Bunch via Hwys 36 and 18, was originally founded in 1926, when the Canadian Pacific Railway built a branch line from Assiniboia through the area. Named after the horse that won the Epsom Derby in England that year, Coronach acquired town status in 1978 after SaskPower established a power station and opened a coal mine here, prompting a rapid increase in the population to approximately 1,000. Anyone interested in free tours of the power station and mine need only phone ahead since they are offered daily.

Most tours of Big Muddy take five to six hours. Visitors are expected to provide a car with a full tank of fuel as there are no filling stations on this 173km (107 mile) circuit, as well as sufficient food and drink. The best time to tour Big Muddy is at the end of June when most of the wild flowers are in full bloom, although there is plenty to see at other times.

One of the most dramatic sights is Castle Butte. Sixty metres (200ft) high and 400m (¼ mile) around its base, this spectacular cliff — formed from a mixture of sandstone and soapstone — is a remnant from the Ice Age. In more recent history it has been a valuable landmark for ranchers, settlers, the North West Mounted Police and outlaws. The climb to the top is short but tricky, since the ground is fairly slippery, even in dry weather. Nonetheless, the view is glorious. Depending on the season the floor of the valley may be a mass of moss flax, scarlet mallow, yellow sage or the flowering prickly pear cacti.

Since the passing of the outlaw era, the nearby hamlet of Big Beaver has clearly reduced in size. Less than forty people live here now, tolerating the feisty sign on Austs, the only store in town, which declares 'If we don't have it, you don't need it!'.

There is little left of the Big Muddy Post. Here the NWMP officers dealt with a diverse range of duties. These ranged from acting as customs officers and jailors to handling a smallpox epidemic and veterinary duties, in addition to overseeing law and order.

Outlaws were not the only inhabitants of Big Muddy. The Plains Indians have left plenty of evidence of their occupation, including burial stones, tipi rings and rare stone effigies of turtles and buffalo. Current wildlife residents include deer, antelope, coyotes, prairie chickens, gophers, and the rare burrowing owl.

To connect with the Central Prairies tour described in Chapter 11, take Hwy 36 then Hwy 2 north for 160km (99 miles) to the city of **Moose Jaw** (population 33,550). Theories on the origin of its name abound, but the leading contender is its derivation from *moosegaw*, a Cree word meaning 'warm breezes'. Airy matters are of considerable consequence in Moose Jaw. The world-renowned Snowbirds' aerobatic team is based here, and every July the city hosts the Saskatchewan Air Show, the largest annual air show on the Prairies.

Moose Jaw's downtown core has an abundance of heritage buildings dating back to the turn of the century. Many are being restored, and historical walking tours are organized by Tourism

Moose Jaw. Murals depicting historical scenes recreate the excitement of the city's earlier years, especially the Roaring Twenties when the likes of Al Capone ordered underground getaway tunnels from some of the downtown buildings.

Wakamow Valley, along the Moose Jaw River, connects six city parks. This lovely tree-filled valley incorporates a wide variety of terrain from marshland to cactus growth, and provides an invigorating environment for walking, cycling, canoeing, camping and rowing. Crescent Park, which offers 12ha (29 acres) of tranquil beauty in the heart of downtown, is home to the rare trumpeter swans and the Moose Jaw Art Museum & National Exhibition Centre. The museum's 3,000 artifacts include period costumes and Sioux and Cree beadwork, as well as a permanent Canadian art collection.

Moose Jaw is also home to one of Saskatchewan's four Western Development Museums. Focusing on the history of transportation, it explores the role transportation has played in the development of the west, from birchbark canoes to automobiles and finally airplanes. One gallery is exclusively dedicated to the 431 Squadron's Snowbirds.

A friendly, vibrant city, Moose Jaw reflects the best that a Canadian prairies town has to offer, with a multitude of facilities to suit the traveller.

Additional Information
— Cattle, Oil & Dinosaurs —

Places to Visit

Assiniboia
Assiniboia & District Historical Museum
506-3rd Avenue West
Open: daily in July and August, rest of year by appointment.
☎ (306) 642-5353/4216

Brooks
Royal Tyrrell Museum Field Station
In Dinosaur Provincial Park (see below)
Open: daily Victoria Day to Labour Day, Monday to Friday rest of year.
☎ (403) 378-4342

Calgary
Fort Calgary Historic Park
750 9th Ave SE
Open: daily May to Thanksgiving, Wednesday to Sunday rest of year
☎ (403) 290-1875

Glenbow Museum
9th Ave and 1st St SE
Open daily
☎ (403) 268-4100

Heritage Park Historical Village
Off Hwy 2, via Heritage Dr
Open daily in summer, weekends only part of year.
☎ (403) 259-1900

Coronach
Coronach District Museum
Centre Street
Open: May to Sept
☎ (306) 267-4923/267-2456

Coronach and District Tours
Open: June to early Sept
☎ (306) 267-3312

Poplar River Power Plant and Mine Site
Open: March to Dec
☎ (306) 267-2078/2157

Drumheller
Royal Tyrrell Museum
Hwy 838, 6km west of Drumheller
Open: daily Victoria Day to Labour Day, Tuesday to Sunday, rest of year
☎ (403) 823-7707

Eastend
Eastend Museum — Cultural Centre
Downtown Eastend
Open: daily late May to early Sept, in winter by appointment
☎ (306) 295-3614/3375

Eastend Paleo Tours/Field Research Station
118 Maple Avenue South
☎ (306) 295-3606

Edmonton
Fort Edmonton Park
Whitemud Dr & Fox Dr
Open: daily Victoria Day to Labour Day, Sundays to Thanksgiving
☎ (403) 496-8787

Provincial Museum of Alberta
12845 102 Ave
Open: daily in summer, closed Mondays rest of year
☎ (403) 453-9100

West Edmonton Mall
170 St & 87 Ave
Open: daily
☎ (403) 444-5300

Fort Macleod
Fort Macleod Museum
25th St & 3rd Ave
Open: daily in summer, Monday to Friday rest of year
☎ (403) 553-4703

Head-Smashed-In Buffalo Jump
Hwy 785
18km (11 miles) northwest of Fort Macleod
Open: daily
☎ (403) 553-2731

Gravelbourg
Elementary School Art Gallery
West of cathedral
Open: June to Sept
☎ (306) 648-3177

Musée de Gravelbourg Museum
133-5th Avenue East
Open: July and Aug
☎ (306) 648-3673/648-3349

Our Lady of Assumption Cathedral
South end of Main Street
Open: daily
☎ (306) 648-3322

Maple Creek
Jasper Cultural and Historical Centre
Jasper Street
Open: May to Sept Mon-Sat, Oct to May daily
☎ (306) 662-2434/2343

The Old Timer's Museum
218 Jasper Street
Open: daily, June to September; Mon to Fri October, April and May.
☎ (306) 662-2474/4159.

Moose Jaw
Moose Jaw Art Museum
& National Exhibition Centre
Crescent Park
☎ (306) 692-4471/3144

Walking Tours of Downtown Moose Jaw
Open: year-round
☎ (306) 692-4471/3144

Western Development Museum
History of Transportation
50 Diefenbaker Drive
Open: daily
☎ (306) 693-5989/6556

Ponteix
Church of Notre Dame D'Auvergne
1st Avenue West
Open: daily
☎ (306) 625-3222

Notukeu Heritage Museum
110 Railway Avenue
Open: Mon-Sat
☎ (306) 625-3340

Val Marie
Perrault Museum and Guided Tour
208-1st Street North
Open: on request
☎ (306) 298-2241

Willow Bunch
Willow Bunch Museum & Heritage Society
8-5th Street
Open: mid-May to mid-Sept; rest of year by appointment
☎ (306) 473-2806/2245

Wood Mountain
Wood Mountain Post Provincial Historic Park
8km (5 miles) south of Wood Mountain on Hwy 18
Open: June to early Sept
☎ (306) 694-3664/2854

Wood Mountain Rodeo and Ranching Museum
Wood Mountain Regional Park
Open: late May to early Sept
☎ (306) 266-4953/4539

Parks

Cypress Hills Interprovincial Park
27km (17 miles) south of Maple Creek on Hwy 21
Box 850
Maple Creek SK
S0N 1N0
☎ (306) 662-4411

Fort Walsh National Historic Park
55km (34 miles) southwest of Maple Creek on Hwy 271
Open: Victoria Day to Thanksgiving, daily. (Farwell's Trading Post closes Labour Day.)
☎ (306) 662-3590/2645

Dinosaur Provincial Park
48km (30 miles) northeast of Brooks via Hwys 873 & 544
Box 60
Patricia AB
T0J 2K0
☎ (403) 378-4342

Polar Bear (Chapter 8)

Preparing dinner in the wilds of the Northwest (Chapter 8)

Recreational vehicles in Banff National Park (Chapter 9)

Lake Louise, Banff National Park, Alberta (Chapter 9)

Elk Island National Park,
RR1 Site 4
Fort Saskatchewan AB
T8L 2N7
☎ (403) 992-6380

Grasslands National Park
PO Box 150
Val Marie SK
S0N 2T0
Open: Park Office is open year-round; the Information centre is open late May to early Sept daily.
☎ (306) 298-2257

St Victor Petroglyphs Provincial Historic Park
Open: year round.
☎ (306) 694-3664/787-2854.

Wood Buffalo National Park
See Northwest Territories

Local Tourist Information Offices

Alberta

Calgary
Calgary Convention and Visitors Bureau
Calgary Tower
9th Ave & Centre St S
Calgary AB
T2G OK8
☎ (403) 263-8510

Edmonton
Edmonton Convention and Tourism Authority
#104 9797 Jasper Ave
Edmonton AB
T5J 1N9
☎ (403) 496-8400 or 1-800-463-4667

Saskatchewan
Saskatchewan Provincial Parks
☎ 1-800-667-2757 (mid-May to August, within Saskatchewan only)
or (306) 787-2700 year-round

Eastend
Eastend Tourism Authority
☎ (306) 295-4144

Moose Jaw
Tourism Moose Jaw
88 Saskatchewan Street East
Moose Jaw SK
S6H 0V4
☎ (306) 693-8097

11 • Land Of The Big Sky

The focus of this tour of the Central Prairies is south and central Saskatchewan, an area rich in natural, cultural and archeological revelations. As in much of the Prairies, the farther *Off The Beaten Track* the visitor strays, the warmer the welcome.

The jumping off point is Moose Jaw, where the Western Prairies itinerary described in Chapter 10 ended. If you are coming from the east, Moose Jaw is 71km (44 miles) west of Regina on Hwy 1. Take Hwy 2 north 18km (11 miles) to Hwy 42, then drive east on Hwy 202 for 16km (10 miles) to **Buffalo Pound Provincial Park**. It is the western gateway to the sweeping views of the Qu'Appelle Valley, a 48km (30 mile) long, east-west gash that drops several hundred feet down below the prairie floor.

The park, which has an extensive campground with sites for both tents and RVs, sits on the southern shores of **Buffalo Pound Lake**, a 60km (37 mile) long reservoir created in 1940. On the north side as you approach the park, St Columba Anglican Church of Canada is a typical Prairie church built by the early settlers 'to the glory of God' in 1898. The 1,900ha (almost 4,700 acre) park was used by Plains Indians for thousands of years to corral wild bison, the largest land mammal in North America. For a time, at least 60 million buffalo lived on the plains, as undisputed lords of the prairies.

Before the advent of guns and horses, natives would capture buffalo by trapping them in a 'buffalo pound'. They would be lured, often by a hunter wearing a buffalo skin, into a coulee. Here the hunters, armed with spears and lances, would line up, ready to frighten the animals into stampeding into a log corral to their ultimate fate.

Several pre-historic pounds have been discovered in the surrounding hills. In 1850 one enormous herd took four days to pass a single point, and Cecil Denny of the North West Mounted Police wrote in 1874: 'We came to places where, as far as the eye could see, untold thousands [of bison] were in sight. The country being fairly

A PRAIRIE TREASURE

Coulees are hidden gems of the prairie landscape. Small ravines or gullies around a stream or natural spring, they are blissfully damp, cool, and lush in the summer yet provide sheltered warmth in the winter. Home to a wide variety of flora and fauna, their trees such as Manitoba maple and green ash provide a dense canopy, allowing moisture-loving plants to grow on the forest floor.

black with them ... these immense herds were moving north and there seemed no end to them.' Since buffalo were capable of speeding along at 50km (31 miles) an hour, the adrenalin-charge from participating in a buffalo hunt can only be imagined.

In 1906 the government of Canada decided to buy some of the last surviving bison herd in Montana. Three years later, $200,000 had been raised to bring 700 bison to Canada. The herd was originally taken to Alberta's Elk Island National Park but in 1972 thirteen were brought to Buffalo Pound Provincial Park. The free-roaming buffalo herd now numbers twenty five. Although captive, they follow the same cycle as their ancestors, rutting in the autumn and calving between April and June.

You may need binoculars to spot them from the 2km (1¼ mile) Bison Trail, but when you do, their appearance is awesome. Despite a diet of only grass, full grown bison stand around 2m (6ft) at the shoulder and weigh almost a ton. In the heat of the day they often disappear into the shaded coulees.

Hikers to Buffalo Pound should come armed with a hat, sunglasses, and binoculars. From early spring to mid-summer, the prairie wood tick (a small, hard insect) is an annoying fact of prairie life that has to be guarded against. The best way to avoid them is to stay on the mowed trails, away from tall grasses and shrubs where the ticks are abundant. Usually you are aware of one of these pests long before it has time to penetrate your skin.

Bird watchers will revel in the 8km (5 mile) trail through the marshes of the park's Nicolle Flats Interpretive Area. An astonishing 80 percent of all North America's waterfowl are hatched in prairie marshes, and over forty different species can be seen here, including mallards, blue-winged terns, yellow-headed blackbirds, grebes and marsh hawks. Above the boardwalk winding through the marsh, the air is thick with birds swirling and soaring, and their shrill songs will ring in your ears.

As the trail leads up into the grasslands, the cacophony tends to diminish, but keep an eye out for larger birds of prey. The steep, eroded slopes of the Qu'Appelle Valley provide almost continual updraughts for large soaring hawks as they patrol the skies in search of any sign of mice, ground squirrels and small birds.

From Buffalo Pound backtrack to Hwy 42, then drive north via Hwys 42, 367 and 19 to Douglas Provincial Park, one of three provincial parks around **Lake Diefenbaker** ('Saskatchewan's Great Lake'). The 100km (62 miles) journey brings you to the southwestern corner of the lake, which was created when the **Gardiner Dam** was built across the Saskatchewan River in the mid 1960s. By flooding a large valley, a reservoir 225km (140 miles) long with almost 800km (500 miles) of shoreline was created. Named in honour of the Rt Hon John G. Diefenbaker (see page 167), it is the largest body of water in southern Saskatchewan. Wildlife viewing opportunities in the nature trails and unique landscapes in the parks around the lake are exceptional.

The reservoir was built to boost prairie economy through water conservation programs. South Saskatchewan has a semi-arid climate, and cycles of drought are common. A long period of drought in the 1930s highlighted the need for a reliable water supply. Building of the dam was an immense, ten-year project. Unfortunately, creation of the lake led to the loss of many cultural and palaeotological sites, since the valley had been home to Plains Indians for thousands of years.

At the three provincial parks (all with campgrounds) around the huge lake you can experience some of the region's wildlife. Plentiful supplies of walleye, lake trout, perch and goldeye, and at least twenty-four other species of fish, keep anglers happy. Located on the north/south migratory path, the area also attracts ardent bird watchers. Ducks, geese and sandhill cranes (over 150,000) live at the upstream end of the lake, which is also a habitat for the endangered piping plover.

Douglas Provincial Park is a family-oriented park. It has a sandy beach, and many of the park activities revolve around the water, boating, waterskiing and board sailing. Sand dunes provide an intriguing look at another side of Saskatchewan, and numerous programs are conducted by park naturalists at the Dunes Interpretive Centre.

Right beside the 5km (3 mile) wide Gardiner Dam is **Danielson**

Provincial Park, which owes its existence to the dam. The 2,400 ha (5,930 acre) park has good camping facilities and offers endless watersport possibilities with its two large sandy beaches. The Visitor Centre has an excellent display on the creation of Lake Diefenbaker and the Gardiner Dam. You can also tour the Gardiner Dam itself.

From here it is a memorable 150km (93 mile) drive through the Coteau Hills via Hwys 45, 342 and 4 to Saskatchewan Landing Provincial Park. Although a substantial detour on the way to the city of Saskatoon, it is well worth the effort. The Coteau Hills are on the edge of the Great Sand Hills, a region where some of the dunes were formed around 14,000 years ago and stand 15 to 20m (50-60ft) high. The Coteau Hills have a sandy, rolling terrain, interspersed with deep ravines and coulees filled with poplar groves and wild fruit shrubs. In parts, the river bed is over 500ft (152m) lower than the surrounding hills. The unusual geography lends itself to a unique blend of grain farming and the more rough and ready cowboy lifestyle. Rodeos are a fixture in many of the smaller towns such as Beechy and Kyle, and hunting and fishing are prime outdoor activities.

Saskatchewan Landing Provincial Park has remnants of the Battleford Trail, a 296km (184 mile) path between Swift Current and Battleford. Originally used by Plains Indians on hunting trips to the north, it was later followed by white settlers and soldiers. Once the railway reached Swift Current in 1883, the trail became the overland link between Battleford and the rest of the world. Oxcarts, horsedrawn wagons, stage coaches and mail carriers used the trail extensively between 1883 and 1890, crossing the river at Saskatchewan Landing by ferry from the 1880s until a bridge was finally built in 1951.

Some of the rugged landscape of the former valley — the deep ravines and razorback ridges — has been preserved. In pre-lake days, cottonwood trees lined the banks of the river and the wooded coulees provided food and shelter for the wildlife. The Visitors Centre of the 5,415ha (13,380 acre) park is in Goodwin House. This old fieldstone house was built around 1900 by Frank Goodwin, a member of the North West Mounted Police. After years of neglect, Goodwin House was eventually restored, and its user-friendly displays provide excellent information on the area. There are two nature trails: the Coulee Trail takes only ½ hour to walk, the Brunyee Ridge Trail at most an hour. Although they are short, there is a 122m (400ft) rise on both trails. A number of ecosystems here include prairie, wooded coulees, sandy beaches and the lake . The sage bush provides nutritious food for the herds of pronghorn that gather here to graze and rest during the winter. In early summer the hillsides are covered with the rich lemon blossom of the prickly pear cactus (one of the prairies' best conservers of moisture), while the grasslands are radiant with the vibrant pink flower of the pin cushion cactus. Airborne predators such as prairie falcons, golden eagles and ferruginous hawks all nest on the steep cliff faces.

There is accommodation in Kyle and Beechy and camping facilities (tents and RVs) in the park, where you can overnight before returning to the Gardiner Dam and continuing north on Hwy 219. A pleasant 95km (59 mile) drive will bring you to Saskatoon. (The key to off-the-beaten-track travel through Saskatchewan is to keep off Hwys 1 and 11 as much as possible. They are fast roads cut through a very flat landscape that does little to improve the Prairies' image.)

Until you reach Hwy 764 the road is straight and surroundings are flat for as far as the eye can see. Giant irrigation systems, with huge spider-like pieces of equipment straddle the fields, looking for all the world like visitors from outer space. After the Hwy 764 turnoff, the road starts to follow the South Saskatchewan River. Although it appears straight as an arrow on the map, the road actually twists and turns through rolling hills, across moorland, past horse and cattle farms, and several Indian reserves.

The city of **Saskatoon** is invariably regarded fondly by all who know it. The city, like the province, has a strong tradition of community involvement, and claims to be the Volunteer Capital of the World.

Its name comes from a Cree word for a succulent berry that grows in much of the Prairies. Founded as a temperance colony in 1883 by settlers from eastern Canada and Great Britain searching for a spiritual Utopia, it is now Saskatchewan's largest city, with a population of 185,000. Arrival of the railway in 1890 cemented its position as the hub of western Canada's transportation system, in the heart of the province's rich grain belt.

Saskatoon's appeal is partly due to the South Saskatchewan River winding through it. A favourite walk or drive is Spadina Crescent, which follows twists and turns through the parkland, known as Meewasin Valley, on the river's west bank. An attractive trail, some 17km (10 miles) long, it is enjoyed by cyclists, joggers, roller bladers and strollers, especially when a concert is taking place in one of the waterfront parks.

One of the valley's (and city's) most prominent landmarks is the castle-like Delta Bessborough Hotel (often referred to as 'the Bess'), with its turrets, dormers, gargoyles and quoins. Built from a variety of Canadian materials — Tyndall stone from Manitoba, tile from Estevan (Saskatchewan), granite from Ontario and bronzes from Toronto and Montreal, it has extensive Elizabethan-style gardens and a commanding riverside location. Actor Charles Laughton reportedly said that his window above the river provided the most pleasing scene that he had known in a lifetime of hotel living. Officially opened in 1935, the Bess was another link in Canadian National Railways' chain of château-like hotels across Canada.

Saskatoon has some superb museums and galleries. The Meewasin Valley Interpretive Centre has excellent hands-on exhibits on Saskatoon's past and this riverside site is a good place to start a visit to Saskatoon. On the University of Saskatchewan campus, the Diefenbaker Centre Museum & Archives has a unique collection of artifacts recording the life of the Rt Hon John G. Diefenbaker (Prime Minister from 1957 to 1963), as well as the politics, government and domestic life of those times.

The Ukrainian Museum of Canada's Pioneer Gallery highlights the story of immigration with regional folk costumes, weaving, woodcarving, *psanky* (Easter eggs), religion and community life. The Mendel Art Gallery collects original art, primarily of Canadian origin, focusing on work from Saskatchewan and western Canada.

Saskatchewan has four Western Development Museums, each presenting a different aspect of the provincial heritage. Saskatoon's museum, known as Boomtown 1910, offers a delightful glimpse of life in a prairie town prior to World War I. Boomtown 1910 is an authentic recreation a mythical Saskatchewan town' main street. The general store overflows with everything from nails to gingham while the pharmacy window is crammed with various medicinal applications such as catarrh balm, Rexall's throat gargle and ointment used for barbed wire poisoning. Mr Wing Lee runs a well-equipped laundry, while the agricultural pavilion is full of vintage farm equipment, from threshing machines to horse-drawn drills.

Saskatoon also has a thriving arts scene. Besides an annual six-week Shakespeare-on-the-Saskatchewan Festival and an International Fringe Festival (over sixty theatre groups from around the world participate), it has some of the country's top theatre companies including Persephone Theatre and Twenty-Fifth Street Theatre.

However brief your stay here, do visit **Wanuskewin Heritage**

Park, 5km (3 miles) north of Saskatoon, off Hwy 11. This 121ha (300 acre) archaeological park, perched on the valley edge above Opimihaw Creek, evocatively showcases Indian culture. The land has been used as a gathering ground for the Northern Plains Indians for some 6,000 years. Now the park, which represents five main Plains Nations, the Saulteaux, Cree, Dakota, Dene and Nakota, is overseen by a Board of Elders with representatives from each tribe.

An excellent slide presentation in the Visitors Centre makes a good introduction to the park. In the adjacent Interpretation Centre, the story of the Northern Plains Indians is told through three themes, namely the First Peoples' relationships with animals, with the earth and with their community.

The Archaeology Theatre represents a typical excavation pit, and a seven-minute film highlights digs in the area that have been taking place since 1932. Artifacts dating back over 6,000 years include a medicine wheel. Only eighty of these have been found on the entire continent. Always located on remote hilltops, their exact purpose is not known, but they continue to have great spiritual significance.

Outdoors, the park is considered to be an archaeological treasure trove, with nineteen pre-contact historic sites. In the amphitheatre you may catch a performance by native dancers who not only perform but explain the significance of the dream catchers, dancing sticks, plumes and bells which are an integral part of their vibrant costumes.

Wanuskewin recently started a Tipi Village program. During an overnight stay in the tipi village, participants can try their hand at early hunting methods, or the gathering of plants and berries. Later, by the campfire, they will eat bannock and drink muskeg tea, while listening to a traditional storyteller or talking about the stars.

Along the trails are old buffalo jumps (one dates back 1,500 years, the other over 2,300 years) and willow-framed lodges covered in hide. On one hill alone there are nine tipi rings — circles of stones which were used as weights to hold the tipis down.

Without a doubt, Wanuskewin (a Cree word for 'seeking peace of mind') will leave an indelible impression.

Time permitting, this is where you can head up to the northern reaches of Saskatchewan. From Saskatoon it is a 158km (98 mile) drive via Hwy 11 north, Hwy 312 east and Hwy 225 north to **Batoche National Historic Site**. In the 1870s, the Métis buffalo hunters and farmers who had been forced to leave Manitoba's Red River Settlement came to live in the village of Batoche. After fifteen years of peaceful existence, the Métis once again felt they had been dealt with unfairly by the Canadian government. Their main issue was land ownership, and they turned for guidance to their old leader, Louis Riel. The central government in Ottawa chose to ignore their petition. Shortly after the local Crees, who had their own grievances, joined forces with the Métis in an armed revolt. This culminated in the North West Rebellion in the spring of 1885. The government forces, led by General Frederick Middleton, hugely outnumbered the Métis, whom they finally overcame at the four-day seige of Batoche. Two Cree chiefs, Poundmaker and Big Bear, were imprisoned and died soon after their release. Riel was tried and hanged in Regina.

In the remains of the old village you can see the trenches used by Middleton's army, the old church and rectory where the Métis held out, a cemetery with the grave of Gabriel Dumont (the Métis military leader), and a mass grave for the Métis killed. The tragic story is brought to life by an unforgettable audio visual presentation in the Visitor Reception Centre.

Continue east along Hwy 225 and then north on Hwy 2 for about 80km (50 miles) through Prince Albert to **Prince Albert National Park**. The most scenic route to enter the park is via Hwy 263, where you will pass one of the few free-roaming herds of plains bison grazing in a paddock just inside the park's southeast boundary.

Within the park's 3,875 sq km (1,496 sq miles) the hills, lakes, streams and bogs bridge the aspen parkland of central Saskatchewan with the province's vast northern boreal forest. An environmental mosaic that fairly teems with wildlife, its grassland region supports prairie animals while the northern forests are home to wolves, elks and bears. Lavallee Lake, on the northern edge of the park, is nesting ground for Canada's second largest pelican colony.

The park's Information Centre in the town of Waskesiu has wonderful exhibits and plenty of pamphlets. Videos and slide shows here include the story of author/conservationist Grey Owl, whose restored cabin and grave can be reached by a hiking trail, and then by boat or canoe. In the early 1900s this legendary figure was considered to be Canada's best-known naturalist. Presenting himself as the son of an Apache woman and a Scot who had served as a scout with the US Cavalry, he lectured widely in England and the United States on the preservation of Canada's wilderness and its inhabitants. As resident naturalist of Prince Albert National Park from 1931 until he died of pneumonia in 1938, he lived in seclusion in a log cabin on Ajawaan Lake. Soon after his death it was revealed that Grey Owl was in fact an Englishman, Archibald Belaney, who had been raised in Hastings by two maiden aunts. He had emigrated to Northern Ontario, where he became a trapper in the Canadian wilderness and created a new identity for himself. Not even his native wife, Anahereo, had an inkling of the truth.

As with most of Canada's National Parks, you do not have to be the most dedicated outdoors person to enjoy a wilderness experience here. Many of the 100km (60 miles) of hiking trails offer gentle walking. Yet along the way you may see some of the tallest white spruce and balsam fir in Saskatchewan, or trek through a black spruce muskeg (or bog). At the day's end you can enjoy all the creature comforts of home, since there are cottages, modern hotels, and a fully serviced campground within the park. For a more remote backcountry experience, consider an overnight hike or canoe trip to Ajawaan Lake and Grey Owl's cabin, or to other wilderness camping areas. With a myriad of lakes and rivers throughout the park, the canoe routes offer trips for all skill levels.

Some of the more organized activities, accompanied by a naturalist, include sunrise or starlight walks, wolf howling, elk bugling and buffalo caravans. Fishing in these cold northern waters is for lake trout, northern pike and walleye, while in winter the special beauty of the park is transformed into 150km (93 miles) of cross-country ski trails through nearly a million acres of unspoiled wilderness.

From here follow Hwy 2 south some 235km (146 miles) to Watrous and **Manitou Beach**.

The wonders of nature take on yet another hue for the first-time visitor to Manitou Beach, 6km (almost 4 miles) northeast of Watrous on Little Manitou Lake. The lake is deeply set in an old glacial spillway, well below the surrounding plains. Manitou is an Indian word meaning God, and area's Natives believed that the lake came from the Great Spirit. Their beliefs were so strong that warring tribes never carried on their feuds when they were in the vicinity of the lake.

The briny water of Little Manitou Lake, fed from underground springs, is three times saltier than ocean water, which makes it denser than even the Dead Sea. A distinct smell of salt hovers in the air much of the time. More than a century ago, Indians came from all over Saskatchewan, bringing their sick and ailing tribesmen to be cured in the waters. Sometimes the patient simply drank from the lake. Others bathed in the cool mineral waters or were treated in sweat lodges, in which lake water was sprinkled on hot stones to

ALL SAINTS ANGLICAN CHURCH

A small agricultural centre, Watrous' main place of interest is All Saints Anglican Church, renowned for its magnificent stained glass window. Numerous Anglican churches scattered over the Prairies incorporated furnishings originally from England, to highlight the church's rich Anglican heritage. The window in the west wall of All Saints Church dates back to pre-Reformation times and was brought to Watrous by the church's first vicar, the Rev F. H. King, in 1912. During the English civil war (1642-48) between Charles I and Oliver Cromwell, the window was removed and buried for safekeeping and later reinstated in the Church of St John the Baptist in the Wiltshire village of Latton. There it remained until the beginning of the twentieth century when it was replaced by another window. The Watrous window, a gift to the Reverend King, arrived (intentionally) in 2,000 pieces and was assembled on the floor of All Saints' Parish Hall. The three-panelled window is typically medieval in design and colour, with a brilliant mix of dark blues, purples, reds, greens and yellows, the dyes created from an ancient art that has been long since lost.

create a steam bath that would purify the body and spirit.

In the 1930s and '40s, Manitou Beach attracted thousands of non-Native visitors from across western Canada who were eager to experience its healing waters. In more recent years, with the addition of a modern hotel and spa, combined with small motels, rental cottages, campsites and even a retreat, tourism is making a comeback in this small village that has only fifty permanent residents. Summer visitors are often content to float in the lake itself, but the waters can be comfortably (and affordably) enjoyed year-round at the spa. In recent years, the resort has drawn a younger crowd, due to the increased interest in holistic health.

From here, continue south down Hwy 2 for 100km (62 miles) to Hwy 11. Last Mountain Lake runs parallel to Hwy 2 and at its north end, a little east of Simpson, is **Last Mountain Lake National Wildlife Area**. The oldest bird sanctuary on the continent, this is a perfect habitat for eight of Canada's twenty-six species of rare, threatened and endangered birds: the peregrine falcon, the piping plover, the whooping crane, the burrowing owl, the ferruginous hawk, the loggerhead shrike, the American white pelican and the Cooper's hawk. In addition, over 260 bird species migrate through the area. During May, August and September, visitors can help protect the province's wildlife by assisting with bird-banding.

From Hwy 2 take Hwy 11 east for 77km (48 miles) to Saskatchewan's capital city. **Regina** (population 177,923) has been the provincial capital since the province's birth in 1905. The early Native Indians knew it by the less regal name, 'Pile o' Bones' since the area had been prime buffalo hunting ground for many tribes. The city has come a long way from the tent settlement on a treeless plain that it was in 1882. Now it is an attractive mix of heritage buildings and gleaming modern architecture.

Regina's most famous attraction is undoubtedly the Royal Canadian Mounted Police. The Mounties were based in Regina from 1882 to 1920, when the headquarters were moved to Ottawa. The force's training academy remains in the city, and within its sprawling headquarters, the RCMP Centennial Museum has a fascinating assortment of uniforms, badges, weapons, snowshoes, maps, wagons and native artifacts. Twice a week, on Mondays and Thursdays at 1pm, recruits drill in the Sergeant Major's Parade on Parade Square.

Wascana Centre, covering 930ha (2,300 acres) in the heart of Regina, is the largest urban park on the continent. On the doorstep of the Saskatchewan Legislative Building, this retreat provides a city oasis for joggers, cyclists, windsurfers, picnickers and nature lovers. Here also are some of Regina's top attractions, including the Royal Saskatchewan Museum, the Saskatchewan Science Centre, former Prime Minister Diefenbaker's homestead, the Saskatchewan Centre for the Arts (equivalent in size to the Lincoln Centre in New York City), and the campus of the University of Regina. There is even a Speaker's Corner, to honour the democratic ideals of free speech and assembly. Centrepiece of the park is the man-made Wascana Lake. Canoes and sailboats skim its water in summer, while ice skaters take over in winter. Its Waterfowl Park is home to both local and migrating waterfowl. Every year around 250 pairs of geese nest on Goose Island, while Tern Island is an annual nesting ground for about twenty-five pairs of terns.

Qu'Appelle Valley

People who live in the Qu'Appelle Valley, also known as the Valley of the Calling Lakes, frequently declare that it is one of Saskatchewan's best-kept secrets. The name comes from an old Indian legend that glorifies the love of an Indian brave who, through mystic echoes in the valley, heard his name called out by his true love. A famous poem by Pauline Johnson, *The Legend of the Qu'Appelle* tells the bittersweet story.

The valley has been described as 'a sunken garden carved by glacial-born waters', sculpted during the recession of the glaciers about 18,000 years ago. Although the valley's first inhabitants lived here over 3,000 years ago, the first white man to arrive in the area was the explorer La Vérendrye, in 1738. Because of its central location, the valley became a trading post and a gateway to the north during the 1800s. A chain of lakes, connected by the Qu'Appelle River, stretches from Round Lake in the east to Buffalo Pound Provincial Park in the west.

Approaching the area from Regina along the Trans-Canada Hwy, the valley's largest town, Fort Qu'Appelle, is only a 72km (45 miles) drive away, but the entire valley has plenty to offer. Follow the Trans-Canada Hwy for 55km (34 miles) east to Qu'Appelle and turn north on Hwy 35. Three kilometre (almost 2 miles) north of Qu'Appelle on Hwy 35 is the Bluenose Country Vacation Farm. Sitting on 890 hectares (2,200 acres), this B & B specializes in 'country elegance' — good home cooking served on fine china with linen napkins and table cloths. The 1904 farmhouse with its 18in-thick walls accommodates a number of guests, and several barns have been converted into charming cottages, some of which are ideal for family groups.

What makes it a B & B with a difference is the adjoining **Bluenose Agricultural Interpretive Centre**. As more and more visitors have shown an interest in learning about farming and rural lifestyles generally, the centre sets out to meet this demand. Here visitors can learn about many aspects of prairie farming, such as the shelter-belting programs (planting trees in the fields to stop soil erosion and to provide protection to farm houses). The inner works of a model grain elevator are totally exposed, giving tourists the only chance they are likely to have of seeing how they function. A tour of the centre is followed with a walk around the farm to inspect their livestock — goats, lambs and pigs — and a small hike down the nature trail to a beaver dam.

The town of **Fort Qu'Appelle** (population 1,974) has a rich history that is well documented in Fort Qu'Appelle Museum. Native peoples, fur traders, missionaries and settlers have all played a significant role in the growth of this town. In the 1800s, explorers and entrepreneurs from the North West Company (erstwhile rivals of the Hudson's Bay Company) were the first white men to arrive in the area. Fort Qu'Appelle began as a crossing point for a number of trails used by the natives, that were later followed by the fur traders.

The museum is on the site of the original Hudson's Bay Company trading post, built in 1864. As the centre that was located nearest the buffalo herds, its primary purpose was to provide supplies for everyone going north. In 1885, during the Riel or North West Rebellion, General Middleton and his 400-odd soldiers stopped at the fort before continuing on to Batoche. As Fort Qu'Appelle was the last supply depot before the inevitable confrontation, the General outfitted all 120 of his wagons here. The building he used is now part of the museum.

The museum provides insight into much more than early pioneer history. Long before the fur traders and settlers moved into the area, Native Indians came to the valley for protection from the harsh winter storms. Through numerous archaeological digs held in the area, over 8,000 artifacts have been found on the fort's site and some are on display here. Arrow heads, hammer heads, bone hide scrapers, even buttons and cooking implements have all been unearthed. Remains of the prehistoric woolly mammoth were also found. In 1880 the North West Mounted Police came to Fort Qu'Appelle, but stayed only seven years before moving on to Regina. While here, their staff of forty were kept busy patrolling trails, checking on the settlers and generally keeping the peace. Many of the early farmers were originally members of the force who had liked the area so much they returned to settle.

Displays on early twentieth-century life include some of the original medical equipment used at the local sanatorium for patients suffering from tuberculosis. The authorities firmly believed that winter or summer, patients needed several hours of fresh air every day. Although winter temperatures can drop to minus 30°C (22°F) they would be put out on their balconies with stone hot-water bottles to keep their blood circulating. A sign for Stiff's Funeral Home always raises a chuckle; the firm was kept busy by the Tuberculosis Treatment Centre for many years.

Fort Qu'Appelle's Treaty Park 4 is extremely significant. Here the First Treaty between the Indians of the North West Territories and Queen Victoria's government was signed on 15 September 1874. Through Qu'Appelle Treaty 4, Indian chiefs from thirty-three bands ceded their rights, titles and privileges over 75,000 sections of land in south Saskatchewan to the British. Every September, a Treaty No 4 Gathering is held in the park to commemorate the signing.

To see local artists at work, stop by the Hansen-Ross Pottery on Bay Avenue. This pottery is made of Saskatchewan clays taken from the Cypress Hills, and no commercial moulds or glazes are ever used. Folmer Hansen's distinctive work can also be seen in galleries across the country, including the National Art Gallery in Ottawa and the Confederation Centre in Charlottetown. In their studio/showroom Hansen and his partner, Don Parker, willingly share with visitors their love for the valley.

Nearby the Qu'Appelle Crafts Store has a good selection of locally produced Indian crafts. Delicate dream catchers crafted from weavings of leather and beads date back thousands of years. They are believed to trap bad dreams but allow good dreams to filter through the feathers into your 'lodge'. Intricately beaded moccasins, sculptures and carvings, baskets made from birch bark, and Ojibwa greeting cards all make unique gifts.

Fort Qu'Appelle has one hotel and several smaller motels. The area also has two campgrounds (both tents and RVs), and several B & Bs and farmhouses that take in guests. In this part of the country, there are numerous opportunities to discover whether you care for buffalo or not — to eat, that is. Both buffalo meat and elk frequently appear on menus.

Just east of Fort Qu'Appelle, south off Hwy 10, take the 7km (4 mile) detour to **Lebret**. The first missions in the Qu'Appelle Valley were established in 1852, and one of the earliest was built here by Bishop Taché, from Winnipeg. It was a base from which missionaries were sent out across the prairies.

The century-old Sacred Heart Roman Catholic Church dominates the town, and for further evidence of the French mission, look up the hill to the Stations of the Cross, with an enormous cross at the very top. The Qu'Appelle Valley has an unusually high percentage of resident artists, including painters, potters, weavers and photographers. Every July art lovers come here for the weekend-long Qu'Appelle Valley Artists Club Annual Show and Sale, held in the basement of Sacred Heart church. Valley life is a common theme to the works, and if you can be here at this time it presents a great opportunity to both view some exceptional art and to experience Lebret's own history.

South of Lebret is Saskatchewan's oldest provincial park, **Katepwa Point Provincial Park**, on Katepwa Lake. Katepwa is the last of a chain of four lakes — Pasqua, Echo, Mission and Katepwa — known as the Calling Lakes or the Fishing Lakes. It has a hotel and camping facilities, and good amenities for boaters and fishing enthusiasts.

Back on Hwy 10, continue east to where it veers to the north. Take Hwy 22 south, then east again. Shortly you will come to Abernethy, an attractive village with century-old fieldstone houses. Just south of Abernethy is **Motherwell Homestead National Historic Site** in the Pheasant Hills. William Motherwell was a prominent Saskatchewan politician who was originally from Ontario. He served as an Agricultural Minister, both provincially and federally, and eventually retired from politics in 1939 at the age of 79. He built his farm, which he called Lanark Place, in the 1890s and the house, barn and outbuildings have been restored by Parks Canada to the 1910-14 period. The fieldstone house was constructed in a dignified Italianate-style, so was typical of nineteenth-century Ontario. Like other Ontarian settlers, he planted extensive treelines to assist in soil conservation and to provide shade and winter shelter. Costumed staff busy themselves at typical pre-war activities. You may chance upon a farmhand operating a 1911 tractor or a maid toiling over the laundry. All of this combined with the home's many original furnishings gives visitors a wonderful sense of what everyday life was like in Lanark Place.

Continue east along Hwy 22 to Hwy 47, and then take Hwy 247 south. As you drive east on the north side of the Qu'Appelle River, the effects of glaciation become stunningly obvious. At this point the valley is quite narrow, and at times, the Qu'Appelle River is more marsh than river.

Crooked Lake Provincial Park captures the spirit of the whole valley, from the lake to the thick aspen groves to open grasslands and some dense, brush-filled coulees. By the water, a canopy of elm, ash and maple trees makes for an idyllic shady campground which has some serviced sites. The park is especially popular with boaters and anglers, lured by the lake's trophy walleye, perch and pike.

On this stretch of the route, the steep-sided valley walls are largely covered in prairie grass, and it is easy to pick out the folds, pucks and creases from all the glacial movement over the centuries. On a lower lake-side road, summer cottages perch at water's edge. Here Bird's Point is a small, family-oriented resort with cabins, trailer sites, little restaurant and even a dance hall.

Round Lake is almost the end of this scenic route through the

The Athabasc Glacier on the Columbia Icefield (Chapter 9)

Approaching Jasper by Via Rail (Chapter 9)

Sandstone hoodoos near Drumheller (Chapter 10)

Rodeo in south-west Saskatchewan (Chapter 10)

MOOSE BAY BURIAL MOUND

Just west of Crooked Lake Provincial Park, Moose Bay Burial Mound is a short, steep but exhilarating climb above the highway. Archaeologists from the Saskatchewan Museum of Natural History excavated here in 1968 and discovered that the mound had been built around 950 years ago by the Plains Indians, as the final stop in a long and complex mourning ritual to honour their dead. After death, the body was wrapped tightly in buffalo hides and then tied to a type of scaffold. In the following months, during various religious rituals, gifts that the donors felt would be needed in the afterlife were presented to the deceased person. A year after the death, a mound was built. Remaining bones were rubbed in ochre and arranged around the central post of the mound, along with other artifacts and some specially prepared grave goods. A low, tipi-like structure was then built over the remains, and tons of earth were pushed on top. Thousands of mounds were built throughout North America between 1,000BC and 1600AD, but the closest to this one is about 161km (100 miles) away.

Qu'Appelle Valley. It was on the shores of Round Lake that the Reverend Hugh McKay established a well-known Presbyterian mission school in the 1850s. A much loved man, he worked for thirty-seven years with the Indians of numerous reserves. Parents were eager to send their children to his school, to have them trained in many areas, and most especially in farming. Since Round Lake is the farthest lake from Regina, it is the least known and least frequented.

This itinerary ends on a unforgettable note as the road dips, curves and climbs up from the verdant valley through the hills to rejoin Hwy 1; a wondrously spectacular interlude between the flat plains of the south and the rolling parkland to the north. From here you may continue east to explore the Eastern Prairies as described in Chapter 12.

Additional Information
— Land Of The Big Sky —

Places to Visit

Abernethy
Motherwell Homestead National Historic Site
Open: late May to early Oct 10am-6pm daily
☎ (306) 333-2115/2128

Batoche
Batoche National Historic Site
Box 999
Rosthern SK
S0K 3R0
Open: daily May, to October
☎ (306) 423-6227

Fort Qu'Appelle
Fort Qu'Appelle Museum
Bay Avenue & Third Street
Open: daily July to early Sept
☎ (306) 332-5941/6443

Lebret
Lebret Art Show and Sale
☎ (306) 334-2250

Sacred Heart Church
Open: year-round
☎ (306) 332-6030/332-4597

Manitou Beach
Manitou Springs Mineral Spa
MacLachlan Avenue
Open: daily
☎ (306) 946-2233

Regina
Diefenbaker Homestead
Lakeshore Drive in Wascana Centre
Open: May 22-Sept 4
☎ (306) 522-3661

RCMP Centennial Museum
Dewdney Avenue West
Open: daily
☎ (306) 780-5838

Royal Saskatchewan Museum
College Avenue & Albert Street
Open: daily.
☎ (306) 787-2815/2810

Saskatchewan Centre of the Arts
Lakeshore Drive in Wascana Centre
Open: year-round
☎ (306) 565-4500/9999

Saskatchewan Science Centre
Winnipeg Street & Wascana Drive
Open: year-round
☎ (306) 791-7914/581
1-800-667-6300 (within Saskatchewan, Montana and North Dakota)

Saskatoon
Western Development Museum/1910 Boomtown
2610 Lorne Avenue South
Open: daily
☎ (306) 931-1910

Diefenbaker Centre Museum & Archives
University of Saskatchewan Campus
Open: daily
☎ (306) 966-8382/8385

Meewasin Valley Centre
402 Third Avenue South
Open: daily
☎ (306) 665-6888

Mendel Art Gallery & Civic Conservatory
950 Spadina Crescent East
Open: daily
☎ (306) 975-7610

Ukrainian Museum of Canada
910 Spadina Crescent East
Open: Sept-June, Mon to Fri & Sun, June to Sept, daily
☎ (306) 244-3800

Wanuskewin Heritage Park
5km (3 miles) north of Saskatoon on Hwy 11
Open: daily
☎ (306) 931-6767

Parks

Buffalo Pound Provincial Park
Open: All-year-round
☎ (306) 693-2678/694-3659

Crooked Lake Provincial Park
Open: Victoria Day to Labour Day
☎ (306) 728-7480

Katepwa Point Provincial Park
Box 790
Fort Qu'Appelle SK
S0G 1S0
Open: May to September
☎ (306) 332-3215/332-3225

Danielson Provincial Park
(Lake Diefenbaker)
Open: All-year-round
☎ (306) 857-2155

Douglas Provincial Park
(Lake Diefenbaker)
Open: All-year-round
☎ (306) 854-2177/854-2002

Saskatchewan Landing Provincial Park
(Lake Diefenbaker)
Open: All-year-round
☎ (306) 375-5525

Last Mountain Lake National Wildlife Area (Simpson)
Open: May to Oct
☎ (306) 836-2022/975-4087

Prince Albert National Park
Box 100
Waskesiu Lake SK
S0J 2Y0
Open: All-year-round
☎ (306) 663-5322

Local Tourist Information Offices

Prince Albert
Northeast Tourism Inc
Northern Shores
3700-2nd Avenue West
Prince Albert SK
S6W 1A2
☎ (306) 922-8662

Qu'Appelle Valley
Valley of the Calling Lakes Tourism Association
Box 279
Qu'Appelle
Saskatchewan S0G 4A0
☎ (306) 699-2224

Regina
Tourism Regina
Box 3355
Regina SK
S4P 3H1
☎ (306) 789-5099 or 1-800-661-5099

Saskatoon
Tourism Saskatoon
6-305 Idylwyld Drive North
Saskatoon SK
S7L 0Z1
☎ (306) 242-1206 or 1-800-567-2444

12 • Fossils, Flowers & Desert Sands

Southern Manitoba and Southern Saskatchewan are often over looked as travellers tear across the country on the Trans Canada Highway (Hwy 1). In doing so, they miss an area rich in ancient and more recent history. Besides countless opportunities for some exhilarating wilderness experiences, you will enjoy discovering more about the Prairies' vibrant cultural mosaic.

Over half Manitoba's population lives in Winnipeg, but as anyone travelling *Off The Beaten Track* will soon discover, no matter where they live, the grandchildren of Manitoba's early immigrant population do not forget their heritage. Descendants of the first settlers, brought here from the Scottish Highlands by Lord Selkirk, celebrate their highland roots at the Manitoba Highland Games hosted each July in the town of Selkirk. In Steinbach, the Mennonites pay homage to their ancestors during Pioneer Days in August, while a *Festival du Voyageur* has as its theme the fur trade era and celebrates the *joie de vivre* of the French-Canadian voyageurs. Lower Fort Garry's Rendezvous relives the times when it was the headquarters for the Hudson's By Company's vast fur trading empire. Also in August, the National Ukrainian Festival is held at Selo Ukraina (Ukrainian Village) south of Dauphin in its 4,000-seat amphitheatre, and Gimli celebrates its beginnings at its summer Icelandic Festival.

The route proposed here is based upon the likely assumption that you will begin this loop from Winnipeg. (If you are approaching this area from the west, the map for Chapter 11 will indicate the best place for you to connect with this itinerary.) Leave Winnipeg along Hwy 3, a wide, two-laned highway, which will take you through the agricultural heartland of Manitoba. Stretching into the far distance, large fields are topped by rich, dark brown soil criss-crossed with ditches and canals so vital in an area that is prone to flooding. Silos tower over solitary clumps of farm buildings. Tall grain elevators, the trademark of the Prairies, preside over small towns.

When the railways reached the Prairies in the late 1800s, a community's fate was decided by the railway barons: if the railway was routed through a town, then its future and economic survival was secure. Countless communities became ghost towns when the railway line was built some distance away.

The thriving town of **Carman**, on the scenic Boyne River, is known for its apple products and its nurseries. Vanderveen Greenhouse is Manitoba's largest greenhouse operation with almost a quarter million square feet under cover. Open for tours, it has flowers blooming the year round. Summer festivities here include the Carman Potato & Blossom Festival at the end of June, an Agricultural Fair in July and the Carman Winston Simpson Fiddle Festival in August, which attracts visitors from across Canada and the northern States. At the south end of Kings Park, the Dufferin Historical Museum captures the feeling of rural life in a bygone era, with its pioneer and native artifacts. Lunch and afternoon teas are served at the Walnut Street Tea Room, in the foyer of a 100-year old former Presbyterian church. The glorious stained glass windows, shipped from Scotland between 1891 and 1898, provide splendid surroundings in which to enjoy 'baked-from-scratch' pastries or a Devonshire tea.

From Carmen, the highway turns sharply south for 33km (20 miles) before changing directions again and heading west towards **Morden**. Morden came into being thanks to the Canadian Pacific Railway. Bypassing several established settlements, the line reached the area that is now Morden in 1882. Since the nearby Mort Cheval Creek provided water for the steam locomotives, the railway built a water tower at the creek crossing.

Besides its annual Corn and Apple Festival in August (it attracts an astonishing 35,000 to 40,000 visitors), the local historical society has organized a self-guided architectural and historical walking tour of some of Morden's heritage buildings. Many are frame homes, built between the late 1800s and about 1930. Others are of Manitoba fieldstone, extracted from the beach of ancient Lake Agassiz. At least four of the finest stone houses in the Central Plains area of Manitoba are in Morden.

Before visiting the Morden District Museum, some regional background is helpful. Millions of years ago mosasaurs (large marine lizards), plesiosaurs (marine reptiles) and great sea turtles lived in the warm and salty waters of the Colorado Sea — a vast body of water that covered most of southern Manitoba, Saskatchewan, Alberta, and extended down to the Gulf of Mexico. Through climactic changes, the sea was replaced by the Wisconsin Glacier and it is thought that the cooling climate contributed to the extinction of the dinosaurs and the great marine reptiles. The glacier eventually melted, to become the freshwater Lake Agassiz. Millions of years later, early inhabitants known as Mound Builders grew corn, squash, pumpkins, beans and tobacco on the shores of Lake Agassiz. After the lake retreated, it left behind a soil rich in nutrients, where saskatoon berries, plums, wild herbs, flowers and shrubs all flourished.

As a result of all this prehistoric activity, Morden District Museum houses the largest collection of marine reptile fossils in North America. Despite their modest surroundings (in the basement of the Morden Recreation Centre), convincing dioramas, excellent interpretive material and the fossils themselves are hugely impressive. Most of the fossils were found in the nearby Bentonite quarries on the Manitoba Escarpment (the long series of highlands in Western Manitoba). Some were on the surface, others over 12m (40ft) below. The museum's largest mosasaur is almost 9m (30ft) long although they averaged 3-6m (10 to 20ft).

With the recent interest in dinosaurs, the museum is especially popular with school-aged children, but it is fascinating to all age groups. Adult visitors are more likely to be intrigued by the methods used to recover the fossils. Since the first view is often the exposure of a tiny fragment or a small bone by a bulldozer working at the mine, it is astounding that so many have been retrieved. Because of their fragility, preparation of the fossils for transportation to the museum is an extremely delicate operation, calling for the patience of Job and the skills of a surgeon.

Other museum specimens include some Jurassic sharks, sea turtles, squid (fossil squids in southern Manitoba are among the largest known, ranging up to 18m or 60ft in length) and two types of birds, *Hesperornis* (a flightless bird, rather like an very large loon) and *Ichthyornis* (a much smaller bird capable of flight).

Hwy 3 follows a significant historic trail, now known as the **Boundary Commission Northwest Mounted Police Route**, which linked communities from the Red River to the Saskatchewan River. In 1874, 274 men of the newly formed Northwest Mounted Police made the 1,257km (781 mile) trek from the Red River in Southern Manitoba to the foothills of the Rocky Mountains in Alberta. The four divisions of scarlet-uniformed police were followed by a mile-and-a-half long supply column of 114 Red River carts, 73 freight wagons, 93 head of cattle, two 99-pounder field guns and two brass mortars. Passing through grasslands, badlands, river valleys, spring-fed lakes, pine forests and gentle hills, they followed a centuries-old trail well known to natives, fur traders, explorers and buffalo hunters. It was also used by the surveyors of the International Boundary Commission, who a year before had trekked across the country establishing the border with the United States.

Although the 49th parallel had been agreed upon as the border between Canada and the USA much earlier, the actual border was not surveyed until 1872, and it took two years to complete. The Boundary Commission, commanded by a Canadian, Captain Donald Cameron and an American, Archibald Campbell, had set up boundary markers every three miles along the newly surveyed border. Many of these were simple earthen mounds, while wooden markers provided directional information. Surveyors on the Canadian Boundary Commission were among the last to witnesses the buffalo herds. A mere ten years later, and the buffalo was virtually extinct.

The next place of note along Hwy 3 is the **Archibald Historical Museum**, north of La Rivière. Nellie McClung, a noted author and pioneer activist for women's rights, led the women of Manitoba in their successful fight for the right to vote (setting the pace for other provinces in the process). Born in the town of Manitou in 1873, she lived for one year in a log house that is now part of the museum.

Getting there is an adventure in itself. Follow the 6.4km (4 mile) track to the two old houses and a three storey barn which create a living museum commemorating the heritage of early pioneers who settled this area. Nellie McClung boarded in the 1878 log house while she taught at Hazel School in 1890-1. The house has been restored to meet the descriptions in her autobiography, *Clearing in the West*. A tin house dating from the 1880s, is crammed with period furnishings like rag carpets made from scraps of old coats, and memorabilia such as handwritten home remedies dating back to 1870 for such afflictions as film on the eyes of man or beast, ingrown toenails, and tapeworm!

Continuing west from La Rivière along Highway 3, **Pilot Mound** is a small town surrounded by farmland, rolling hills and wide valleys along the Pembina River. A little over 3km (2 miles) north of the town is a 35m (116ft) high elevation called The Old Mound. It was used as a pilot, or directional guide, to the early settlers travelling west across the Prairies. The last stand of the Sioux Indians on British territory took place on the slopes of the Mound in 1854, in a battle against the buffalo hunters. Some years later, Sir John A.

Macdonald (Canada's first prime minister) is said to have addressed a political rally from the Mound during his western tour. Originally the town was built on the Mound, but later it was moved to be close to the railway.

Killarney is a small community at the east end of Killarney Lake. A popular holiday spot, it has both permanent homes and vacation cottages nestled along the shoreline amidst the oak, maple and poplar trees. In town, the original post office, built in 1889, has been converted into the J. A. V. David Museum. On display are native and pioneer artifacts including a collection of early cameras.

The small town of **Boissevain**, just north of the junction of Hwys 3 and 10, makes a pleasant base for visiting Turtle Mountain Provincial Park and the International Peace Garden. Two museums of interest here are Beckoning Hills Museum (dedicated to pioneer life) and the Moncur Gallery of Prehistory, which houses one of the finest archaeological collections in Manitoba. It depicts the life and work of the people who lived in the Turtle Mountains from the time of the great glaciers until the land was divided up by government surveyors for agricultural purposes. Some of the artifacts here belonged to the hunters of the woolly mammoths who roamed in the area 11,000 years ago. St Paul's United Church on Johnson Street, completed in 1893, is considered to be an excellent example of nineteenth-century fieldstone construction. There are several small hotels, bed and breakfast establishments and a vacation farm in the area.

Turtle Mountain Provincial Park rises 245m (804ft) above the surrounding prairie, and is said to be named after the area's large population of painted turtles. As this was the first dry land to appear after the glacial period, it is the oldest inhabited part of Manitoba.

Between 1810 and 1870, Métis hunters from the Red River Settlement conducted huge annual hunting trips in the area. Up to 2,500 men, women and children participated, travelling west in their sturdy Red River carts. The women prepared pemmican from the meat. This highly nutritious form of dried meat, mixed with herbs and fat, often saved the settlers and traders from starvation. As the herds diminished, Métis set up homesteads around Turtle Mountain. As well, during the Sioux Wars of the 1860s and 1870s in the United States, many of them escaped north of the 49th Parallel to find safety in Turtle Mountain.

The French explorer and trader, La Vérendrye, described Turtle Mountain as the 'blue jewel' of the Prairies. Unfortunately the

Assiniboine Indians, who were based in the area when the first explorers arrived, ultimately suffered terribly from their dealings in the fur trade. As suppliers of pemmican to the traders, they played an integral role in the fur trade. But then, susceptible to the numerous diseases that the Europeans had brought with them, they were largely wiped out by major epidemics of smallpox, scarlet fever and diphtheria.

Although most of the hunting trails skirted Turtle Mountain, the Dunseith Trail crossed the central part and was heavily used for smuggling alcohol into the dry states during Prohibition (from 1920 to 1933) in the USA.

Well-marked scenic trails, from 5km to 15km (3-9 miles) long within the park are wide enough for hikers and mountain bikers. Some are also used for horse riding and fitness. With over 200 lakes in the park, canoeing and fishing (for rainbow trout and brown trout, pike, walleye, and perch) are other leisure opportunities. The hills of Turtle Mountain are thick with trembling aspen, black poplar ash, birch, maple, elm and oak, which provide a rich habitat for the moose, elk, deer, fox, coyote, rabbits, squirrels and the many smaller animals that live here. The best time for sighting moose is in the early morning or late evening, in the marshes or along the lakeshore trails.

There are campsites at Adam, William and Max Lakes. Through the Manitoba Parks Department you can also arrange to stay overnight in a cabin at Emma Lake. It is free of charge and sleeps up to eight people. The Parks Department even supplies the wood — you simply have to take your own sleeping bags and food.

At the south-east corner of Turtle Mountain Provincial Park, are the formal, fragrant gardens of the **International Peace Garden**. A mass of colour every summer, there are over 120,000 annuals on show, while perennials such as the purple bush clematis and the orange and yellow Asiatic lilies are dazzling from mid-July to mid-August. Straddling the world's longest undefended border, the garden has 586ha (1460 acres) in Manitoba and 360ha (900 acres) in North Dakota.

This largest garden, dedicated to peace, was the dream of Henry Moore, a horticulturalist from Islington, Ontario. He managed to raise funds from both sides of the border to establish the park in 1932, as a tribute to lasting peace between the two countries. Every year over 2,000 students from the United States, Canada and other countries (including Japan, Jamaica, Norway and Singapore), attend an International Music Camp Summer School of Fine Arts during June and July. In August training for young athletes is provided by the Canadian Legion Sports Camp.

Footpaths lead to the 36.6m (120ft) Peace Tower, its four pillars representative of people from the four corners of the earth. Ponds around the tower represent the world's oceans while the bridges across them symbolically connect North America and the rest of the world.

The Peace Chapel is open at all times, with services on Sundays. On its stone walls, inscriptions quoting such masters as Shakespeare, Confucius and Einstein focus on a common theme of peace, love, and faith in the human spirit.

There are two self-guided driving tours within the garden: the Canadian Natural Drive and the United States Cultural Drive, both 5.6km (3½ miles) long. As the name suggests, the Canadian drive is largely wilderness, through land inhabited by deer, beaver, moose, muskrat, and fox. Lake Stormon is a delight to bird watchers as ducks, blue heron and many smaller birds nest and make their homes in the trees and rushes around the lake. The drive through the United States passes more of the park's formal buildings including a large amphitheatre, Masonic Auditorium, Music Camp and various picnic areas.

On the way to the eastern Saskatchewan section of this tour, there are several major and minor routes to choose from. If you take Hwys 3, 21 and 2 to the Saskatchewan border, do make a short 22km (14 mile) detour to the town of **Souris**. Here, Canada's longest single span suspension bridge (582ft, or just over 177m) straddles the Souris River. Walking across it is somewhat reminiscent of trying to remain upright during a rough ferry crossing, but the water below is considerably calmer and the surroundings could not be more serene. Charming old homes shaded by huge trees grace both sides of the river.

Originally known as Plum Creek, Souris is on the traditional buffalo trail from the south and was a favourite camping ground for Indians. The first settlers came from Ontario, arriving by river boat up the Assiniboine River and then overland to the town site. The swing bridge was originally built in 1904 to give a local bigwig, Squire Nowden, access to his properties on either side of the river. His former home is now the Hillcrest Museum, with local artifacts on show in the furnished period rooms, while the Pioneer Days Museum features household and agricultural tools. South of Souris, the Souris Agate Pits hold the largest variety of semi-precious stones in North America, including agates, jasper, epidote, petrified wood and dendrite. Anyone wanting to have a go at rock-hounding can pay a minimal amount for a permit at the Rock Shop on 1st Street South.

From the Saskatchewan border, it is close to 150km (93 miles) via Hwy 13, plus another 70km (44 miles) via Hwy 9 to Moose Mountain Provincial Park and **Cannington Manor Provincial Historic Park**.

Moose Mountain Provincial Park, 27km (almost 17 miles) north of Cannington Manor, is an island forest in a sea of grass. Rolling hills, lakes and lush aspen forest make up this 40,000 hectare park on the highest plateau in southeast Saskatchewan.

Home to herds of moose, elk and white-tailed deer, it is also a nesting place for many species of migrating birds. Wood ducks, bald eagles, golden eagles, ruffed grouse and sharp-tailed grouse hang around the lakes and woods while common goldeneye, bufflehead, great blue heron, double-breasted cormorant and terns share the sloughs with beaver and muskrat.

A popular area for vacationing Prairie families, its recreational facilities include golf, tennis, horse-back riding, swimming, boating and water slides. The park has fully-serviced campgrounds, a resort and restaurant, and in nearby Kenosee Lake Village there is a night club of sorts.

Returning to Manitoba via Highway 1, you will come to a significant archaeological site, the Stott Site, in the Grand Valley Provincial Recreation Park, 12km (7½ miles) west of Brandon. Native hunters periodically stampeded bison down the valley slope onto the flood plain, where they could be trapped and killed. Making it easier to visualize, a viewing platform has been built over a reconstructed pound and encampment.

Manitoba's second largest city, **Brandon** (population almost 40,000) came into being in 1793 when a Hudson's Bay Company post was established here. Fifty years or so later, settlers from Ontario and the Atlantic provinces moved into the area, and in 1881 the arrival of the Canadian Pacific Railway cemented Brandon's position as an important distribution and administrative centre. Agriculture, though, is the backbone of the local economy, with two-thirds of Manitoba's farmland in a 128km (80 mile) radius of the city. Its name comes from the nearby Brandon Hills, an immensely popular getaway for locals.

Brandon's agricultural roots are reflected in numerous annual events. The Royal Manitoba Winter Fair at the end of March is the largest agricultural show in Western Canada. A Summer Fair and

CANNINGTON MANOR PROVINCIAL PARK

For 18 years, between 1882 and 1900, an idealistic band of English men and women were lured by advertisements about a place where they could 'live like princes on the money required in England just for taxes'. The advertisements had been placed by one Captain Edward Pierce, a retired English army officer. He promised instruction in the rudiments of farming, and invited families to come and operate small industries and businesses. Those who answered the call arrived with their old school ties and cricket togs, and the social rituals so dear to them back home.

Pierce and three partners formed the Moose Mountain Trading Company to provide freighting services, mortgages, a school and other essentials, including an agricultural college to train young bachelors who had responded. By the 1890s, Cannington Manor had 200 homesteads, a fine hotel, general store, blacksmith and carpenter's shop.

Now six of the original buildings have been restored, and the small museum's photographs and exhibits give us a peek into the extraordinary lifestyle created here. Some houses were as grand as English manor houses with French windows, billiards rooms, and stables as modern as their European counterparts at the time. Women dressed up for a night out in London rather than a small town in the Prairies; afternoon tea and formal dances were two of the many treasured Victorian rituals.

The community had its own Sketch Club, Literary Society and Glee Club, and in 1888 Cannington Manor Hunt Club was formed.

Pro Rodeo is held each June, while in October the Ag Ex and Rodeo is Manitoba's largest livestock show.

The military has had a strong presence in the Brandon area for many years, and three museums symbolize these tight connections. The Commonwealth Air Training Plan Museum, with its displays of World War II aircraft and air force memorabilia, is Canada's only museum dedicated solely to those who trained and fought for the British Commonwealth during World War II. Also thirteen aircraft and several Royal Canadian Air Force vehicles of 1940 vintage are on display in the authentic wartime hangar at the municipal airport north of the city.

East of Brandon off Highway 340, at the Canadian Forces Base in Shilo, the Royal Regiment of Canadian Artillery Museum has some

'Ladies wore ample pleated habits and rode side saddle' reported the *Moosomin News* after one of the hunts. The first hounds brought in were from Isle of Wight stock imported from Iowa. Proper dress was, naturally enough, important to community residents. Rifle hunters wore Norfolk jackets and breeches, and cricket and tennis called for traditional whites.

The location of their newfound Shangri-la worked sorely against them, and their vision of utopia did not survive the harsh realities of the Prairies. The death knell for the community was a decision of the Canadian Pacific Railway Company to build its tracks 16 km (10 miles) south of town, isolating Cannington farmers from their potential markets. Frost, drought, and all-time low wheat prices in 1894 speeded up their demise. Some families moved to British Columbia while many of the young bachelors headed north in search of gold. By 1900 the community was deserted.

The ultimate fate of Cannington Manor was described succinctly by Inglis Sheldon-Williams, one of the village's residents: 'Built upon a raw new country, on unstable foundations, the anomaly could not endure, but the short life was a merry one .... If we did nothing else, we contributed a piquant chapter to the literature of pioneering.'

Although the park provides a fascinating glimpse of an unusual community, the dwellings here belonged to trades and crafts people, and the meagre accommodation given to the bachelors. They do not reflect the flamboyant lifestyles of the more interesting 'upper crust' immigrants.

10,000 artifacts including over 150 major pieces of equipment ranging from 1796 to the present day. Then, back in the city, there is a 26th Field Artillery Regiment Museum.

The journey north from Brandon takes you up Hwy 10 via Minnedosa, an area rich in the history of fur traders and pioneers, to **Riding Mountain National Park**. The only national park in Manitoba, this huge tract of land, some 1,867 sq km, (1,160 sq miles), was designated as an International Biosphere Reserve in 1986. It is a crossroads where the habitats of eastern, western and northern Canada meet harmoniously in forest and grasslands, hills and valleys. Riding Mountain once acted as a barrier to the great glaciers, and as a result it created a northern oasis for boreal plants and animals in the middle of the prairie landscape. Part of the

Manitoba Escarpment, it was named by fur traders because of its elevation of 350m (1,500ft) above the surrounding lands. Here they exchanged canoes for horses before continuing their journey west.

The preserve was declared a national park in 1933, when it became a popular retreat for nature lovers, yet offers enough home comforts to visitors not committed to a total wilderness experience. As well as campsites varying from fully-serviced to primitive, there are cottages, motels and hotels and restaurants to meet all tastes and budgets around Wasagaming on the southern shores of Clear Lake. One, the Wigwam Restaurant, was frequented by Grey Owl, the famous conservationist and author who lived here before moving to Saskatchewan. He was responsible for initiating a beaver conservation program here in the 1930s. Many of Wasagaming's buildings are built from logs because of the availability of local Scandinavian craftsmen skilled in log-building techniques. The community claims to have the largest movie theatre built of logs in North America.

The stone and log Interpretive Centre is an excellent place to orient yourself before setting off to explore. There are over 400km (250 miles) of trails within the park, all designed for walking. Some can be undertaken by mountain bike or on horse back. One of the most popular trails, 18km (11 miles), return is to Beaver Lodge Lake where Grey Owl lived in a log cabin.

You can stroll through a mixed forest to an island where loons nest, or through meadows thick with prairie wild flowers. Some trails follow roads used by pioneers, others are original Indian paths. The trek up the escarpment is arduous but well rewarded with a panoramic view. More species of wildlife live here than in any other part of Manitoba. They include elk, moose, deer, wolves, coyotes, lynx, even a herd of around thirty bison in an enclosure besides Lake Audy (best viewed in the early morning or evening hours). 180 species of birds nest in the park, 68 kinds of butterflies flutter about and over 500 types of exotic plants cover the hills and valleys.

Organized activities run from lectures on Native history to river rambles through prime moose and elk habitat, to stories around the camp fire. Leisure facilities include an 18-hole golf course, tennis courts and lawn bowling greens. Many of Riding Mountain's visitors come to enjoy the natural environment and the countless opportunities to explore the backcountry. Fishing for northern pike, walleye, whitefish and trout is excellent in Clear Lake and other lakes within the park. Dotted around the lakes, secluded campsites have thick carpets of pine needles, ensuring a blissfully comfortable and fragrant night's sleep.

If you have time for explorations further north, head up Hwy 10 towards the city of **Dauphin**. A short distance east of the city, Lake Dauphin was discovered by La Vérendrye in 1739. He established a fur trading outpost, Fort Dauphin, not far from the present town site, and named it in honour of the French king's son. The first settlers arrived in the 1870s, including a large contingent from the Ukraine. One of the town's main attractions is Selo Ukraina, or Ukrainian Heritage Village, which incorporates a restored homestead, a church, and a 4,000-seat amphitheatre that hosts Canada's National Ukrainian Festival.

Take Hwy 5 west out of Dauphin, and turn off at Grandview onto Hwy 366, which leads into **Duck Mountain Provincial Park**. Another segment of the Manitoba Escarpment, Duck Mountain's hilly terrain is often referred to as 'the Ducks'. It includes Baldy Mountain, the highest elevation in Manitoba, at 831m (2,726ft) above sea level. From the observation tower at the top you can look out over a great forest of spruce and aspen, to Riding Mountain in the south. Madge Lake, in the heart of the park, offers a wide variety of recreational opportunities.

Fur trading figured prominently in the lives of the Duck Mountain natives, who hunted elk and moose, and trapped beaver and other fur-bearing animals. In 1899 when the Canadian Northern Railway completed its line to Swan River, just north of Duck Mountain, settlers from other parts of North America and many more from Europe poured into the area. During the winter, settlers would work in the various timber operations within the thick forests. From their earnings, they were able to buy the sorely needed equipment, seed and stock for their farms.

The park's pristine lakes and ponds are a legacy of glacial times. East Blue Lake, at 60m (200ft) deep, is one of the province's clearest lakes. An angler's paradise, its plentiful fish stocks include brook, speckled, rainbow, brown and lake trout, salmon, splake, pickerel, northern pike and whitefish.

The upland meadows in the Roaring and Shell river valleys are brilliant with wildflowers during spring and summer, and are also important feeding grounds for the area's 1,200 elk population. Moose, white-tailed deer, black bear, fox, lynx, coyote and timber wolf all live on Duck Mountain. At night, campers are often serenaded by the haunting call of loons over the lakes, the howling of coyotes and wolves, or the bugling elk. As well as six major hiking

NEEPAWA'S LITERARY CONNECTIONS

As well as its natural beauty and history, Neepawa holds a particularly significant place in Canadian literature. Margaret Laurence, one of Canada's most beloved authors and a world-acclaimed writer, was born here in 1926. As an adult she lived in Africa, England, Vancouver and finally, in Lakefield, Ontario, but her prairie roots were of immense importance to her. Her five Manawaka books (her fictional name for Neepawa), including *The Stone Angel*, *A Jest of God* and *The Diviners*, all owe a great deal to her deep attachment to the Prairies.

Five months after Laurence died in January 1987, the Margaret Laurence Home was opened in Neepawa, in her Grandfather Simpson's 100-year-old house on First Avenue, where Margaret and her mother and brother had lived during her youth. Purchased with her approval and blessing in 1986, the Margaret Laurence Home is now a cultural centre, hosting events such as writers' workshops and book launchings. Personal possessions on display include her typewriter, doctoral robes, and award certificates. Books, papers, magazines, letters, videos and tapes are all available for research or to peruse. On the main floor's Manawaka Gallery, the work of other Manitoba artists is on display. Margaret Laurence's remains are buried in the Riverside Cemetery near the Davidson Memorial, an evocative sculpture that is believed to have been the inspiration of *The Stone Angel.*

trails through the boreal and deciduous forests and upland meadows, Duck Mountain offers canoeing, boating, fishing and camping, with the main campgrounds located around Blue, Wellman, Singush and Childs lakes.

On the return leg of the route to Winnipeg, skirt Riding Mountain National Park along Hwy 5 and you will come to **Neepawa**, (a Cree word for 'plenty'). When Manitoba was formed in 1870, its western boundary ran through Neepawa, which was then called Beautiful Plains. The first settlers found an area rich in fertile land, water and game. Incorporated in 1882, the first train of the Manitoba and Northwestern Railway steamed into town in 1883, ensuring Neepawa's future prosperity as an administrative and business centre. Its 1884 court house and jail are the oldest municipal buildings in Manitoba, and the Beautiful Plains County Court Building

The Big Muddy Valley, Saskatchewan (Chapter 10)

Sam Kelly Caves, the hideout of one of the Big Muddy's infamous outlaws (Chapter 10)

Buffalo Pound Provincial Park near Moose Jaw includes Buffalo (above) and the St Columba Anglican Church, 1898 (below), a typical early prairie church (Chapter 11)

has been maintained as a historical landmark by the citizens of Neepawa.

Spruce Woods Provincial Park lies east of Hwy 5, about 30km (19 miles) south of Hwy 1. Within the park's 248 sq km (96 sq miles) are some of Western Manitoba's most breathtaking landscapes. Besides a forest of white spruce trees on the rolling sand hills, the park has an unusual combination of forest and grassland. Also an especially fascinating and fragile feature, a desert-like area called Spirit Sands. As informative displays within the Visitor Centre explain, Spirit Sands is not a genuine desert since it receives from 300 to 500mm of moisture annually, which is almost twice as much as a real desert. This section of the park is extremely fragile, eroding and scarring easily. Originally 6,500 sq km (2,509 sq miles) of 'deltaic' sand, it has reduced over the last 12,000 years to only 5 sq km (almost 2 sq miles).

Hiking through Spirit Sands highlights the park's rich cultural history. On carefully marked trails, visitors learn about the area's religious significance to the native peoples. According to their beliefs, sand is one of the first elements of creation, and is therefore closer to the Great Spirit than any other living thing. Because of its religious significance, early inhabitants would perform rituals and make offerings before entering Spirit Sands. Even early explorers held the area in awe. In 1806 the fur trader Alexander Henry the Younger wrote about the dunes (then called Devil's Mountain) as a place where 'many strange noises were heard in its bowels .... In crossing those hills, our horses sank up to their knees in many places.'

Trails encompass a variety of terrain, plants and animal life. In the dunes, you may come across the non-poisonous Western hognosed snake, which uses scare tactics such as imitating a rattlesnake to frighten off humans. (If that does not work, it plays dead.) Its main prey is Manitoba's only lizard, the northern prairie skink. The slow-growing pin-cushion cactus is unique to the dunes and creates a sensational blanket when the brilliant magenta, star-shaped flowers bloom in June. Walking through the sand is not easy at the best of times, and is most challenging in summer when the air temperature is around 30°C (86°F), while the sand is around 55°C (131°F). The few hardy creatures who can survive in this harsh climate are wolf spiders, digger wasps, tiger beetles and velvet ants.

The rest of Spruce Woods is a relict boreal forest, the remains of a forest established across southwest Manitoba in the wake of the receding glacier 12,000 years ago. Parts of it succumbed to prairie grasses as the climate became drier, but tamarack and black spruce are still found in cool, boggy places. White-tailed deer and elk live deep in the forest, while ruffed grouse, raccoons and weasels stay closer to the river banks in the shade of American elms and Manitoba maples.

The Assiniboine River winds through Spruce Woods. Originally both natives and traders travelled along the river in birch-bark canoes, but eventually the paddle wheel river boats took over. These carried freight and passengers down the Assiniboine river between 1879 and 1885, and were nicknamed the 'Prairie Navy'. They travelled west as far as Saskatchewan and north up the Red River from Winnipeg to Lake Winnipeg. Nowadays, the Assiniboine River is used largely for recreational purposes and has reverted to being an enjoyable canoe route.

Excellent trails for bicycling, horseback riding and hiking await the visitor to Spruce Woods. The four main hiking trails range from a little over 1km (¾ mile) to 40km (25 miles) and can be combined to take in the various terrains. A return trip to the sand dunes and the scenic Devils Punch Bowl can take as little as one hour or as long as three. Covered wagon rides are also available.

The closest town to Spruce Woods is **Carberry**, just south of the Trans Canada on Highway 5. Home to Ernest Thompson Seton, a world-famous artist, writer and naturalist (1860-1946), Spruce Woods were a continual source of fascination to him. His books and artwork can be seen at the Seton Centre in Carberry. The Carberry Plains Museum is dedicated to the life of Manitobans from the early settlements to the present day.

As you drive back to Winnipeg, the town of **Portage la Prairie** deserves more than a passing glance. The French-Canadian explorer Pierre Gaultier de La Vérendrye arrived here in 1738 and used it as his base for fifteen years while he explored the Prairies to the south, west and north. The name dates back to when it was a resting area in the short portage between the Assiniboine River and Lake Manitoba. A cairn south of the town commemorates Fort la Reine, one of the four trading posts built by La Vérendrye in 1738. Most trading posts did not last more than two seasons, but La Reine remained in operation for eleven years. Ultimately it was destroyed, and succeeding French posts were built farther to the west, to take better advantage of the normal buffalo migration paths.

Fort La Reine Museum and Pioneer Village is a replica of the original, and contains the private railway car of William Van Horne, a driving force in the construction of the Canadian Pacific Railway. The city's architectural heritage is exceptional, and guided walking tours starting from the Chamber of Commerce are offered twice daily during July and August.

A short distance north of the Trans Canada off Hwy 26 is **St François Xavier**, the oldest permanent Métis community in Manitoba. It was established in 1823 by Cuthbert Grant, a famous buffalo hunter who was the son of a Scottish father and a Cree mother. The Grey Sisters in St Boniface sent two sisters to St François Xavier in 1850 to set up a convent school. Although the convent was destroyed by fire in 1915, a replacement nunnery was built on the same site a year later, and has been designated as a historical site. Now converted into a café and market, the Nuns' Kitchen is the original kitchen of the Grey Nuns. Also within the complex is an art gallery, antiques and crafts stores, and a bakery. All of which adds up to a pleasing break before embarking on the final leg of the journey back to Winnipeg.

Additional Information
— Fossils, Flowers & Desert Sands —

Places to Visit

Boissevain
Moncur Gallery
Boissevain Civic Centre
Open: Monday to Saturday
☎ (204) 534-6478/2433

Beckoning Hills Museum
425 Mill Road South
Open: Victoria Day weekend to Sept
☎ (204) 534-7118/6718

International Peace Garden
Box 419
Boissevain MB
R0K 0E0
Open: daily, year-round
☎ (204) 534-2510

Brandon
Commonwealth Air Training Plan Museum
No.1 Hangar, McGill Field
Open: daily
☎ (204) 727-2444

26th Field Artillery Regimental Museum
Brandon Armoury
116 Victoria Avenue
Open: Sunday afternoons, or by appointment
☎ (204) 725-2372

Carberry
Carberry Plains Museum
520-4th Avenue
Open: daily Mid-June to mid-Sept
☎ (204) 834-2195/3295

The Seton Centre
116 Main Street
Open: mid-June to Labour Day, Tues, Thurs and Sun afternoons
☎ (204) 834-2509

Carman
Dufferin Historical Museum
South end of Kings Park
Open: afternoons daily Victoria Day weekend to Labour Day Sun,
☎ (204) 745-3597

Dauphin
Fort Dauphin Museum
140 Jackson Street
Open: daily May-Sept
☎ (204) 638-6630

La Rivière
Archibald Historical Museum
north-east of La Rivière
Open: mid-May to Labour Day, 12 noon-7pm. Closed Wed and Thur
☎ (204) 242-2825/242-2554

Killarney
J. A. V. David Municipal Museum
414 Williams Avenue
Open: summer, and by appointment
☎ (204) 523-7325

Manor
Cannington Manor Provincial Historic Park
☎ (306) 577-2131/2854
Open: daily Victoria Day to Labour Day

Morden
Morden & District Museum
Morden Recreation Centre
2nd Street and Gilmour Avenue
Open: daily June to Aug, weekends Sept to May
☎ (204) 822-3406/4150

Neepawa
Beautiful Plains Museum
Hamilton Street
Open: daily, in summer
☎ (204) 476-3896/2016

Margaret Laurence Home
312 First Avenue
Open: May to Oct, Mon to Fri afternoons, Oct to May, by appointment.
☎ (204) 476-3612(summer)
(204) 476-2926 (winter)

Portage la Prairie
Fort La Reine Museum and Pioneer Village
Hwy 1A, 1.6km (1 mile) east of Portage
Open: daily May-mid-Sept
☎ (204) 857-3259

St François Xavier
Thee Olde Nunnery Cafe and Market
North of Hwy 1 on PTH#26
Open: daily
☎ (204) 864-2306

Shilo
Royal Canadian Artillery Museum CFB Shilo
Open: daily Victoria Day to Labour Day, Winter: Mon to Fri
☎ (204) 765-3534

Souris
Hillcrest Museum
Crescent Avenue East
(by Swinging Bridge)
Open: daily Victoria Day to Labour Day
☎ (204) 483-3138

Pioneer Days Museum
41 Oak Avenue West
Open: May to Oct
☎ (204) 483-3216

Wasagaming
Pinewood Museum
154 Wasagaming Drive
Open: daily June-Labour Day
☎ (204) 735-2205/7622

Parks

Duck Mountain Provincial Park
Open: All-year-round
☎ (204) 622-2104

Moose Mountain Provincial Park
Box 220
Kenosee Lake SK, S0C 2S0
Open: All-year-round
☎ (306) 577-2131

Spruce Woods Provincial Park
☎ (204) 827-2543 (May to Sept)
(204) 834-3223 (Sept to May)

Turtle Mountain Provincial Park
Box 820
Boissevain MB
R0K 0E0
Open: daily, year-round
☎ (204) 534-7204/7205

Riding Mountain National Park
Wasagaming MB
R0J 2H0
☎ (204) 848-7275/7272
Open: year round (most Wasagaming attractions are seasonal)

Local Tourist Information Offices

Brandon
Brandon Economic Development Tourism & Convention Services
1043 Rosser Avenue
Brandon MB
R7A 0L5
☎ (204) 728-3287

Parks Manitoba
(comprehensive information on all provincial parks)
☎ 1-800-214-6497 (toll free Manitoba only)
(Can request *Manitoba Magic, Provincial Parks Guide* from Travel Manitoba)

Saskatchewan
☎ (306) 787-2700 year-round
1-800-667-2757, mid-May to Aug within Saskatchewan only

13 • Winnipeg — Where The West Was Born

One of Canada's most diverse cities, Winnipeg constantly amazes first-time visitors. When Canadian-born Hollywood star Keannu Reeves, agreed to take on the role of Hamlet at Manitoba Theatre Centre it caused more than a frisson of surprise and even disbelief across the country. Theatre critics and fans from around the world descended on the city — in winter, no less — to discover that not only had Reeves met the challenges of the role, but also that Winnipeg has a lot to offer, both culturally and historically.

With nineteen theatre companies, two dance companies, eight ethnic theatres and three orchestras, Winnipeg is a performing arts paradise. The Royal Winnipeg Ballet, established in 1939, is Canada's oldest professional ballet company and regularly tours the globe. Le Cercle Molière is Canada's oldest continuously running theatre company, presenting a five-play season in French, from October to May. The Winnipeg Symphony Orchestra, the Manitoba Chamber Orchestra and Contemporary Dancers are all outstanding companies.

Winnipeg grew up at the junction of the Red and Assiniboine Rivers, in an area now known as The Forks. Here, in 1823, the Hudson's Bay Company built Fort Garry, the trading post that became the hub of the nineteenth-century settlement. After years of neglect, a $100 million redevelopment plan has brought life back to the area, and the Forks National Historic Site is an excellent starting point for first-time visitors to begin their city explorations.

The Forks is on the doorstep of the venerable Union Station, an impressive structure built in 1909 on the site of the original Fort Garry. Designed in the Beaux Arts tradition by the same New York architects who designed Grand Central Station, its Tyndall limestone blocks still have some ancient fossils imbedded in the rock.

At the junction of the two rivers there is a lovely walk, the River Promenade, which skirts the north shore of the Assiniboine River and the west bank of the Red River. The discovery of spearheads and copper tools from numerous archaeological digs show that various native groups had camped at the Forks up to 6,000 years ago. They harvested fish from the Red and Assiniboine rivers, and hunted bison and deer frequenting what used to be a heavily wooded area. In 1738 the first small fur-trade post, Fort Rouge, was built by the French following the discovery of this area by the French explorer La Vérendrye and his sons. The French traders used their various trading posts to redirect the flow of furs from the English in Hudson's Bay, east to New France (Quebec) through the Great Lakes.

With the formation of the North West Company in 1775, a bitter battle was begun between them and the Hudson's Bay Company over control of the fur trade. This led to a competition in the construction of forts, including the building of The Fork's second fort, Fort Gibraltar, in 1810, by the NWC.

In 1812, Lord Selkirk established the Red River Settlement (as The Forks was then known), and gradually farming replaced fur trading as the main way of life. Among other things, Selkirk built an HBC-sponsored settlement near The Forks, at Fort Douglas. The conflict between the two rival fur companies led, in 1821, to the Hudson's Bay Company absorbing the North West Company and changing Fort Gibraltar's name to Fort Garry.

Steamboats first made their way up the Red River from Minnesota in 1859. Replacing the canoe and oxcart they became a vital link in the transportation of both merchandise and passengers between north and south. By the 1870s, hundreds of immigrants were arriving in Winnipeg by steamboats, which then returned laden with grain.

In 1869 the Canadian government purchased an immense tract of land from the Hudson's Bay Company, through largely secret negotiations. This led to the Natives and Métis of the Red River Settlement rebelling and forming their own provincial government. Under Louis Riel's leadership, they were able to negotiate terms when Manitoba entered the Confederation as a province in 1870. However, the terms of the Manitoba Act that guaranteed rights to land, language and religion were not respected and by the late 1870s, many Manitoba Natives left for Saskatchewan and Alberta.

Winnipeg, and specifically The Forks, became a key site in early railway development. The buildings at The Forks today are visible reminders of a national railway system connecting the country coast to coast. At one point, twenty-four rail lines converged on the city.

Now, in revitalizing The Forks, the Grand Trunk Pacific Railroad's stable building has been turned into the **Forks Market**, where you will find a tantalizing array of fresh produce in an airy atrium, or can sample food from around the world. The second floor has arts and crafts stores, boutiques and some good restaurants which include the excellent Sandpiper. Close by are the Johnston Terminal, with more shops, restaurants and the Manitoba Sports Hall of Fame, with the Manitoba Children's Museum in the former Boiler and Brake Building. An outdoor amphitheatre besides the river is a congenial setting for historical pageants, concerts and special events.

A local landmark close to the Forks and Union Station is the Hotel Fort Garry, which has played a major role in Winnipeg's social and cultural life since it was built between 1911 and 1913 by the Grand Trunk Pacific Railway. In the *château* design of most of Canada's railway hotels prior to World War 1, its exterior has the Romanesque and Gothic elements of a medieval French palace. For all its old-world elegance, the hotel is meeting late twentieth-century demands, and has a lavish in-house casino on its seventh floor.

Winnipeg's historic areas are best explored on foot. Not far from Hotel Fort Garry, along Main Street, is Fort Garry Gate, the only remnant of Upper Fort Garry. Built in 1835 by the Hudson's Bay Company, it served as Louis Riel's headquarters during the 1870 Provisional Government. Follow the River Promenade beside the Assiniboine, to the Manitoba Legislature, a splendid neo-classical edifice built from local Manitoba Tyndall stone, and topped by a glittering statue of the Golden Boy sheathed in 23.5 carat gold.

An extension of The Forks, Winnipeg's **Exchange District** is renowned for its turn-of-the-century heritage buildings. Huge warehouses built in the Chicago and Romanesque architectural style used to accommodate some 200 wholesale businesses in the area. Many of this exceptional collection of terra cotta and cut stone buildings have been converted into vibrant business and arts organizations, galleries, book stores, restaurants and cabarets. Old Market Square opened in 1877 as Winnipeg's first market. Now it is the site of an outdoors market on summer weekends and in early July much of the Winnipeg Fringe Festival takes place here. Some of the city's cultural icons — the Manitoba Museum of Man and Nature, the centennial Concert Hall, and the Manitoba Theatre Centre are all found in the Exchange. In July and August, guided walking tours focusing on the area's history and architecture leave from the museum.

The winner of a coveted rating in the *Michelin Green Guide*, the fundamental theme of the **Manitoba Museum of Man and Nature** explores the relationship of Manitobans to their environment. Displays range from the vivid diorama of the Métis Buffalo Hunt (the big hunts that were held twice a year in the spring and autumn had around 1,000 participants) to the survival skills taught to the tiniest of children in Manitoba's sub-Arctic. There is an authentic replica of *Nonsuch*, the seventeenth-century ketch that sailed from England into Hudson Bay, and a fascinating display on the Red River colony's 'Plural society' of Scots, Métis and French, who peacefully coexisted, sharing the resources of the forest, the rivers and the plain. In an engrossing Urban Gallery, Winnipeg is shown as the 'gateway to the west' in the early 1920s during this 'boomtown' era.

The collection at **Winnipeg Art Galley** ranges from sixteenth-century Flemish tapestries to the world's largest agglomeration of contemporary Inuit art and a magnificent collection of pre-1960 art produced by Manitoban and other Canadian artist. European artists such as Corot, Chagall, Bonnard and Miro as well as Britain's Henry Moore, Augustus John and many more are also represented.

Between the Assiniboine and Red rivers are two of Winnipeggers' favourite neighbourhoods. Historic **Osborne Village** in the Fort Rouge district is minutes from downtown and easily accessible, even by water. It has six blocks of restaurants and a wide variety of both standard and more eclectic stores and boutiques. A *Historical Walking Tour* guide can be picked up at any Village business. It identifies some of the eighteen architectural landmarks, including churches and stately homes.

Nearby, **Corydon Avenue** is a combination of restaurants, sidewalk cafes and boutiques. The European flavour is accented by hanging baskets blooming on turn-of-the century gaslights and flower urns lining the streets. At Heaven Art & Book Café, a popular local book store, you can enjoy cappuccino, congenial conversations, and attend weekly readings by acclaimed authors, including local resident and recent Booker and Pulitzer prize winner, Carol Shields.

There's even a **Chinatown**, on the periphery of the Exchange District, west of Main Street. Initially a small settlement for Chinese immigrants brought to Winnipeg to work on the railway, it gradually expanded to an impressive selection of authentic restaurants and shops peddling a wondrous variety of exotic medicinal herbs, spices and Oriental silks. Its focal point is the Dynasty Building, which houses the Winnipeg Chinese Cultural & Community Centre. In its Coffee and Snack Station the decor is less than noteworthy, but the food is exceptionally good and the price is right.

St Boniface has the largest French-language community in Western Canada. It dates back to the French-Canadian fur traders who first settled here,in the eighteenth century. Later, Lord Selkirk arranged for two priests to be sent from Quebec to establish a mission in the part of his colony where most of the residents were Métis and French. He donated 52 sq km (20 sq miles) of land on the east side of the Red River to the mission, which was then named St Boniface. The view over to St Boniface from the River Promenade is unforgettable. Early evening is a particularly lovely time to explore. Cross the Provencher Bridge, amble back down Promenade Taché, and enjoy the sun setting over the towers and turrets of downtown Winnipeg. Pause to explore the Basilica, rebuilt in 1968 after the former Basilica (built in 1908) was burnt down. The Romanesque façade (on the side facing the river), has arches, pillars and a statue of St Boniface, which survived the fire and now provides a dramatic counterpoint to the present basilica. In the grounds is the tomb of Louis Riel, who in 1992 was finally recognized as the founder of the province of Manitoba.

Further along Promenade Taché is the St Boniface Museum, built in 1846, and Winnipeg's oldest building. Originally a convent erected for the Grey Nuns who came from Montreal in 1844, it is the largest oak-log construction in North America. The museum commemorates the Prairies' French-Canadian and Métis culture and the Red River colony's early history in the 1800s.

All-year round, the Centre Culture Franco-Manitoban offers a lively mixture of theatre, music and dance programs, celebrating largely, but not exclusively, French Canadian heritage. Jazz lovers should drop by on any Tuesday, for the weekly 'Mardi Jazz'. French Canadian fare is the speciality of several St Boniface restaurants.

When heading out to **Assiniboine Park**, on the west side of the city, make sure to approach it via Wellington Crescent, one of the city's most exclusive residential streets with gracious mansions bordering the Assiniboine River. Assiniboine Park is 376 acres of woodlands and prairie on the south side of the river, originally bought by the City in 1904. In its zoo (over 1,200 animals) the emphasis is on northern creatures such as the European bison, the Siberian tiger and the Snow Leopard. Find the Leo Mol Sculpture Garden to see the entire works of this local, but internationally renowned sculptor. Many an unsuspecting visitor virtually stumbles across this stunning collection of religious, wildlife, and human sculptures in its magical woodland setting.

THE WEST'S FIRST WHITE SETTLERS

Close to the grave of Louis Riel in the grounds of the St Boniface Cathedral, is the grave of Jean-Baptiste Lagimodière and his wife, Marie-Anne Gaboury. Not only were they Louis Riel's grandparents on his mother's side, but Marie-Anne Gaboury was the first white woman to settle in the West, and hers is an incredible story.

Born in Trois Rivières, Quebec, in 1782 Marie-Anne led a very sheltered life for the first twenty-five years of her life. From the age of 14 she worked as a live-in assistant to a priest's housekeeper, and for the next eleven years her life revolved around the church.

In 1806 a young Canadian voyageur, Jean-Baptiste Lagimodière, who had already spent five years in the North West, came to visit his family in Quebec. After their paths crossed, they had a whirlwind romance and married in April 1807. Marie-Anne and her family all assumed he had come back to Quebec for good. To everyone's astonishment, Jean-Baptiste announced he intended to return to the North West. Although her family were adamantly opposed to her accompanying her husband, Marie-Anne consulted with her priest, who surprisingly advised her that if she had the courage and strength to face the adversities ahead — which would undoubtedly be immense — then she should follow her husband.

Two weeks after their marriage, they left for Lachine, near Montreal, and travelled by canoe, with the voyageurs carrying supplies for the fur trade and provision for the forts in the North. As the only woman in the group, she was not expected to paddle or carry heavy loads, but the days were long and the journey treacherous. On the vast inland sea of Lake Superior they experienced at least two terrible storms. It took them two months to reach Lake Winnipeg.

No other French Canadian women ventured to the West for another eleven years, and Marie-Anne never returned home. Her experiences included warding off a murder attempt by the Native woman her husband had previously lived with, giving birth in the wilderness to four children, and surviving attacks by bears, poverty, locust plagues and flooding. Much of her time was spent on her own while her husband was trapping. Eventually the Lagimodière family settled in St Boniface, and her husband continued to hunt for the rest of his life. Eventually Marie-Anne died in 1879, at the age of 96. Throughout her action-packed life, she remained devoted to her religion and her family.

Assiniboine Forest Nature Park is a well-kept secret, even in Winnipeg. You can reach its 283ha (700 acres), just south of Assiniboine Park, from the corner of Chalfont and Grant Avenues. The forest is a mixture of meadow and forest, and suits a variety of wild life. Set aside by concerned citizens as a refuge for parklands wildlife, it is designed to restore disturbed areas to native prairie species.

Dawn and dusk are the best times to spot some of the herd of white-tailed deer that resides here (look for signs such as droppings, browsed twigs, tracks in the mud or snow). Trembling aspen is the dominant tree, so called because the slightest breeze makes the leaves tremble, and on a breezy day it sounds like a rushing stream. A wilderness within a city, Assiniboine Forest is a cherished retreat for Winnipeg's nature lovers.

More widely promoted but worth a visit anyway, is the **Fort Whyte Centre**. In their award-winning interpretive centre, the Aquarium of the Prairies reveals what lurks in Manitoba's lakes and rivers. You can also feel the coats of wolves, weasels and waterfowl on special taxidermy displays, encounter a considerable number of waterfowl, and learn about the prairie landscape. Winter activities sound like fun: snowshoeing along powder-white trails, visiting bird and deer feeding stations, or having a go at ice-fishing.

The rivers continue to play a dominant role in Winnipeg. With over 100km (62 miles) of them winding through the city, thirty major bridges make it easier to travel around. The river banks and streets are shaded by lovely old trees with splendidly gnarled trunks and sprawling branches. Indeed, Winnipeg has the largest collection of publicly owned elm trees on the continent, 60,000 on the streets and 120,000 on other public lands.

Riel House in the Winnipeg suburb of St Vital is a clapboard-faced log house surrounded by a modern subdivision of bungalows and split-level houses. It is easy to miss the small Parks Canada sign as you drive along River Road. Although Louis Riel never lived here and only visited briefly on a few occasions, this is where his body lay in state for two days in December 1885 prior to his burial in the grounds of St Boniface Cathedral. He had been hanged at the North West Mounted Police Jail in Regina in November for his involvement in a Métis uprising in Batoche, Saskatchewan.

The house was lived in by the Riel family from 1880 to 1968, although Louis Riel had already left home at age 14, after the death of his father, to study in Montreal. By 1868 he was an extremely articulate and determined young man, who had been heavily influenced by both his parents. His father, also Louis, had been a champion of Métis rights (he was one-quarter Métis) and his mother was a devout Christian.

The house has been restored to as it was in the spring of 1886, six month's after Riel's death, when it was lived in by twelve people. The six adults and six children included Riel's Métis wife, Marguerite Monet, and their two children.

Costumed guides describe the cultural, social and economic aspects of the lives of the Riel and Lagimodière families, and the Métis culture generally, with its own *mitchif* language, laws and the seigneurial system of dividing land, as in New France. Life was hard for the Métis of St Boniface and the other communities along the Red and Assiniboine rivers. With the decline of the great buffalo herds they had turned to raising crops and cattle, but by the late 1860s they were plagued by drought, grasshoppers, and the threat of displacement by land-hungry settlers from Ontario.

A short distance south down the Pembina Highway (Hwy 75) is **St Norbert Provincial Heritage Park**, at the junction of the Red and La Salle rivers. Visitors here learn how a natural landscape was used by native peoples hunting, fishing and camping up to 8,000 years ago, evolved into a French-speaking Métis settlement, and then into a French-Canadian agricultural community by World War I. Two houses from the 1870s, Turenne House and Bohemier House, have been restored using original materials and techniques.

A self-guided trail just 1km (½ mile) long leads to the river, where you can get a strong sense of the area described by fur trader Alexander the Younger in 1800 as: 'thickly wooded countryside overgrown with poplar and interspersed with small meadows. Beyond lies the vast plains of North America'. Moose, elk and bison wintered here and fish in the two rivers were plentiful.

Nearby, the **St Norbert Arts and Cultural Centre** produces a range of multi-disciplinary exhibitions, performances, and lectures beside the ruins of a former Trappist Monastery. The dramatic setting lends itself to some tremendously exciting performances.

Excursions from Winnipeg

Lower Fort Garry National Historic Park and River Road

On the banks of the Red River south of Selkirk and about 32km (20 miles) north of Winnipeg on Hwy 9, Lower Fort Garry is a limestone fort that has seen several reincarnations since it was first built in 1830 by the Hudson's Bay Company. Replacing an earlier fort at the Forks that had been subjected to regular flooding, it is the oldest stone fur-trading post in North America still intact.

Lower Fort Garry was originally commissioned by George Simpson, the Hudson's Bay Company's governor, who decided that the rowdy commercial life of the Red River Settlement did not meet his more delicate requirements. Additionally, as a prospective groom, he wanted to provide an elegant lifestyle for his new bride. The flooding of the fort at the Red River Settlement in 1826 gave him a perfect excuse to relocate to higher ground. Construction got under way in 1830 but the Simpsons never lived here, and they moved to Montreal after the death of their first child.

Progress was slow until Duncan McRae, a 24-year old Scottish stone mason from the Hebrides, joined the company in 1837; even so the complex was not finished until 1848. Ironically, the fort's distance from the Red River Settlement worked against it. Ultimately, the Hudson's Bay Company switched their operations back to the original fort, which they rebuilt and named Upper Fort Garry. After HBC sold its land to the new Dominion of Canada, the Lower Fort became in turn a penitentiary to serve the west, the first training and winter headquarters for the North West Mounted Police, an asylum, and then a country club retreat.

Given to the federal government in 1951, Lower Fort Garry was carefully restored to recreate the mid-nineteenth century fur-trading period. Costumed guides provide a lively interpretation of that period. For example, on the front porch of his elegant home Eden Colville, Associate Governor of the Hudson's Bay Company, delights in telling visitors about his charming wife at home and his Métis mistress in town, and about life in general at Lower Fort Garry in the 1850s. Inside the house, Mrs Colville expands upon lavish dinner parties she has to arrange for visiting dignitaries. Indeed, the Big House held social functions that were sufficiently grand to be reported upon in detail in Toronto and London newspapers.

It is the role-playing of the costumed interpreters representing the actual people who lived here that makes a visit to Lower Fort Garry so memorable. No matter what is happening in the outside world, in Lower Fort Garry it is always 1851. Among the twenty exhibits and restored buildings is one of the famed York boats, backbone of the transportation system between the far-flung trading posts of the Hudson's Bay Company. Nine men per boat, nine boats per brigade left the fort each spring for the arduous journey to Hudson Bay to collect pelts from the fur-rich grounds of the

Athabasca and Mackenzie. Elsewhere you will spot some of the oxcarts, known as Red River carts. The fort's shop is crammed with every possible commodity, from glass panes to Perry David Pain Killer and Lea and Perrin sauce.

Lower Fort Garry's military fortifications were built by soldiers of the Royal Warwickshire (6th Foot) Regiment between 1846 and 1848. The soldiers' presence was ostensibly to prepare against a possible American invasion, although their real purpose was to suppress trade with the Hudson's Bay Company's rivals. Historical displays and audio-visual presentations on the fur trade and the Red River Settlement can be seen in the reception centre.

Combine a visit to Lower Fort Garry with **Lockport Heritage Park**, on the east bank of the Red River, where archaeological evidence from 3,000 years ago has been discovered, and you will learn a lot about Manitoba history. Displayed in the museum, known as Kenosewun (which means 'there are many fishes') is evidence from the camps of the early nomadic plains hunters and later cultures who farmed, hunted and fished here.

Parallel to Highway 9 is the historic River Road, much travelled by Chief Peguis and his Saulteaux band, Selkirk's settlers, and numerous other Métis and Europeans during the nineteenth century. Seventeen historic sites along this road invite you to discover more about old Manitoba. For instance, south of Lockport, St Andrew's Anglican Church is the oldest stone church in western Canada (built between 1845 and 1849) where the kneelers are still covered with buffalo hide, and classical music concerts are held each June. A short distance north of the church is Kennedy House. Built in 1866 by Captain William Kennedy, a Hudson's Bay Company fur trader and Arctic explorer, it has been converted to a museum that depicts his lifestyle in the late 1800s. Of even more interest are the glorious prairie gardens, which have been lovingly restored to plans based upon an old photograph taken in the 1920s.

Mennonite Heritage Village, Steinbach, Manitoba

The Mennonite Village Museum was founded by the children and grandchildren of Manitoba's Mennonite settlers. A labour of love to preserve and share their heritage with outsiders, these descendants continue to work the land, serve in the shop, look after the horses and serve Mennonite meals to visitors.

Over twenty heritage buildings in the 16ha (40 acre) village were moved here to commemorate the Mennonites who came to Canada from the Ukraine in 1874. Located 16km (10 miles) south of the Trans-Canada on Hwy 12, and 68km (40 miles) southeast of Winnipeg, the village is laid out in a traditional Mennonite pattern, and furnished in period style.

The long and arduous road from sixteenth-century Holland where Menno Simons first broke with the Catholic church doctrine, to twentieth-century Manitoba is well documented at the museum. Most of Canada's Mennonites came from South Russia (what is now the Ukraine). The first group arrived between 1874 and 1880, more in the 1920s, and a third group after World War II.

Persecuted for their beliefs, the Mennonites found religious freedom in the Ukraine for almost a century. The exodus began when the government ruled that Russian had to be taught in all schools, and that there would be no exemption from military conscription on the grounds of religious belief. Hoping to entice more settlers into the newly acquired North West, the Canadian government reserved eight townships in southeastern Manitoba for the Mennonite immigrants, and in 1874 the first Mennonites to arrive in this area included eighteen families who founded Steinbach (named after the German words for 'stone' and 'creek'). By 1880 their numbers had increased to some 7,000, which was more than 10 percent of the total provincial population at that time.

The houses were identical, with large gardens for growing fruit and vegetables, and a barn attached to each house by a corridor to prevent animal odours from reaching the family quarters. Naturally, every village had a school and a church. Initially farming was the sole occupation of the Mennonites.

The Village Centre traces the progress of Manitoba's settlers through different types of houses, from the first primitive sod huts (known as semlin) to log cabins with thatched roofs (with Roman numerals punched into the logs to permit easy dismantling and reassembly). Later, frame houses of the late 1800s were so uniform in design that, according to the guide, 'If everyone opened his side door, you could see the entire street'.

Steinbach's nineteenth-century church is decidedly modest, with no stained glass windows or any other ornamentation. Centrally located to symbolize religion as the core of their lives, Mennonite churches were also kept simple for reasons beyond religious beliefs. In times of persecution, it was prudent to be unobtrusive.

Within the large and modern Village Centre (incongruous in its pioneer setting, but designed by the grandson of an early settler) you will see turn-of-the-century clothes and period furniture. And Russian wicker trunks, used to store a family's valuable possessions or food during the long voyage to Canada, when the trans-

A dancer at Wanuskewin Heritage Park (Chapter 11)

Grey Owl's cabin, Prince Albert National Park (Chapter 11)

Camping in the Qu'Appelle Valley, Saskatchewan (Chapter 11)

Morden Corn & Apple Festival (Chapter 12)

Atlantic steamers offered no dining facilities on the emigrant decks.

Over the years, closer contact with Canadian culture began to impact upon the Mennonites' lifestyle. Nonetheless, their traditions are still richly entrenched in this area.

Hecla Provincial Park

Hecla Island provides an opportunity to see more of Manitoba's wildlife in its natural habitat, and an introduction to the province's Icelandic community. On the 177km (110 mile) journey up Hwy 8 to Lake Winnipeg's Hecla Island (joined by a causeway to the mainland) you will pass Gimli, the largest Icelandic community outside Iceland.

In 1875 the disappearance of cod and the eruption of the volcanic Mount Hecla in southern Iceland encouraged hundreds of Icelanders to risk the hazardous journey to Canada. They packed their few belongings and came to Manitoba where the Canadian government had established Hecla Island as a republic of New Iceland, for exclusive settlement by the Icelanders. Hecla Village became part of Manitoba in 1887, but the Icelandic community continued to thrive.

To all intents, the environment on this small, 439 sq km (169sq mile) island must have seemed inhospitable, with its marshes and thin rocky soil. Yet the Icelanders were convinced that the fish in the cold waters of Lake Winnipeg were the key to a secure livelihood. They had to learn to ice fish since the waters around Iceland seldom froze, and were obliged to build ice houses as Canadians preferred fresh fish to the dried fish that was popular in their former land. Through sheer perseverance, the Icelanders pioneered commercial fishing on Lake Winnipeg, with whitefish, goldeye and pickerel, the most sought-after fish.

Theirs was not an easy life. The men spent months on end in fishing camps at the northern end of the lake, where there were more plentiful supplies of whitefish. On Hecla, women and children looked after the log homesteads. Flooding and early frosts made farming difficult, but they managed to survive by raising enough cattle to meet their needs, and by fishing.

The Icelandic population on Hecla reached 500 by the 1920s. At its peak, they had a well established social life, based around the church and the community hall — the island's social centre, where dances would often continue until dawn.

Over the years the island's trees were used up and then, in 1947, the sawmill burned down. With the closure of the two-room school in 1966, families with children were forced to move to the mainland. Fishing became unprofitable as the stocks depleted, and the lake was even closed to fishing in 1970 for two years because of mercury pollution.

However, in 1969 Hecla's renaissance began with the conversion of the island into a provincial park. A campground, cabin accommodations, nature trails and interpretive programs were set up for visitors and the ferry service was replaced by a causeway. Some of the original buildings have been restored to form a pioneer village-type of museum which is easily explored along the 1km (½ mile) self-guiding trail.

Nature enthusiasts will find plenty to enjoy on Hecla, provided that the mosquitoes are not too much in evidence. Its revitalized aspen forest is home to twenty-four animal species including wolves, foxes, lynx and a large moose population. A footpath from the West Quarry Trail leads to a 20ft (almost 7m) high viewing platform from which moose can often be sighted at sunset or sunrise as they cross between the marshlands and forests. If you are out of luck with the moose, head down to the boardwalk over the marshes. With Hecla's location on the continent's Central Flyway, the marshes are home to 50,000 migrating wildfowl every summer.

Gull Harbour Resort Hotel offers a comfortable, Scandinavian-styled base for visitors who prefer not to camp. Its recreational facilities are exceptionally good, with tennis courts, an 18-hole golf course, badminton courts, a swimming pool, a sauna and access to the lake for swimming and sailing. In winter, Winnipeggers head up here with their cross-country skis.

Whiteshell Provincial Park

Ensconced in Precambrian Shield country, Whiteshell Provincial Park is one of Manitoba's largest parks, and is much favoured by the outdoors, nature-loving crowd. It is an easy 1½-hour drive, 118km (73 miles) east of Winnipeg along the Trans-Canada Hwy, passing from flat prairie, through woodland, to the craggy, rock-hewn landscape of the Canadian Shield. The name 'Whiteshell' comes from the small, white sacred seashell, known as the *megis*. According to Native beliefs, the Creator breathed life through this shell into the first human.

The 2,590 sq km (1,000 sq mi)le park is part of the historic Winnipeg River system. During the mid-1700s, the Winnipeg River became an important fur trade route for the Montreal-based North West Company. Each spring brigades of voyageurs such as La Vérendrye took their canoes laden with furs from the inland posts to Fort William (Ontario), and returned with trade goods later in the summer. The canoe era in western Canadian history ended in the 1870s with the development of the railways. By 1883 the line between Winnipeg and Fort William, which went through Whiteshell, was fully operational. At the turn of the century gold was discovered near Keewatin which sparked a mini gold rush. Attempts were also made to farm in the area but the land proved to be unsuitable.

During the 1920s, the first summer cottages were built in Whiteshell close to the railway, and a road-building program was initiated to make the area even more accessible. As well as providing easier access to cottages, the roads made a huge difference to fire-fighting efforts. (Forest fires continue to be a real hazard during dry summers.)

With around 200 sparkling lakes, sandy beaches and mixed-wood forests, Whiteshell offers endless opportunities for *Off the Beaten Track* vacationers. Jack pines straddle the rocky ridges, black spruce and tamarack thrive in the wetter areas while aspen and balsam fir grow in abundance throughout the woods. Resident wildlife includes the bald eagle, spruce grouse, red fox, black bear, moose, deer, coyote, wolf, mink and weasel.

One of Whiteshell's most challenging hikes is the 60km (37 miles) Mantario Hiking Trail. The longest trail in the Canadian Shield of Western Canada, it is intended for only the experienced hiker and can take from three to six days to complete. However there are many shorter trails, from 1.5km to 12.6km (1 to 8 miles) to suit every level of physical endurance.

The most developed part of Whiteshell is around West Hawk and Falcon Lakes, which have campgrounds, motels and resorts, a golf course and riding stables. To find a more remote spot, head north a little farther. Caddy Lake, for example, has only two resorts, on different sides of the lake. Some of the park's resorts are fairly rustic, with small, simply furnished cabins, that are often self-catering. Others have out-camps so that their guests can take advantage of the hunting and fishing even farther afield. Fishermen delight in the Northern pike, walleye, perch, smallmouth bass and goldeye in the Winnipeg River system. In autumn, Natives from across Manitoba and Ontario come to Whiteshell to harvest the wild rice that fills the bays of some of the lakes and the banks of the Whiteshell River.

The Alfred Hole Goose Sanctuary in Whiteshell was started in 1938 when a railway worker presented four goslings that he had found on the railway track to Alfred H. Hole, a mink rancher and outdoorsman. From this simple beginning the sanctuary, now owned by the Manitoba government, has become an island of safety for hunted animals and for its permanent breeding population of around 160 Canada geese. A 1.5km (one mile) self-guiding trail takes you to more remote parts of the sanctuary. Spring, when the gosling are still keeping close to their mothers, is an excellent time to visit.

To find out more about the history of the Shield, you can study an excellent geological display in the Visitors Centre at West Hawk Lake. Evidence of human presence in the Whiteshell area has been traced back at least 8,000 years, through various archaeological excavations. There are rock alignments (petroforms) throughout Whiteshell, such as the Bannock Point Petroforms, an ancient spiritual site for the Algonquin-speaking natives. Arranged in the forms of snakes, turtles, humans and other geometric shapes, they were used as a source of spiritual healing power. If you come across some during your travels, you are asked to respect their significance and leave them untouched.

Whiteshell caters to all tastes, whether you prefer 'soft adventure' with a comfortable bed to sleep in after a day's hiking or canoeing, or to camp in the bush for days at a time.

Churchill

Without a doubt, the train journey from Winnipeg to Churchill (1,609km or 1,000 miles) is one of North America's last great rail adventures. Churchill is sometimes described as the 'accessible' Arctic because this is where you can have a true Arctic experience with all the comforts you want. Here on Hudson Bay you can watch the northern lights, listen to the all-enveloping silence, and be deafened by wild geese touching down on the ice flows as they head south.

Churchill, Canada's only Arctic seaport, is known as the Polar Bear capital of the world. Inaccessible by road, it can be reached by air (a flight of just over two hours) or by a tri-weekly Via Rail train service from Winnipeg. The train journey takes 36 hours.

Far north of the treeline, the region has a gorgeous array of wild flowers in summer. The two main attractions though are beluga whales swimming in the bay (sometimes as many as 3,000 are sighted in one day) each summer, and the annual migration of the polar bears each fall, as they wait for the ice to form on Hudson Bay. Nature safaris mount half and full-day expeditions, by 'tundra buggies' (armoured vehicles with 100-150cm [36-60in] diameter wheels) to look for the bears in October and early November, and by boat to see the whales in July and August. Caribou, Arctic fox, polar bear, ptarmigan and thousands of geese and swans summer here. Other birds of the more than 200 species that nest here or pass through on their annual migrations include the rarely-seen Ross' Gull, as well as loons, terns, and a wide variety of shorebirds.

Although wildlife viewing is the main reason for visiting Churchill, it has an interesting history, starting with the Pre-Dorset inhabitants of 1,700BC. The local Inuit Museum has a magnificent selection of their carvings, many collected by the Oblate fathers over a forty-year period. It also explains the cultures of native peoples in the region from 1,700BC to the present-day Inuit, and traces the local history of the fur trade.

Discovered by a Dane, Jens Munk, in 1619, Churchill was first inhabited by Europeans in 1685. The Hudson's Bay Company's Fort Churchill, named after John Churchill, a company director who later became the Duke of Marlborough, was the first permanent settlement. After a second fort was built and destroyed by the French in 1782, the original Fort Churchill was re-established as a trading post. Present-day Churchill, however, traces its origins to the completion of the railway and harbour facilities in 1931. Although the ice-free season is limited to three months, the port's proximity to Europe — 1,600km (1,000 miles) closer than Montreal — is a considerable advantage when shipping prairies wheat.

Life was tough at Fort Prince of Wales, built in the 1700s by the Hudson's Bay Company. The 40ft (12m) wide walls and forty cannons were not enough to prevent its destruction by the French in 1782. Now a National Historic Park, it can be reached by boat between June and September, and by dog team during the winter. A trip to this part of the world must be booked far in advance, since Churchill has a short tourist season, and transportation, tours and accommodation is limited.

Additional Information
— Winnipeg, Where The West Was Born —

Places to Visit

Churchill

Cape Merry National Historic Park
PO Box 127
Churchill MB
R0B 0E0
Open: Guided tours daily, June to mid-Sept.
☎ (204) 675-8863

Fort Prince of Wales National Historic Park
Open: Guided tours Tues-Sat, depending on tides and weather
☎ (204) 675-8863

Inuit Museum
Open: year-round, closed Sundays
☎ (204) 675-2030

River Road

Captain Kennedy House
River Road Heritage Parkway
Open: daily mid-May to Sept
☎ (204) 334-2498

St Andrew's Church
Open: daily, Victoria Day to Labour Day, weekends in Sept
☎ (204) 334-5700

Selkirk

Lower Fort Garry National Historic Site
Open: Mid-May to Labour Day, weekends in September
☎ (204) 785-6050

St Andrew's Rectory Historic Park
5km (3mi) south of Selkirk on Hwy 9
Open: daily Mid-May to Labour Day
☎ (204) 334-6405
1-800-442-0600 (toll-free within Manitoba)

Steinbach

Mennonite Heritage Village
Open: daily from May to Sept, Oct to Apr, Mon to Fri
☎ (204) 326-9661

Winnipeg

Centre Culture Franco-Manitoban
340 Provencher Blvd
☎ (204) 233-8972

Fort Whyte Centre
1961 McCreary Road
Open: daily
☎ (204) 989-8353

Legislative Building
Broadway & Osborne
Guided tours available
☎ (204) 945-5813

Leo Mol Sculpture Garden
Assiniboine Park
Open: daily, year-round
☎ (204) 986-3823

Manitoba Children's Museum
45 Forks Market Road
Open: daily
☎ (204) 956-5437

Manitoba Museum of Man and Nature
190 Rupert Avenue
Open: daily Victoria Day-Labour Day. Sept to May, closed Mondays
☎ (204) 956-2830

Riel House National Historic Site
330 River Road
Open: daily mid-May to Labour Day, and next four weekends
☎ (204) 257-1783/233-4888

St Boniface Basilica
190 de la Cathedrale Avenue
Open: All-year-round

St Boniface Museum
494 Taché Avenue
Open: year round
☎ (204) 237-4500

St Norbert Arts and Cultural Centre
Box 175
St Norbert MB
R3V 1L7
Open: daily
☎ (204) 269-0564/261-5126

Winnipeg Art Gallery
300 Memorial Boulevard
Open daily: Mid June to Labour Day, closed Mondays, rest of year

Assiniboine Park, Zoo, Conservatory and Pavilion
2799 Roblin Avenue
Open: All-year-round
☎ (204) 986-3130

Assiniboine Forest Nature Park (Living Prairie Museum)
2795 Ness Avenue
☎ (204) 832-0167

The Forks National Historic Site
45 Forks Market Road
Open: year-round
☎ (204) 983-2007 (May to Sept)
983-6757 (off-season)

St Norbert Provincial Heritage Park
☎ (204) 269-5377 (in season)
(204) 945-4375 (off season)
Open: June to September,

Parks

Hecla Provincial Park
Open: year-round
☎ (204) 279-2056/378-2945

Lockport Heritage Park
Open: daily June to Aug
☎ (204) 757-2864

Whiteshell Provincial Park
Open: year-round
☎ (204) 348-2203/369-5232/349-2245

Local Tourist Information Offices

Churchill
Churchill Visitor Reception Centre
Bayport Plaza
Open: All-year-round
☎ (204) 675-8863

Gimli
Municipality of Gimli
Box 1246
Gimli MB
R0C 1B0
☎ (204) 642-8593

Selkirk & Lockport
☎ (204) 482-3320
Mon to Fri, 8.30am-5pm

Winnipeg
Tourism Winnipeg
320-25 Forks Market Road
Winnipeg MB
R3C 4S8
☎ (204) 943-1970/1-800-665-0204

Accommodation & Eating Out

Accommodation

Every province and territory has complimentary tourism information available on request, and this includes lists of visitor accommodation, campgrounds and restaurants. Information centres located throughout the country distribute extra local information. The Canadian and American Automobile Associations jointly operate an inspection and rating system of between one and five diamonds for accommodation. These establishments display the organizations' distinctive signs.

Hotels in all price ranges are available in cities and large towns. Canadian chains include Delta, Four Seasons and Canadian Pacific hotels and resorts. Representatives of the major international groups include Sheraton, Hilton, Ramada, Best Western, Holiday Inn and Choice Hotels. Hotel prices are similar to those in the United States, and often a little lower than in western Europe.

The Comfort Inn and Econo Lodge chains have modest (and affordable) accommodation in most towns, often handy to main highways. They provide fairly new and consistently clean, spacious rooms for up to four persons. There are also many smaller chains and individually-managed motels.

Hotels and campgrounds are mentioned throughout this guide to ensure that visitors have a bed for the night. In almost all cases the authors are personally familiar with these places. Where we are not, we list hotels belonging to chains we are comfortable in recommending.

Bed and breakfast lodgings, available across western Canada, are detailed in provincial, territorial and regional tourist guides. In the Prairies many farms welcome paying guests. These, as well as dude ranches, fishing and hunting camps and the heritage hotels can give you a uniquely Canadian experience.

Often colleges and universities offer accommodation to tourists during the summer months. Elderhostel Canada, for people in their mid-50s and beyond, provides a wide range of educational experiences along with university or hotel accommodation in many western Canadian locations. Their address is: 308 Wellington Street, Kingston ON, K7K 7A7, ☎ (613) 530-2222.

The Canadian Hostelling Association, with hostels in every western province as well as Yukon Territory imposes no age limit on its guests. Many hostels have individual and family rooms. Address: 1600 James Naismith Drive, Suite 608, Gloucester ON, K1B 5N4, ☎ (613) 748-5638.

Whatever your accommodation preference, advance reservations by telephone or fax are advised. Most establishments will hold a room until 6pm, later if you give them a major credit card number.

Western Canada has nearly 2,000 campgrounds, some of the best located in national, provincial, territorial and municipal parks where sites can be hedged with tall trees and velvety deer come visiting at dawn. Facilities range from paved sites with electricity, water and sewage hook-ups suitable for large recreational vehicles to unserviced campground spaces. Many parks invite hikers and canoeists to set up camp wherever they choose.

Provinces have parks with RV campsites close to the Trans-Canada and other main highways. The Yukon has a number of RV campsites right beside its highways. KOA Kampgrounds is a commercial chain which provides RV operators with predictably clean sites, full services and facilities. Such RV campgrounds may not accommodate those with tents. RV campsite costs range up to $30 per night, sometimes more in commercial operations. Where appropriate, we have also listed adventure outfitters and similar organizations which often include sleeping arrangements in their programs.

We have indicated the approximate cost of a double hotel or B & B room for a night in the high season, including taxes, using the following scale:

$ = less than $70
$$ = $70 - $100
$$$ = $100 - $150
$$$$ = over $150
B & B rates include breakfast.

Eating Out

Often in small communities the best meals are served in hotels. Even so we have attempted to recommend alternatives. Many Canadian motorist keeps Anne Hardy's *Where to Eat in Canada* guide (published by Oberon Press, Ottawa) in their car, ready for handy reference. Restaurants listed there are recommended by readers, and then checked out by the authors. Nobody pays to be included in the book, so unless something disastrous has happened in an establishment since the most recent printing, you are assured of a good meal when heeding its recommendations.

For highway motorists there are usually two options. Roadside service centres have limited menus, but food can be nutritious, service fast and facilities are invariably clean. Or you can follow exit signs directing you to nearby small community restaurants. Distances are so great in Canada, it is wise to stop when you have the chance if you are feeling hungry.

Price of an evening meal in a restaurant, including a modest wine, taxes and tip, for two people, is listed as:

$ = less than $50
$$ = $50
$$$ = $100 -$150
$$$$ over $150.

Chapter 1 • Vancouver & Excursions From The City

Accommodation

CHILLIWACK
Comfort Inn by Journey's End $
45405 Luckakuck Way
Sardis BC, V2R 3C7
☎ (604) 858-0636/1-800 228-5150

HARRISON HOT SPRINGS
Harrison Hot Springs Hotel $$$
100 Esplanade Ave
Harrison Hot Springs BC
V0M 1K0
☎ (604) 796-2244

Harrison Village Motel $$
1280 Esplanade Ave
Harrison Hot Springs BC
V0M 1K0
☎ (604) 796-2616

VANCOUVER
Delta Place Hotel $$$$
645 Howe St
Vancouver BC, V6C 2Y9
☎ (604) 687-1122/1-800-268-1133

CP Waterfront Centre $$$$
900 Canada Place Way
Vancouver BC
V6C 3L5
☎ (604) 691-1991/1-800-441-1414

Quality Inn Airport $$
725 SE Marine Dr
Vancouver BC
V5X 2T9
☎ (604) 321-661/1-800-228-5151

Capilano RV Park
295 Tomahawk Ave
North Vancouver BC
V7P 1C5
☎ (604) 987-4722

Eating Out

VANCOUVER
Grouse Nest $$$
6400 Nancy Green Way
North Vancouver
☎ (604) 984-6378

Mulvaney's $$
1535 Johnston St
Granville Island
Vancouver
☎ (604) 685-6571

Seasons in the Park Restaurant $$$
Queen Elizabeth Park
Vancouver
☎ (604) 874-8008

HARRISON HOT SPRINGS
The Black Forest $$
180 Esplanade
Harrison Hot Springs
☎ (604) 796-9343

STEVESTON
Charthouse Restaurant $$
3866 Bayview St
Steveston
☎ (604) 271-7000

The Sleigh's $$
3711 Bayview St
Steveston
☎ (604) 275-5188

Chapter 2 • Pacific Islands & The Sunshine Coast

Accommodation & Adventure Outfitters

GIBSONS
Gibsons Motor Inn $
Hwy 101 & Park Rd
Gibsons BC
V0N IV0
☎ (604) 886-4638

Bonniebrook Lodge (also RV park) $$
1532 Ocean Beach Esplanade
Gibsons BC
V0N 1VO
☎ (604) 886-2887

LUND
Lund Hotel $
Lund BC
V0N 2G0
☎ (604) 483-3187

Good Diving and Kayaking
Box 47
Lund BC
V0N 2G0
☎ (604) 483-3223

Eagle Kayaking Adventures
General Delivery
Lund BC
V0N 2GO
☎ (604) 483-4012

PORT HARDY
Pioneer Inn $
4965 Byng Rd
Port Hardy BC
V0N 2P0
☎ (604) 949-7271

North Shore Inn $ - $$
7370 Market St
Port Hardy BC V0N 2P0
☎ (604) 949-8500

Wildwoods Campsite
Forestry Road, south of ferry terminal
☎ (604) 949-6753

POWELL RIVER
Beach Gardens Resort Hotel $$
7074 Westminster Ave
Powell River BC
V8A 1C5
☎ (604) 485-6267

Hyatt Motor Lodge $
6255 Marine Ave
Powell River BC
V8A 4K6
☎ (604) 483-9113

Seaside Villa Motel and Trailer Park $
7274 Hwy
Powell River BC
V8A 4Z2
☎ (604) 485-2911

TOFINO
Pacific Sands Beach Resort $$
1421 Pacific Rim Highway
Box 237
Tofino BC, V0R 2Z0
☎ (604) 725-3322

Best Western Tin Wis Resort $$
1119 Pacific Rim Hwy
Tofino BC
V0R 2Z0
☎ (604) 725-4445

UCLUELET
Canadian Princess Resort $-$$
Peninsula Road
Ucluelet BC
V0R 3A0
☎ (604) 726-7771

Crow 'n' Eagle B & B and Charters $
232 Albion Crescent
PO Box 194
Ucluelet BC
V0R 3A0
☎ (604) 726-4407

Majestic West Coast Wilderness Adventures Ltd
PO Box 287
Ucluelet BC
V0R 3A0
☎ (604) 726-2868

VICTORIA
The Empress Hotel $$$$
721 Government St
Victoria BC
V8W 1W5
☎ (604) 384-8111/1-800-441-1414

Quality Inn Harbourview $$
455 Beleville St
Victoria BC
V8V 1X3
☎ (604) 386-0450/1-800-228-5151

Haterleigh B & B $$
243 Kingston St
Victoria BC
V8V 1V5
☎ (604) 384-9995

Fort Victoria RV Park
340 Island Highway
Victoria BC
V9B 1H1
☎ (604) 479-8112

Eating Out

GIBSONS
Chez Philippe
1532 Ocean Beach Esplanade
Gibsons
☎ (604) 886-2188 $$

PORT HARDY
Snuggles Dining Room
Byng Rd, adjacent to Pioneer Inn
Port Hardy
☎ (604) 949-7575 $$

POWELL RIVER
Jitterbug Café
4643 Marine Ave
Powell River
☎ (604) 485-7797 $$

TOFINO
Alley Way Café
305 Campbell St
Tofino
☎ (604) 725-3105 $

Blue Heron Restaurant
Weigh West Marine Resort
634 Campbell St
Tofino
☎ (604) 725-4266 $$

UCLUELET
Stewart Room Restaurant
Canadian Princess Resort
Peninsula Rd
Ucluelet
☎ (604) 726-7771 $$$

Wickaninnish Restaurant
Long Beach
Pacific Rim National Park
☎ (604) 726-7706 $$

VICTORIA
The Sooke Harbour House $$$$
1528 Whiffen Spit Road
Sooke (north on Trans-Canada Hwy)
☎ (604) 624-3421

Herald Street Caffe $$
546 Herald St, Victoria
☎ (604) 381-1441

Oak Bay Marina $$$
1327 Beach Ave
Oak Bay
☎ (604) 598-8555 $$$

Chapter 3 • By Gold Rush Trails To The Yellowhead

Accommodation & Adventure Outfitters

BELLA COOLA
Cedar Inn $
Mackenzie St
Bella Coola BC
V0T 1C0
☎ (604) 799-5316

Bay Motor Hotel $
Hwy 20 Hagensborg
PO Box 216
Bella Coola BC
V0T 1C0
☎ (604) 982-2212

Tweedsmuir Lodge $$
(In Tweedsmuir Park, open mid-March to mid-November)
RR#1
Bella Coola BC
VOT 1CO
☎ (604) 982-2402

CLEARWATER
Wells Grey Inn $
Village Road
Clearwater BC
V0E 1N0
☎ (604) 674-2214

Wells Grey Guest Ranch ($$ inc meals)
Wells Grey Park Rd
RR#1, Box 1766
Clearwater BC
V0E 1N0
☎ (604) 674-2792

Interior Whitewater Expeditions
Box 24015
Scotch Creek BC
V0E 2L0
☎ (604) 674-3727

KAMLOOPS
Hospitality Inn $$
500 W Columbia St
Kamloops BC
V2C 1K6
☎ (604) 374-4164

Panorama Inn $$
610 W Columbia St
Kamloops BC
V2C 1l1
☎ (604) 374-1515

Kamloops View Campsite/RV Park
1-4395 E Trans-Canada Hwy (10km east)
Box 1
Kamloops BC
V2C 4S4
☎ (604) 573-3255

LYTTON
Kumsheen Raft Adventures
281 Main St
Lytton BC
V0K 1Z0
☎ (604) 455-2296

PRINCE GEORGE
Coast Inn of the North $$ - $$$
770 Brunswick St
Prince George BC
V2L 2C2
☎ (604) 563-0121

Holiday Inn Prince George $$
444 George St
Prince George
BC V2L 1R6
☎ (604) 563-0055/1-800-HOLIDAY

Spruceland KOA Kampground
Kinball Rd
Hwy 16, 6km west of Hwy 97
☎ (604) 964-7272

QUESNEL
Cariboo Hotel $
1254 Front St
Quesnel BC
V2J 2K2
☎ (604) 992-2333/1-800-665-3200

Good Knight Inn $
176 Davie St
Quesnel BC, V2J 2S7
☎ (604) 992-2187

SPENCES BRIDGE
Steelhead Inn $-$$
Box 100
Spences Bridge BC, V0K 2L0
☎ (604) 458-2398

WHISTLER
Château Whistler Resort $$$$
4599 Château Blvd
Whistler BC, V0N 1B4
☎ (604) 938-8000/1-800-268-9411

Eating Out

KAMLOOPS
Chapters Viewpoint $$
Columbia Ave, adjacent to Panorama Inn
Kamloops
☎ (604) 374-3234

Sinbad's $$
1502 River St
Kamloops
☎ (604) 372-1522

PRINCE GEORGE
Rosel's Restaurant $$
1624 7th Ave
Prince George
☎ (604) 562-4972

Da Moreno $$
1493 3rd Ave
Prince George
☎ (604) 564-7922

QUESNEL
The Vaughan House Restaurant $$
714 Front St
Quesnel
☎ (604) 992-6852

WHISTLER
Rimrock Café $$$
Highland Lodge
Whistler
☎ (604) 932-5565

Val d'Isère $$$
4433 Sundial Place
Whistler
☎ (604) 932-4666

Chapter 4 • The Fabulous North

Accommodation

FORT ST JAMES
Chundoo Motor Inn $
290 East Stuart Drive
Box 130
Fort St James BC
V0J 1P0
☎ (604) 996-8216

Stuart Lodge $
Stones Bay Rd
Box 838
Fort St James BC
V0J 1P0
☎ (604) 996-7917

NEW HAZELTON
28 Inn $
4545 Yellowhead Hwy
Box 358, New Hazleton BC
V0J 2JO
☎ (604) 842-6006

Robbers Roost Lodge $
Yellowhead Hwy,
Box 555, New Hazleton
BC V0J 2JO
☎ (604) 842-6916

'Ksan Campground
'Ksan Village (Hazelton)
c/o Box 440
Hazelton BC
V0J 1Y0
☎ (604) 842-5940

PRINCE RUPERT
Crest Motor Hotel $$$
222 1st Ave W
c/o Box 277
Prince Rupert BC
V8J 3P6
☎ (604) 624-6771/1-800-663-8150

Best Western Highliner Inn $$
815 1st Ave W
Prince Rupert BC
V8J 1B3
☎ (604) 624-9060/1-800-627-7759

Park Avenue (Municipal) Campground
1750 Park Ave
(1km east of ferry terminals)
☎ (604) 624-5861

TERRACE
Coast Inn of the West $$
4620 Lakelse Ave
Terrace BC, V8G 1R1
☎ (604) 638-8141

Eating Out

HAZELTON
The Hummingbird $$
Hwy 16
Old Hazelton
☎ (604) 842-5628

PRINCE RUPERT
Smile's Seafood Café $$
113 Cow Bay Rd
Prince Rupert
☎ (604) 624-3072

The Waterfront Café $$$
Crest Motor Hotel
222 First Ave
☎ (604) 624-6771

TERRACE
Don Diego's $$
3212 Kalum St
Terrace
☎ (604) 635-2307

Chapter 5 • Through Okanagan Orchards To The Rockies

Accommodation

GOLDEN
Prestige Inn $$$
1049 Trans-Canada Hwy
Golden BC
V0A 1H0
☎ (604) 344-7990

KELOWNA
Lake Okanagan Resort $$$$
2751 Westside Road
Kelowna BC
V1Y 8B2
☎ (604) 769-3511/1-800-663-3273

Siesta Motor Inn $$
3152 Lakeshore Rd
Kelowna BC
V1W 3T1
☎ (604) 763-5013

Lakeside RV Park
654 Cook Rd
Kelowna BC
V1W 3G7
☎ (604) 860-4072

OSOYOOS
Bella Villa Resort Motel $
6904 64A Ave
Osoyoos BC
V0H 1V0
☎ (604) 495-6751

Safari Beach Resort $$
1609 89th St
Osoyoos BC
V0H 1VO
☎ (604) 495-7217

Haynes Point Provincial Park
(camping & RVs)
Hwy 97 South
(2km south of Osoyoos)
☎ (604) 494-0321

PENTICTON
Coast Lakeside Resort $$$
21 Lakeshore Dr W
Penticton BC
V2A 7M5
☎ (604) 493-8221

Happy Hour Resort (camping and RVs)
RR2 (6km S on Hwy 97)
Penticton BC
V2A 6JR
☎ (604) 493-8506

VERNON
Swiss Hotel Silver Lode Inn $$
Silver Star Mountain Road
Box 5 Vernon BC
VOE 1GO
☎ (604) 549-5105

Lord Aberdeen Hotel $$$
139 Main St
Silver Star Mountain
Box 1, Silver Star Mountain BC
V0E 1GO
☎ (604) 542-1992

Travelodge Vernon $
3000 28th Ave
Vernon BC V1T 1W1
☎ (604) 545-2161

Silver Star RV & Trailer Park
Stickle Road
1km north of Vernon on Swan Lake
☎ (604) 542-2808

Eating Out

KELOWNA
Le Papillon Restaurant $$
375 Leon Ave
Kelowna
☎ (604) 763-3833

Williams Inn $$
526 Lawrence Ave
Kelowna
☎ (604) 763-5136

OSOYOOS $$
The Chalet Helvetia
8312 74th Ave
Osoyoos
☎ (604) 495-7552

PENTICTON
Granny Bogner's $$$
302 Eckhart Ave W
Penticton
☎ (604) 493-2711

Salty's Beach House $$
1000 Lakeshore Dr
Penticton
☎ (604) 493-5001

VERNON
Avonlea Dining Room $$$
Prestige Inn
4411 32nd St
☎ (604) 558-3900

Chapter 6 • Discovering The Kootenays

Accommodation

CRANBROOK
Inn of the South $$
803 Cranbrook St N
Cranbrook BC
V1C 3S2
☎ (604) 489-4301

Ponderosa Motel and Campground $
500 Van Horne St S
Cranbrook BC
V1C 4H3
☎ (604) 426-6114

Bull River Ranch $$
(a working ranch with log cabins)
15km north on Hwy 95
Box 133, Cranbrook BC
V1C 4H7
☎ (604) 429-3760

CASTLEGAR
Fireside Motor Inn $$
Hwys 3 & 22
Castlegar BC
V1N 2Y2
☎ (604) 365-2128

Mountain Retreat Guest House $$
RR1 Castlegar BC
V1N 3H7
☎ (604) 365-6578.

Castlegar RV Park and Campground
1725 Mannix Rd
Castlegar BC, V1N 3R8
☎ (604) 365-2337

FAIRMONT HOT SPRINGS
Fairmont Hot Springs Resort $$
Box 10, Fairmont Hot Springs BC
V0B 1L0
☎ (604) 345-6311

A typical prairie landscape, wheat field and canola field (Chapter 12)

Auctioning cattle at Brandon's Royal Manitoba Winter Fair (Chapter 12)

Brown bears make an occasional appearance in prairie parkland (Chapter 12)

Red foxes frequent many of Manitoba's parks (Chapter 12)

KIMBERLEY
Inn of the Rockies $
300 Wallinger Ave
Kimberley BC
V1A 1Z4
☎ (604) 427-2266

Inn West $$
880 North Star Drive
Kimberley BC
V1A 2Y6
☎ (604) 427-7616

NAKUSP
The Selkirk Inn $
Box 370
Nakusp BC
V0G 1R0
☎ (604) 265-3666

Nakusp Recreation Park Campsite
8th Ave W
c/o Box 280
Nakusp BC
V0G 1R0
☎ (604) 265-4234

NELSON
Heritage Inn $
422 Vernon St
Nelson BC
V1L 4E5
☎ (604) 352-5331

Inn the Garden B&B $$
408 Victoria St
Nelson BC
V1L 4K5
☎ (604) 352-3226

City Tourist Park (RV facilities)
90 High St
Nelson BC
V1L 4E8
☎ (604) 352-9031

RADIUM HOT SPRINGS
Radium Hot Springs Resort $$$
Box 310
Radium Hot Springs BC
V0A 1M0
☎ (604) 347-9311

Alte Leibe Motel & Restaurant $$
Box 104
Radium Hot Springs BC
V0A 1M0
☎ (604) 347-9548

Eating Out

CASTLEGAR
Gabriel's Restaurant $$
1413 Columbia Ave
Castlegar
☎ (604) 365-6028

KIMBERLEY
Bauernhaus Restaurant $$
280 Norton Ave
Kimberley
☎ (604) 427-5133

NELSON
Fiddlers Green Restaurant $$
Lower 6 Mile Rd
(10km north of Nelson on Hwy 3a)
☎ (604) 825-4466

The Wild Onion $$
536 Stanley St
Nelson
☎ (604) 352-6800

RADIUM HOT SPRINGS
The Old Salzburg Restaurant $$
4943 Hwy 93
Radium Hot Springs
☎ (604) 347-6553

Chapter 7 • The Legendary Yukon

Accommodation & RV Rental

BEAVER CREEK
Westmark Inn Beaver Creek $$$
Mile 1202 Alaska Hwy (1934km)
Beaver Creek YT
Y0B 1A0
☎ (403) 862-7501

DAWSON CITY
Dawson City B & B $$
451 Craig St
Dawson City YT, Y0B 1G0
☎ (403) 993-5648

Eldorado Hotel $$$
3rd Ave and Princess St
Dawson City YT
Y0B 1G0
☎ (403) 993-5256

Westmark Inn Dawson $$$
5th Ave & Harper St
Dawson City YT
Y0B 1G0
☎ (403) 993-5542

Gold Rush Campground
5th Ave and York St
Box 198
Dawson City YT
Y0B 1G0
☎ (403) 993-5247

DESTRUCTION BAY
Talbot Arm Motel $$
Box A, Destruction Bay YT
Y0B 1H0
☎ (403) 841-4461

HAINES JUNCTION
Mountain View Motor Inn $$
Box 5479, Haines Junction YT
Y0B 1L0
☎ (403) 634-2646

Kathleen Lake Campground
Kluane National Park
27km south on Hwy 3
Box 5495, Haines Junction YT
Y0B 1L0
☎ (403) 634-2251

WHITEHORSE
Westmark Whitehorse $$$
201 Wood St
Whitehorse YT
Y1A 3T3
☎ (403) 668-4700

Best Western Gold Rush Inn $$$
411 Main St
Whitehorse YT
Y1A 2B6
☎ (403) 668-4500

Sourdough City RV Park
2nd Ave
c/o 411 Main St
Whitehorse YT
Y1A 2B6
☎ (403) 668-4500

Robert Service Campground
South Access Road
c/o City of Whitehorse YT
Y1A 1C2
☎ (403) 668-3721

Klondike Recreational Rentals Ltd
(RVs & campers)
Box 5156, Whitehorse YT
Y1A 4S3
☎ (403) 668-2200

Eating Out

DAWSON CITY
Jack London Grill $$$
Downtown Hotel
2nd Ave & Queen St
Dawson City
☎ (403) 993-5346

Klondike Kate's Restaurant $$
3rd Ave & King St
Dawson City
☎ (403) 993-6527

WHITEHORSE
The Cellar $$$
Edgewater Hotel
101 Main St, Whitehorse
☎ (403) 667-2573

No Pop's $$
312 Steele St, Whitehorse
☎ (403) 668-3227

Chapter 8 • Adventuring In The Northwest

Accommodation & Adventure Outfitters

FORT SMITH
Anna Hodgkins B&B $
12 Pine Crescent
Fort Smith NT , X0E 0P0
☎ (403) 872-2639

Linda Calder Guesthouse $
13 Cassette Crescent
Fort Smith NT
X0E 0P0
☎ (403) 872-5787

Queen Elizabeth Park Campground
c/o Economic Development & Tourism
Box 1320
Yellowknife NT
X1A 2L9
☎ (403) 872-7244

Subarctic Wilderness Adventures Ltd
Box 685, Fort Smith NT
X0E 0P0
☎ (403) 872-2467

RAE-EDZO
Sah Naji Kwe Camp $$
Box 98, Rae-Edzo,
NT X0E 0Y0
☎ (403) 371-3144

YELLOWKNIFE
The Explorer Hotel $$$$
Box 7000
Yellowknife
NT X1A 2R3
☎ (403) 873-3531

Blue Raven B & B $
37-b Otto Drive
Yellowknife NT
X1A 2T9
☎ (403) 873-6328

Captain Ron's B & B $
8 Lessard Drive
Yellowknife NT
X1A 2G5
☎ (403) 873-3746

Cygnus Ecotours
Box 682
Yellowknife NT
X1A 2N5
☎ (403) 873-4782

Frontier RV Rentals
Box 1088
Yellowknife NT, X1A 2N7
☎ (403) 873-5413

Raven Tours
Box 2435
Yellowknife NT
X1A 2P8
☎ (403) 873-4776

Yellowknife Outdoor Adventures
904 Findlayson Court
Yellowknife NT
X1A 3A6
☎ (403) 873-5751

Eating Out

YELLOWKNIFE
Bullock's Fish and Chips $
4 Lessard Dr
Yellowknife
☎ (403) 873-3474

The Office Lounge $$$
4915 50 Street
Yellowknife
☎ (403) 873-3750

The Wildcat Café $$
Wiley Rd
Yellowknife
☎ (403) 873-8850

Chapter 9 • Alberta's Fabled Rockies

Accommodation & Adventure Outfitters

BANFF
Banff Springs Hotel $$$$
Spray Ave
Box 960, Banff AB
T0L 0C0
☎ (403) 762-2211/1-800-441-1414

Banff Ptarmigan Inn $$$
337 Banff Ave
Box 1840, Banff AB
T0L 0C0
☎ (403) 762-2207/1-800-661-8310

Inns of Banff Park $$$
600 Banff Ave
Box 1077, Banff AB
T0L 0C0
☎ (403) 762-4581/1-800-661-1272

Warner Guiding and Outfitting Ltd
(horseback vacations)
Box 2280
Banff AB
T0L 0C0
☎ (403) 762-4551

White Mountain Tours
(hiking, cross-country skiing)
Box 2294
Canmore AB
T0L 0M0
☎ (403) 678-4099

LAKE LOUISE
Château Lake Louise $$$$
Lake Louise AB
T0L 1E0
☎ (403) 522-3511/1-800-441-1414

JASPER
Jasper Park Lodge $$$$
5km north via Hwy 16 and Maligne Rd
Box 40
Jasper AB
T0E 1E0
☎ (403) 852-3301/1-800-441-1414

Lobstick Lodge $$$
94 Geikie St
Box 1200
Jasper AB
T0E 1E0
☎ (403) 852-4431

WATERTON LAKES PARK
Prince of Wales Hotel $$$
Waterton AB
Open May-Oct
for reservations write to:
Mail Station 5570
Phoenix AZ 85078, USA
☎ (406) 226-5551

Bayshore Inn $$$
Main St
Box 38
Waterton Park AB
T0K 2M0
Open May-Oct
☎ (403) 859-2211

Eating Out

BANFF
Le Beaujolais $$$
212 Buffalo St
Banff
☎ (403) 762-2712

Coyote's $$
206 Caribou St
Banff
☎ (403) 762-3965

JASPER
Hava Java $
407 Patricia St
Jasper
☎ (403) 852-5727

Becker's $$
8km south of Jasper on Hwy 93
☎ (403) 852-3535

WATERTON LAKES PARK
Kilmorey Lodge $$
Waterton Park
Open all year
☎ (403)859-2334

Chapter 10 • Cattle, Oil & Dinosaurs

Accommodation

BROOKS
Heritage Inn $
1303 2nd St W, Hwy 873
1m south of Trans-Canada Hwy
Box 907
Brooks AB
T1R 1B8
☎ (403) 362-6666

CALGARY
Delta Bow Valley Inn $$$$
209 4th Ave SE
Calgary AB
T2G 0C6
☎ (403) 266-1980 1-800-268-1133

Sandman Hotel Downtown Calgary $$
888 7th Ave SW
Calgary AB
T2P 3J3
☎ (403) 237-8626 1-800-726-3626

Calaway Park RV Campground
Jct Trans-Canada Hwy & Springbank Rd
(10km west of city)
RR#2 - Site 25, Comp 20
Calgary AB
T2P 2G5
☎ (403) 249-7372

KOA Kampground Calgary West
Trans-Canada Hwy, 2km west of city limits
Box 10, Site 12, SS #1
Calgary AB
T2M 4N3
☎ (403) 288-0411

CORONACH
Country Boy Motel (facilities for RVs) $
Box 459
Coronach SK
S0H 0Z0
☎ (306) 267-3267

Country Flavor Bed & Breakfast $
Box 427
Coronach SK
S0H 0Z0
☎ (306) 267-4507

CYPRESS HILLS
Cypress Hills Four Seasons Resort $$
30km south of Maple Creek
Box 1480, Maple Creek SK
S0N 1N0
☎ (306) 662-4477

Cypress Hills Interprovincial Park Campsite
28km south of Maple Creek on Hwy 21
Box 850, Maple Creek SK
S0N 1N0
☎ (306) 662-4411

DRUMHELLER
Drumheller Inn $$
100 S Railway Ave
Drumheller AB
T0J 0Y0
☎ (403) 823-8400

The Lodge at Drumheller $
48 N Railway Ave
Box 1810
Drumheller AB
T0J 0Y0
☎ (403) 823-3322

Dinosaur Trail RV Resort
Hwy 838
11km west of town
Box 1300
Drumheller AB
T0J 0Y0
☎ (403) 823-9333

EDMONTON
Hotel Macdonald $$$$
10065 - 100 St
Edmonton AB
T5J 0N6
☎ (403) 424-5181/1-800-441-1414

Comfort Inn by Journey's End $$
17610 - 100 Ave
Edmonton AB
T5S 1S9
☎ (403) 484-4415/1-800-228-5150

Delta Edmonton Centre Suite Hotel $$$
10222 - 102 St
Edmonton AB
T5J 4C5
☎ (403) 429-3900/1-800-661-6655

Klondike Valley Campground
1660 Calgary Trail SW
(west of West Edmonton Mall)
Edmonton AB
TW6 1A1
☎ (403) 988-5067

MANKOTA
Grassland's Inn $
Box 152
Mankota SK
S0H 2W0
☎ (306) 378-2909/(306) 478-9200

McCORD
Horse Creek Vacation Farm $
Box 89, McCord SK
S0H 2T0
☎ (306) 478-2682/(306) 478-2635

MOOSE JAW
Best Western Downtown Motor Lodge $
45 Athabasca Street East
Moose Jaw SK
S6H 0L3
☎ (306) 692-1884/1-800-528-1234

Latimer's on Oxford B & B $
37 Oxford Street
Moose Jaw SK
S6H 2N2
☎ (306) 692-5481

Prairie Oasis Campground
9th Avenue NE, off Hwy 1E
☎ (306) 692-4894/(306) 693-8888

River Park Campground
300 River Drive
Open: mid-April to mid-Oct
☎ (306) 692-5474

VAL MARIE
Paradis Place Country Vacation Farm $
Box 141, Val Marie SK
S0N 2T0
☎ (306) 298-2061

Val Marie Campground
Box 178, Val Marie SK
S0N 2T0
Facilities: tents, trailers, RVs
☎ (306) 298-2022

WILLOW BUNCH
Jean Louis Legaré Regional Park
Box 114
Willow Bunch SK
S0H 4K0
Open: mid-May to Sept
Facilities for tents and RVs
☎ (306) 473-2624/9372

Stage Coach Motel and Restaurant $
Box 61, Willow Bunch SK
S0H 4K0
☎ (306) 473-2362

WOOD MOUNTAIN
Bar F Country Vacations $
Box 82, Wood Mountain SK
S0H 4L0
☎ (306) 266-4310/2011

Wood Mountain Regional Park Campground
Box 7
Flintoff SK
S0H 1R0
Open: mid- May to early Sept
☎ (306) 266-4322

Eating Out

CALGARY
Florentine $$
1014-8th Street SW
Calgary
☎ (403) 232-6028

DRUMHELLER
The Sizzling House $
160 Centre Street
Drumheller
☎ (403) 823-8098

EDMONTON
Jack's Grill $$
290 Saddleback Road
Edmonton
☎ (403) 434-1113

MAPLE CREEK
Currah's Bakery $
107 Maple Street
☎ (306) 662-3811

MEDICINE HAT
Barney's $$
665 Kingsway Avenue SE
Medicine Hat
☎ (403) 529-5663

RAVENSCRAIG
The Country Tearoom $
At Spring Valley Ranch
☎ (306) 295-4124

Chapter 11 • Land Of The Big Sky

Accommodation

BEECHY
K Bar Country Vacation & Bed & Breakfast $
Box 221, Beechy SK
S0L 0C0
☎ (306) 859-4509

Prairie Lake Regional Park Campground
Box 84
Beechy SK
S0L 0C0
☎ (306) 859-2181

BUFFALO POUND
Buffalo Pound Provincial Park Campground
☎ (306) 693-2678/694-3659

CROOKED LAKE
Crooked Lake Provincial Park Campground
Open: May to September
☎ (306) 728-7480

FORT QU'APPELLE
Company House $
172 Company Avenue
Fort Qu'Appelle SK
S0G 1S0
☎ (306) 332-6333

Country Squire Inn $
Hwy 10 & Bay Street
Box 699
Fort Qu'Appelle SK
S0G 1S0
☎ (306) 332-5603

Echo Valley Provincial Park Campground
Box 790
Fort Qu'Appelle SK
S0G 1S0
Open: all-year-round
☎ (306) 332-3215

Harman's Country Vacation Farm $
Box 265
Fort Qu'Appelle SK
S0G 1S0
☎ (306) 332-5228

MANITOU BEACH
Best Bed'n Breakfast $
Box 996
Watrous SK
S0K 4T0
☎ (306) 946-2495

Manitou Springs Resort $$
Box 610, Watrous SK
S0K 4T0
☎ (306) 946-2233/1-800-667-7672

Delwood Campground
Box 77
Watrous SK
S0K 4T0
☎ (306) 946-2318/(306) 946-2168

PRINCE ALBERT
Comfort Inn by Journey's End $$
3863 2nd Avenue West
Prince Albert SK
S6W 1A1
☎ (306) 763-4466 1-800-228-5150

PRINCE ALBERT NATIONAL PARK
Lakeview Hotel $
Open: mid-April to mid-Oct
☎ (306) 663-5311

Waskesiu Lake Lodge $$
Open: all-year-round
☎ (306) 663-6161

Prince Albert National Park Campgrounds
(four)
Box 100
Wasskesiu Lake SK
S0J 2Y0
☎ (306) 663-5322

QU'APPELLE
Bluenose Country Vacation Farm $
Box 173, Qu'Appelle SK
S0G 4A0
☎ (306) 699-7192/(306) 699-2328

REGINA
Comfort Inn by Journey's End $$
3221 East Eastgate Drive
Regina SK
S4Z 1A4
☎ (306) 789-5522/1-800-228-5150

Hotel Saskatchewan Radisson Plaza $$
2125 Victoria Avenue
Regina SK
S4P 0S3
☎ (306) 522-7691/1-800-333-3333

King's Acres Campground
Box 168 , Regina SK
S4P 2Z6
Open: year-round
☎ (306) 522-1619

Buffalo Lookout Campground
Box 3884, Regina SK
S4P 3R8
Open: May to mid-Sept
☎ (306) 525-1448

ROUND LAKE
Bird's Point Store & Pavilion $
(cabins and campsites)
Box 301, Stockholm SK
S0A 3Y0
☎ (306) 793-2888

Lakeside Bed & Breakfast $
Box 178, Broadview SK
S0G 0K0
☎ (306) 793-4499

Maple Grove Resort $
Box 857, Whitewood SK
S0G 5C0
☎ (306) 793-4365

SASKATOON
Comfort Inn by Journey's End $$
2155 Northridge Drive
Saskatoon SK
S7L 6X6
☎ (306) 934-1122 1-800-228-5150

Delta Bessborough $$$
601 Spadina Crescent East
Saskatoon SK
S7K 3G8
☎ (306) 244-5521

Eating Out

PRINCE ALBERT
Amy's on Second $$
2990 2nd Avenue W
☎ (306) 763-1515

REGINA
Saje $$
2330 Albert Street
☎ (306) 569-9726

SASKATOON
St Tropez Bistro $$
243-3rd Avenue South
Saskatoon
☎ (306) 652-1250

ST-ISADORE de BELLEVUE
Le Rendezvous $
Highway 225
St-Isadore de Bellevue
☎ (306) 423-6264

WATROUS
Paul's Place ($45)
Highway 2
Watrous
☎ (306) 946-3933

Chapter 12 • Fossils, Flowers & Desert Sands

Accommodation & Adventure Outfitters

BOISSEVAIN
The Blue Jewel Inn $$
Box 445, Boissevain MB
R0K 0E0
☎ (204) 534-6258

Oak Valley Bed and Breakfast $
Box 938, Boissevain MB
R0K 0E0
☎ (204) 534-2389

BRANDON
Casa Maley Bed & Breakfast $
1605 Victoria Avenue
Brandon MB
R7A 1C1
☎ (204) 728-0812

Comfort Inn By Journey's End $$
925 Middleton Avenue
Brandon MB
R7C 1A8
☎ (204) 727-6232/1-800-228-5150

CARBERRY
Seton Trails Guest Lodge $
Box 579, Carberry MB
R0K 0H0
☎ (204) 466-2783

CARMAN
Walnut Street Bed & Breakfast $
77-2nd Avenue SW
Carman MB
R0G 0J0
☎ (204) 745-6787

DUCK MOUNTAIN PROVINCIAL PARK
Duck Mountain Provincial Park Campgrounds
☎ (204) 622-2104

Childs Lake Lodge and Outfitters
Box 13
Baggy Creek MB
R0L 0G0
Open: all-year-round
☎ (204) 546-2746

Wellman Lake Lodge & Outfitters
Box 249
Minitonas MB
R0L 1G0
Open: May to Sept
☎ (204) 546-9936

KILLARNEY
Emerald Isle Motel & Resort $
(includes camping facilities)
Box 1600
Killarney MB
R0K 1G0
☎ (204) 523-4215

Erin Inn $
Box 1418
Killarney MB
R0K 1G0
☎ (204) 523-4651

Molly O'Malley's Inn $
Box 119
Killarney MB
R0K 1G0
☎ (204) 523-8575

MORDEN
Valley View Farm Bed and Breakfast $
Box 140, RR 1
Morden MB
R0G 1J0
☎ (204) 822-3731

Colert Beach Campground
Box 1696
Morden MB
R0G 1J0
Open: May to Sept
☎ (204) 822-4991

MOOSE MOUNTAIN
Moose Mountain Provincial Park Campground
Box 220
Kenosee Lake SK
S0C 2S0
Open: year-round
☎ (306) 577-2131/2144

NEEPAWA
Vivian Motor Hotel $
236 Hamilton Street
Neepawa MB
R0J 1H0
☎ (204) 476-5089

PORTAGE LA PRAIRIE
Manitobah Inn $$
South Service Rd on Trans-Canada Hwy
Box 867
Portage La Prairie MB
R1N 3C3
☎ (204) 857-9791

RIDING MOUNTAIN NATIONAL PARK
Aspen Ridge Farm $
General Delivery
Lake Audy MB
R0J 0Z0
☎ (204) 848-2964

Elkhorn Resort $$$
Box 40
Onanole MB
R0J 1N0
☎ (204) 848-2802

Lee's Holiday Bungalows $$
Box 156
Wasagaming MB
R0J 2H0
Open: May to Sept
☎ (204) 848-2511

Wasagaming Campground
Open: May to mid-Sept
☎ (204) 848-7221

Trailhead Outfitters
Lake Audy MB
R0J 0Z0
☎ (204) 848-7649

SANFORD
Destination Adventure
Box 28
Sanford MB
R0G 2J0

SOURIS
Victoria Park Campground
Box 634
Souris MB
R0K 2C0
Open: May to Sept
☎ (204) 483-4074

SPRUCE WOODS PROVINCIAL PARK
Kiche Manitou Campground
Open: May to Sept
☎ (204) 827-2458

Eating Out

BRANDON
Kokonas $$
1011 Rosser Avenue
Brandon
☎ (204) 727-4395

WAWANESA
Kurt's Schnitzel House $
123 4th Street
Wawanesa
☎ (204) 824-2472

Chapter 13 • Winnipeg — Where The West Was Born

Accommodation, Adventure Outfitters & Tour Operators

CHURCHILL
Polar Inn $$
15 Franklin Street
Box 1031, Churchill MB
R0B 0E0
☎ (204) 675-8878

Seaport Hotel $$
299 Kelsey Boulevard
Box 399
Churchill MB
R0B 0E0
☎ (204) 675-2795

Churchill Wilderness Encounter
PO Box 9
Churchill MB
R0B 0E0
☎ (204) 675-2248

HECLA
Gull Harbour Resort & Conference Centre $$
General Delivery
Riverton MB
R0C 2R0
☎ (204) 279-2041/1-800-267-6700

Gull Harbour Campground
Open: May to Sept
☎ (204) 378-2945

Solmundson Gesta Hus Bed & Breakfast
Box 76
Hecla Island MB
R0C 2R0
☎ (204) 279-2088

ST BONIFACE
Voyageur House Bed & Breakfast $
268 Notre Dame Street East
Winnipeg MB
R2H 0C6
☎ (204) 231-1783

WHITESHELL PARK AREA
Caddy Lake Resort $$
Whiteshell Post Office MB
R0E 2H0
☎ (204) 349-2596
off-season: (204) 668-4253

Falcon Beach Riding Stables & Guest Ranch $$$
Falcon Lake MB
R0E 0N0
☎ (204) 349-2410

Whiteshell Provincial Park Campgrounds
Open: May to Sept
☎ (204) 349-8247

WINNIPEG
Comfort Inn Airport by Journey's End $
1770 Sargent Avenue
Winnipeg MB
R3H 0C8
☎ (204) 783-5627/1-800-228-5150

The Delta Winnipeg $$$
288 Portage Avenue
Winnipeg MB
R3C 0B8
☎ (204) 956-0410/1-800-268-1133

Frontiers North
774 Bronx Avenue
Winnipeg
MB R2K 2E9
☎ (204) 949-2050/1-800-663-9832

Hotel Fort Garry $$
222 Broadway
Winnipeg MB
R3C 0R3
☎ (204) 942-8251/1-800-665-8088

West Gate Manor Bed & Breakfast $
71 West Gate
Winnipeg MB
R3C 2C9
☎ (204) 772-9788

KOA Winnipeg, East Campground
Box 11, Group 612, SS6
Winnipeg MB
R0C 1W0
☎ (204) 253-8168

Eating Out

ST BONIFACE
La Vieille Gare $$
630 Des Meurons at Provencher
St Boniface
☎ (204) 237-7072

STEINBACH
The Dutch Connection ($45)
88 Brandt Road
Steinbach
☎ (204) 326-2018

WINNIPEG
The Sandpiper $$$
& *The Prairie Oyster* $$
1 Forks Market Road
Winnipeg
☎ (204) 942-0918

Canada Fact File

Climate & Clothing

For a first-time visit, we recommend you come between the end of May and late September. Air-conditioning is virtually universal in commercial buildings throughout Canada. Southern sections of the prairie provinces can be very hot and humid in July and August. May and June are usually very pleasant in these regions, although warm clothes will be required at night. Biting insects such as mosquitoes and black flies can be a nuisance during summer. Insect repellant and cover-up clothing helps.

Mountain ranges west of the Rockies make western Canada's temperatures and rainfall extremely variable. The prairies are more predictable, with warm summers and cold winters and moderate rainfall. Sub-Arctic regions of the Yukon and Northwest Territories can be warm in summer.

Overall, September is perhaps the best month for mild days and cool nights and colourful autumn foliage. Temperatures can be very low between December and late April all over the country, except in the southern and coastal areas of British Columbia. Heavy outdoor clothing is necessary at this time of the year. It is, of course, the season for skiing, snow-shoeing, ice skating and a host of other winter activities.

Canadians dress fairly informally. Visitors from Europe and the United States will be comfortable with the leisure clothes they bring from home. Outdoors clothing suitable to local conditions may be purchased virtually anywhere in Canada. In the cities, hotels and more formal restaurants usually expect men to wear jackets and ties in the evening, and women to be appropriately attired.

Crime

Although Canada has its share of crime, particularly in the larger cities, it is generally safe to walk the streets at night. Visitors should take the same precautions against pickpockets, and other petty criminals, as they would at home. Put valuables in your hotel safe, and keep your belongings out of sight when leaving your car in tourist areas, parks and public places.

Handguns are prohibited and the use of other firearms strictly controlled. Buying or selling illicit drugs is severely dealt with by the police and courts. Some aboriginal communities prohibit alcoholic beverages.

Currency, Banking & Credit Cards

Canada's currency is dollars and cents. Coins consist of copper-coloured cents, silver-coloured 5, 10, 25 and 50 cent denominations, gold-coloured dollars and bi-metal two dollars. Bills in 5, 10, 20, 50, 100 and 1,000 dollar denominations are all the same size but different colours. United States currency is widely accepted at the prevailing exchange rate. Currently, the Canadian dollar is worth approximately 72¢ US and 45p sterling.

Most communities have branches of the large national banks. Hours of operation are, at the minimum, 10am to 3pm on weekdays, and much longer in cities. Banks are closed on legal holidays, but then exchange bureaus in cities, airports and at border crossings are usually open. Automated teller machines are widespread and accept bank cards issued by most foreign banks. The major credit cards issued by American Express, Master Card and Visa are accepted, as are American Express, Thomas Cook, Mastercard and Visa travellers cheques.

Customs, Immigration & Health Regulations

Vacationers will find Canada's entry requirements simple and usually Customs and Immigration officials are courteous. United States citizens or permanent residents do not need passports or visas. Visitors from all other countries require a valid passport. Citizens of Great Britain and many other British Commonwealth and European Community countries do not need a visa. If in doubt your status can be clarified by your travel agent or a Canadian consulate before departure. Non-Canadians who want to go to the United States will require a visa obtained through a United States consulate before leaving home.

Personal effects for use during your stay are allowed without restriction. Duty-free limits for adults are 1,125cl (40oz) of spirits or wine, or 48 x 355cl (12oz) bottles of beer, and 200 cigarettes or 50 cigars or 1kg (2.2lb) of tobacco.

All plants and foodstuffs of any kind must be declared to Customs on arrival and may be subject to inspection and possible confiscation. Regulations on the importation of plants, pets and firearms can be obtained from Canadian consulates.

There are no health restrictions to visitors from most western countries. Travellers from outside Canada are not covered by government-operated medical insurance plans and are strongly advised to purchase health and accident insurance before leaving home.

Disabled Visitors

Shopping centres, public buildings, national, provincial and territorial parks and most hotels and restaurants are required by law to accommodate the physically challenged. If you anticipate problems we suggest you consult tourist information officials before setting out.

Driving

Current driving licences from most countries are accepted. All drivers must have accident liability insurance. Cars can be rented at airports and in most urban centres from the international chains: Hertz, Avis, Budget and Dollar, as well as Tilden and other Canadian companies.

Driving is on the right-hand side of the road. Highways are excellent and well-maintained. Some lesser-used roads have a gravel surface. Speed limits, posted and fairly strictly enforced, are usually 100 km/hour on major highways, less on secondary roads or in urban areas.

Seatbelts are mandatory for both drivers and passengers. Babies and young children must be secured by approved seats. Radar detectors are illegal in the Yukon and Northwest Territories and in Manitoba, but permitted elsewhere in western Canada. Later model cars have daytime running lights which turn on when the engine is started. Drivers of older cars should use headlights outside the cities during daylight, and always at night.

Well-equipped automobile service stations (gas stations) operate in all but the remotest areas. On major highways they often have restaurants or fast-food establishments attached. Highway signs frequently show the distance to the next service station so you can know when it's prudent to refuel (even if it means turning back.) Currently, gasoline is 60¢ to 75¢ per litre depending on grade, a little higher in the far north. In case of breakdown, lift the hood as sign of a problem, then stay with the vehicle to wait for a police or highways department patrol. Truck-drivers will often stop and help or radio for assistance. In remote areas, almost any driver will offer help.

Electricity

Canada's systems are identical to those in the United States, operating on 110 volt, 60 cycle current. Transformers and adaptors are necessary to use 220 volt appliances.

Emergencies

Dial 911, without charge to telephone police, fire or ambulance services.

Food & Drink

Restaurant food is similar to what you will find in the United States and Great Britain, with additional national and regional specialities. Heritage fare handed down from times preceding refrigeration and modern cooking facilities lean towards meat (especially venison and pork), fish and vegetables, baked goods, with a selection of preserves and chutneys. Corn and bean soups are part of the aboriginal heritage.

The coastal regions are justifiably renowned for fresh sea-foods such as salmon and crab, oysters and clams, as well as halibut, Arctic char and most other cold-water fish. Their rich chowders are a meal in themselves. Excellent grain-fed beef is usually served in very large portions.

Immigrant restauranteurs provide an interesting variety of ethnic dishes. In most cities you will find traditional cuisine familiar to anyone from Argentina to New Zealand as well as European and Asian countries. All of this, of course, plus the international hamburger and pizza chains and home grown varieties of 'fast food' outlets.

Holidays

Legal holidays common to all parts of western Canada are:

New Year's Day
Good Friday
Easter Monday
Victoria Day — May 24th or the Monday before
Canada Day — July 1st
August — 1st Monday except Yukon Territory, where Discovery Day is 3rd Monday
Labour Day — the first Monday in September

Thanksgiving Day — the 2nd Monday in October
Remembrance Day — November 11th
Christmas Day
Boxing Day — December 26th

Language

Canada's two official languages are English and French, but English is dominant everywhere in western Canada. French-language services are available in federal government offices. French, German and Japanese are spoken in many tourist areas. English-language spelling is somewhere between British and American usage.

Maps & Brochures

These are readily available and complementary from provincial and territorial tourism information centres listed below. Limited tourism information can be provided by Canadian consulates in the United States and from high commission offices or embassies in other countries. In Canada, tourism bureaus are located in most cities and on main highways close to provincial and US border points. Smaller communities often support regional or local information offices. Hotels and motels also offer a selection of area attraction brochures.

Hikers, canoeists and other back country adventurers can obtain detailed maps from park authorities and local tourism offices.

National, Provincial & Territorial Parks

Currently a daily vehicle permit in the more developed national parks ranges between $5 and $8 per day. In some parks, there is an additional charge of $3 or $4 per person per day, with discounts for children and Canadian seniors. Admission to less developed parks may be free. Annual permits for all western national parks cost $60, and for the Rocky Mountain area parks, $50. Fully serviced campsites vary up to $20 a day; wilderness camping is usually free. Parks may require registration by anyone using specific hiking and portage trails. Some limit access to a stated number of users at any one time, and charge a usage fee. Before setting off on a wilderness hiking or canoeing trip, it is wise to pick up a topographic map showing secondary paths, creeks and rivers.

A fishing permit, valid for any national park, can be bought at a visitor centre, warden's office or campground. Hunting is not permitted and most national parks prohibit firearms.

Drive with caution, especially at dawn or dusk when wildlife

Gardens outside Chinatown's Dynast Pavilion, Winnipeg (Chapter 13)

Leo Mol Sculpture Garden, Winnipeg (Chapter 13)

Baking bread the traditional way at Lower Fort Garry National Historic Park (Chapter 13)

Mennonite Heritage Village, Steinbach (Chapter 13)

can be on the roads, and do heed bear precautions listed in pamphlets given out at park entrances.

In addition to the national system, the provinces and territories as well as some municipalities operate parks and recreation areas, often with overnight camping, and sometimes motel and resort accommodation as well. User fees are comparable with those in national parks. Provincial fishing permits are required in these parks, and in fact anywhere else within the individual provinces.

Some parks accept advance reservations for campsites and limited access trails so a telephone call in advance of your arrival can be useful.

Park wardens serve a variety of roles. They are there to help and advise visitors, but are also responsible for protection of the environment and its plant and wildlife. Because they know their own park intimately, you are well advised to heed their warnings about personal safety. While they rarely need to remind visitors, they do have police powers so their word is, in fact, law.

Newspapers & Magazines

Local newspapers, as well as *The Globe and Mail* and *The Financial Post* are available across the country. International magazines are sold everywhere, as are *Maclean's*, *Chatelaine* and smaller Canadian magazines. Newspapers from the United States and Britain are available in most cities.

Outdoor Adventures

Outdoors enthusiasts can obtain the addresses of organizations which may be of interest through provincial and territorial tourism authorities.

National or regional organizations include:

Alpine Club of Canada
278 St Barbara's Terrace,
Canmore AB
T0O 0M0
☎ (403) 678-3200

Canadian Camping Association
1806 Avenue Rd
Suite 2
Toronto ON
M5M 3Z1
☎ (416) 781-4717

Canadian Parks and Wilderness Society
160 Bloor St E
Toronto ON, M4W 1B9
☎ (416) 972-0868

Canadian Recreational Canoeing Association
1029 Hyde Park
RR Hyde Park ON
N0M 1Z0
☎ (519) 473-2109

Sierra Club of Western Canada
620 View St
Suite 314
Victoria BC
V8W IJ6
☎ (604) 386-5255

Manitoba Naturalists Society
401-63 Albert Street
Winnipeg
MB R3B 1G4
☎ (204) 943-9029.

Outdoors equipment and clothing of all kinds are readily obtainable across the country. Mountain Equipment Co-op, which has a mail order service as well as retail outlets in Vancouver, Calgary, Toronto and Ottawa, is an excellent source. The Co-op's mail order catalogue is available from the Vancouver retail location:

130 W Broadway
Vancouver BC
V5Y 1P3
☎ (604) 876-6221.
A lifetime membership fee of $5 must accompany the first order.

Radio & Television

The Canadian Broadcasting Corporation (CBC) provides am and fm radio and television services in both official languages across the country. CTV is an independent national television network; various cities have their own independent tv stations. Private radio stations are numerous and American services are received in most communities. Highway signs show the frequency of radio transmitters within reception distance.

Recreational Vehicles (RVs)

Campgrounds that provide full RV services are included in all our itineraries. Camper and motorhome rentals are available across Canada. It is essential to make reservations well in advance, and to ensure your vehicle is totally reliable it is a good idea to insist on one no more than two years old. Rental agencies can usually supply bedding, dishes and cookware, though it is often cheaper to buy inexpensive items and simply discard them at the end of the trip. Make sure the rental people demonstrate operation of stoves, furnaces, refrigerators and plumbing systems. If you are unused to operating large vehicles, or driving on the right-hand-side of the road, you should allow time to become familiar with the vehicle before setting off down a highway.

Provincial and territorial tourism literature includes RV rental companies. We have listed some in the more remote areas.

Of the larger RV rental organizations, Go Vacations is probably the best known. The head office address is:

129 Carlingview Drive
Rexdale
Ontario
M9W 5ET
☎ (416) 793-8763.
Western Canada branches include Winnipeg, Edmonton, Calgary and Vancouver, as well as some in California and Arizona.

Another company with branches in Vancouver, Whitehorse, Edmonton and Calgary is:

Canada Campers Inc
2720 Barlow Trail NE
Calgary
Alberta
T1Y 1A1
☎ (403) 250-3209

Shopping

Canada has a broad range of retail establishments. Typically stores are open from 10am to 6pm, six days a week, but most shopping malls are open until 9pm from Monday to Friday. Increasingly, cities have Sunday shopping with restricted hours. In tourist areas, shops are generally open every day to dusk during summer.

Clothing sizes follow the American system rather than the Imperial or Continental systems.

While Canada has adopted metric, the old Imperial system is still used informally in food stores and markets or in areas much frequented by United States visitors.

One kilometre = 0.62 miles. One metre = 3.3 feet. One litre = 0.22 Imperial gallons or 0.26 US gallons. One kilogram = 2.2 pounds.

The Federal government levies a 7 percent Goods and Services Tax on most purchases. In addition, the provinces of British Columbia and Manitoba levy their own 7 percent sales tax compounded on top of the federal tax. Saskatchewan has a similar, 9 percent tax. Alberta and the Yukon and Northwest Territories have no sales taxes of their own.

Sales taxes are added to the advertised price at the cash register, so be prepared to pay at least 7 percent and perhaps 14 to 16 percent more than what the price tag reads. Refunds of federal Goods and Services Tax available to foreign visitors can be arranged through Canada Customs when leaving the country, so keep all the invoices which show taxes charged. Provincial tax refunds are also available in some provinces, so consult merchants on refunds available and methods to be followed.

Sports & Outdoor Events

The major spectator sports are baseball, (Canadian) football, and ice hockey (described simply as 'hockey'). Rodeos, often called 'stampedes' which can last an entire weekend, are well attended throughout the west. Soccer, cricket and other sports have their adherents. Golf and tennis, walking and cycling on both country and city trails are popular. In summer, canoeing, kayaking and hiking, often combined with fishing, are common weekend and vacation activities. Snowmobiling, ice-skating, snow-shoeing and both Nordic and Alpine skiing are popular in winter. Dog-sled races are a feature of northern life.

Telephones

Canada's telephone system is identical to that in the United States. Numbers consist of a 3-digit area code (omitted in local calls) followed by the 7-digit local number. When calling long distance dial 1 first. If you require operator assistance, as when using a telephone company credit card or to call collect, dial O. Detailed instructions are in the front of telephone directories. Cost of a local call (unlimited length) from a public box is currently 25c. Toll-free numbers are prefixed by 1-800. Their use may be limited to certain sections of the country.

Time & Time Zones

The 24-hour clock is used on air, train and bus schedules.

Canada stretches over six time zones, three of them in western Canada. Manitoba is on Central Standard Time (6 hours behind GMT). Saskatchewan, Alberta and a section of British Columbia are on Mountain Standard Time, and most of British Columbia and Yukon Territory are on Pacific Standard Time. The western section of the Northwest Territories stretches across the Central and Mountain time zones.

Daylight saving time is in effect from the last Sunday in October (when the clock is put back one hour) to the last Sunday in April. Saskatchewan and northeast British Columbia do not use daylight saving time.

Tipping

Service charges are not usually added to the bill, except in resorts. In most hotels, tipping is optional. Gratuities of 10 to 15 percent before taxes are customary for good service in restaurants, hairdressers, taxis, etc. Hotel porters and bellmen customarily receive a dollar per bag, the room-maid a dollar or two per night.

Toilets

Public toilets are known as restrooms or washrooms. While there are very few on-street public facilities, you can always find them in shopping centres, department stores, restaurants, service stations, parks and roadside rest areas. Most are accessible to the physically challenged; some provide facilities for changing babies. With few exceptions, they are free, and clean.

Tourist Information Sources

Toll-free numbers can be used in both Canada and the United States.

Alberta
Travel Alberta
10155 102nd St
Edmonton
Alberta
T5J 4L6
☎ (403) 427-4321
or 1-800-661-8888

British Columbia
Tourism British Columbia
1117 Wharf St
Victoria BC
V8W 2Z2
☎ (604) 685-0032
or 1-800-663- 6000

Manitoba
Travel Manitoba
155 Carlton St
Winnipeg
Manitoba
R3C 3H8
☎ (204) 945-3777
or 1-800-665-0040

Northwest Territories
Department of Economic
Development and Tourism
Yellowknife
X1A 2L9
☎ (403) 873-7200
or 1-800-661-0788

Saskatchewan
Tourism Saskatchewan
Suite 500 1900
Albert St
Regina
Saskatchewan
S4P 4L9
☎ (306) 787-2300
or 1-800-667-7191

Yukon
Tourism Yukon
PO Box 2703
Whitehorse
Yukon
Y1A 2C6
☎ (403) 667-5340

For useful, comprehensive tourism information, it is always best to contact the provincial tourist offices in Canada. However, tourism sections of some Canadian Consulates may be able to provide limited material. Major Canadian Consulates are:-

Australia
Consulate General for Canada
5th Level
Quay West
111 Harrington St
Sydney
NSW 2000
☎ (2) 364-3000

Ireland
Canadian Embassy
65 St Stephen's Green
Dublin 2
☎ (1) 478-1988

New Zealand
Canadian High Commission
61 Molesworth St
Thornton
PO Box 12049
Wellington
☎ (4) 473-9577

United Kingdom
Canadian High Commission
Macdonald House
1 Grosvenor Square
London
W1X 0AB
☎ (0171) 258-6600

United States
Canadian Embassy
501 Pennsylvania Ave, North West
Washington
DC 20001
☎ (202) 682-1740
Also in Atlanta, Boston, Buffalo, Chicago, Dallas, Detroit, Los Angeles, Miami, Minneapolis, New York and Seattle.

Transport

Air Travel

Major international airlines, in addition to the flag carriers, Air Canada and Canadian Airlines International, operate services into Vancouver, with more limited services to Calgary and Edmonton. There are also numerous connections with United States points and within Canada. Both of Canada's flag carriers are associated with feeder airlines which service smaller communities. In the more remote areas, there are also small independent carriers and charter services.

Rail Travel

Via Rail has a daily service between Toronto and western Canada, with connections to Montreal, Quebec City and Halifax. The Toronto to Vancouver trip via Winnipeg, Saskatoon, Edmonton and Jasper takes 3½ days if you stay on the same train all the way. This is one of the world's great rail adventures, carrying passengers into northern wilderness not accessible by road, across great plains once filled with buffalo herds, through spell-binding scenes of snow-capped mountains reflected in turquoise lakes, and finally farmlands leading to the coast.

Via Rail also operates a service between Prince Rupert and Jasper, and between Vancouver and Seattle. Its Esquimalt & Nanaimo Railway runs one train daily on weekdays between Victoria, Nanaimo and Courtenay.

Sleeping accommodation on Via Rail's trains comes in various styles: single and double bedrooms with toilet and sink ensuite, 'sections' or bunk beds which convert to seats, and the basic reclining daynighter seats. Meals on board are good, housekeeping efficient.

Since railway stations are usually located downtown, train travel can be very convenient. Sleeper reservations should be made well in advance of summer travel, especially on the ever-popular Jasper to Vancouver segment.

Tour packages, travel passes, group, seniors' and youth fares, and reduced car-rental rates are offered. Reservations may be made through travel agents. Or telephone Via Rail direct, at 1-800-561-8630.

In British Columbia, BC Rail has a daily service between North Vancouver, Whistler and Lillooet, and in summer to Quesnel and Prince George (where it connects with Via Rail). The service between Lillooet and Prince George is less frequent at other times.

For information on BC Rail services contact:

BC Rail
Box 8870
Vancouver BC
V6B 4X6
☎ (604) 984-5246

The privately-operated Great Canadian Railtour Co (Rocky Mountaineer Railtours) operates during summer on the original Canadian Pacific line between Vancouver and Kamloops and Banff, and on the Via Rail line to Jasper. Because this is a tourism-oriented service, the most scenic sections of its journeys are reserved for daylight viewing. For more information contact the company at:

1150 Station Street, 1st Floor
Vancouver BC
V6A 2XJ
☎ 1-800-665-7245

Bus Travel

Greyhound Lines of Canada operate throughout western Canada. Services connect with a number of points in the United States and as far east as Toronto, Ontario. There are also many regional lines, some of which connect with Greyhound and municipal services. Greyhound Lines, as well as the other long-distance companies have seven-, fifteen- and thirty-day passes for unlimited travel, often with student, youth or senior's discounts. While savings may vary with the season, there is seldom any reason for an informed regular bus traveller to pay the listed fare. For more information on Greyhound Lines of Canada, contact them at:

877 Greyhound Way SW
Calgary
Alberta
T3C 3V8
☎ 1-800-752-4841

Ferries

BC Ferries, which link British Columbia's coastal communities, provide one of Canada's great travel bargains. They are fast, clean and efficient. They have modest dining facilities and most carry vehicles of all sizes. For more information, contact:

British Columbia Ferry Corporation
1112 Fort St
Victoria BC
V8V 4V2
☎ (604) 386-3431 in Victoria
(604) 669-1211 in Vancouver.

There are also a number of private lines, including services to the United States.

Alaska Marine Highway System has a terminus at Prince Rupert for services to Seattle and various ports in Alaska, including Skagway, which has connections to the Yukon. For information, contact their Prince Rupert terminal at:
Box 458
Prince Rupert BC
V8J 3R2
☎ 1-800-642-0066 (toll free).

Provincial and territorial highways departments operate free ferries across a number of lakes and rivers where there are no bridges, and they can accommodate the largest vehicles using that road.

Water

Tap water is safe to drink all over the country. In parks, rest areas, etc, warning notices usually indicate where untreated water is intended only for washing.

Acknowledgements

So many people shared their knowledge and expertise in our travels to research this book, it simply is not possible to name them all. However, we particularly want to thank the following:

Shannon Ohama of Canadian Airlines International for getting us to places where even we, veterans of Canadian travel, had not ventured before.

Ann Checkley of Canadian Pacific Hotels and Resorts, Tara White of Choice Hotels and Marilotte Bloemen at Delta Hotels and Resorts, for some comfortable sleeps along the way.

Western Canada's provincial, territorial, regional and community tourist office staff for so readily sharing their knowledge. With special thanks to Jamie Smyth of the Northwest Territories, Mireille Carefoot of Yukon Tourism, Chris Dadson, Mary Ann French, Rhoda Morton and Geoff Sturgeon all of British Columbia's regional offices. Gerard Makuch, Saskatchewan Tourism Authority and Colette Fontaine of Travel Manitoba.

Maureen C. Cumming, British Columbia Ferry Corporation.

And a special thanks to Joanna's husband, Arthur Samuel, for infinite patience, overall assistance with ideas and research and providing endless cups of tea.

Picture credits:

The authors and publisher would like to thank the following for the use of illustrations:

Joanna Ebbutt (Jasper National Park, Kelly Caves, St Columba church, Wanuskewin Park, Winnipeg); Economic Development & Tourism NWT (Dene girl, Inukshuk, polar Bear, skidoos, Tourism Saskatchewan (buffalo, Grasslands National Park, Prairie landscape, bear, fox, rodeo, Big Muddy, Prince Albert National Park, Qu'Appelle Valley, sunset at Wanuskewin); Travel Manitoba (Brandon, Lower Fort Gary, Morden, Steinbach); Yukon Government (Alaska Hwy, Dall Ram, Dempster Hwy, Kluane National Park, Yukon).

All the remaining illustrations were taken by Michael Algar.

Index

A
Abbotsford 42
Abernethy 176
Agassiz 41
Alaska Highway 21, 75, 110, 111
Alberta 22-23, 27, 127-153
Allison Pass 81
Anthony Island 56
Armstrong 87
Ashcroft 66
Assiniboia 154
Assiniboine River 194, 199
Athabasca Falls, Glacier, Parkway, River and Valley137, 138

B
Babine Lake and Mountain 78
Badlands 145, 147, 151
Balfour 96
Bamfield 50, 52
Banff 23, 92, 131, 134
Banff National Park 19, 131-137
Banks Island 125
Barkerville 19, 27, 65, 67-68
Batoche 168
Battleford 32, 165
Bear Cove 55
Bear Glacier 75
Beaver Creek 111
Beaver Hills 145
Beaverdell 100
Beechy 166
Bella Coola 26, 66
Bennett Lake 104
Bertha Falls 131
Big Beaver 157
Big Muddy 155, 157
Big White Mountain 101
Birds Hill Park 25
Blackcomb Mountain 62
Blue Lake 192
Boissevain 184
Bonanza Creek 21, 106, 109, 110
Boundary 111
Bow Lake and Valley 134, 136, 137
Bowron Lakes Park 68
Boyne River 181
Brandon 187-188
Brisco 93
British Columbia 19-20, 27, 34-102
Broken Group Islands 52
Brooks 146
Buffalo Pound Park 162-164
Bugaboo Glacier 93
Bulkley River 77, 78
Burns Lake 79
Burwash Landing 111
Buttle Lake 54

C
Cache Creek 66
Caddy Lake 211
Calgary 31, 145-146
Cameron Lake 131
Campbell River 53, 54
Cape Mudge 54
Cape Scott Park 55
Carberry 194
Carcross 106
Cariboo 26, 66, 68
Cariboo Mountains 67
Cariboo Road 42, 63, 64, 65
Carmacks 108
Carman 181
Carmi 101
Cascade Mountains 42, 81, 82
Cassair Hwy 75
Castle Butte 157
Castlegar 98
Cathedral Lakes and Mountain 82, 89, 90
Cavell Glacier 138
Chemainus 49
Chilcotin Hwy 66, 67
Childs Lake 192
Chilkoot Pass and Trail 21, 104, 105, 106
Chilliwack 42
Chimney Coulee 150
Churchill 24, 212-213
Clear Lake 25
Clearwater 70
Coalmount 82
Columbia Lake 93
Columbia River 26, 89, 93, 98
Comox 53, 57
Conkle Lake 100
Coquihalla Hwy 42
Coronach 156
Coteau Hills 165
Courtenay 53, 57
Cowichan Valley 49
Craigellachie 31, 88
Cranbrook 94
Creston 96
Crooked Lake 176
Crowsnest Hwy and Pass 81, 94, 147
Cultus Lake Park 42
Cypress Hills 32, 148, 149, 150

D
Danielson Park 164
Dauphin 191
Dawson City 109-111
Della Falls 54
Dempster Hwy 21, 109
Desolation Sound Marine Park 57
Dewdney Trail 99
Dinosaur Park 146
Dome Glacier 137
Donjek River 112
Douglas Park 164
Doukhobour 98
Driftwood Canyon 78
Drumheller 145
Duck Mountain 191

Duffey Lake 63
Duncan 48
Dunseith Trail 185

E
Eagle Pass and River 31, 88
Earl's Cove 58
East Blue Lake 191
Eastend 150
Edmonton 23, 142-143
Edzo 122
Elk Falls Park 54
Elk Island National Park 143
Ellison Park 86
Emerald Lake 89
Enderby 87

F
Fairmont Hot Springs 93
Falcon Lake 211
Fernie 94
Field 89
Five Finger Rapids 108
Forbidden Plateau 54
Fort Calgary 32
Fort Garry 24
Fort Good Hope 21
Fort La Reine 194
Fort Langley 26, 42
Fort Macleod 29, 32, 33, 146
Fort Qu'Appelle 173, 173-175
Fort Rouge 24
Fort Smith 115, 122, 123
Fort St James 79
Fort Steele 93, 94
Fort Victoria 26
Fort Walsh 32, 33
Fort Whoop-up 32
Fraser Canyon, Lake, River and Valley 20, 26, 27, 32, 40-43, 63, 69, 79
Fred Henne Territorial Park 119
Frenchman River 24, 150, 152

G
Gabriola Island 50
Galiano Island 40
Ganges 39
Gardiner Dam 164
Garibaldi Park 41, 61
Gibraltar Island 52
Gibsons 58
Glacier National Park 88
Gold Rush Trail 65-72
Golden 89
Golden Ears Mountain 41
Golden Hinde 54
Grand Beach 25
Granite Creek 82
Granville 27
Grasslands National Park 151-153
Gravelbourg 153
Great Slave Lake 114, 115, 122
Green Point 52
Grenville Passage 55
Gwaii Haanas National Park Reserve 56

H
Hagensborg 67
Haines Junction 112
Harrison Hot Springs 41
Harrison Lake 41
Hay River 122
Head-Smashed-In Buffalo Jump 29, 128, 146
Hecla Island 209
Hell's Gate 64
Helmcken Falls 70
Hope 41, 72
Horseshoe Bay 46, 58
Houston 78
Hudson Bay 24
Hudson Bay Mountain 78

I
Icefield Parkway 23, 136, 137, 138
Icefield Ranges 112
Ingraham Trail 119
Inkaneep Provincial Park 83
Inside Passage 55
Inuvik 21, 109, 115, 125
Invermere 93

J
Jackass Mountain 64
Jasper 23, 70, 138-139, 140
Jasper National Park 137-140
Joffre Glacier and Lakes 63
Johnson Peak 42
Johnston Canyon 133

K
Kalamalka Lake 87
Kamloops 70, 72
Katepwa Lake 175
Kathleen Lake 112
Kelowna 85-86
Keremeos 82
Kettle River 100
Kicking Horse Pass 32, 90, 136
Kicking Horse River 89, 90
Killarney 184
Killdeer Badlands 151
Kimberley 94
Kitimat 75
Kitwanga 75
Klondike Hwy 106, 108
Klondike River 109
Kluane National Park 111
Kootenay Bay, Park, Pass and River 92, 96, 98
Kruger Lake 69
'Ksan Village 77
Kyle 166

L
La Rivière 183
Lac Beauvert 139
Lake Agnes 136
Lake Cowichan 49
Lake Diefenbaker 164
Lake Kinbasket 70
Lake Louise 136
Lake Manitoba 194
Lake Minnewanka 134
Lake Okanagan 87
Lake Windermere 93
Lakelse Lake Park 75
Langdale 58
Last Mountain Lake 171
Lebret 175
Lillooet 62, 63, 65
Little Manitou Lake 170
Lockport Heritage Park 207
Long Beach 50
Lougheed Hwy 40
Lower Fort Garry 32, 205-207
Lund 57
Lytton 63, 65

M

Mackenzie Hwy, Mountains and River 21, 22, 109, 122
Macmillan Park 50
Maligne Canyon and Lake140
Manitoba 24-25, 27, 180-213
Manitou Beach 170, 171
Mankota 152
Manning Park 81-82
Maple Creek 148
Maple Ridge 41
Mayne Island 40
Mayo 109
Medicine Hat 94, 147
Meewasin Valley 166
Meziadin Junction 75
Midway 100
Miette Hot Springs 140
Miles Canyon 106
Minter Gardens 41
Miquelon Lakes 145
Mirror Lake 136
Mission 41
Montague 108
Moose Jaw 157, 158
Moose Mountain 187
Moraine Lake 134
Morden 181-182
Moricetown Indian Reserve 78
Mount Baker 36
Mount Currie 62
Mount Custer 131
Mount Edith Cavell 138
Mount Fryatt 138
Mount Garibaldi 61
Mount Layton Hot Springs 75
Mount Logan 111
Mount Norquay 133
Mount Ogden 90
Mount Revelstoke 88
Mount Robson Park 70
Mount Rundle 133
Mount Seymour 36
Mystic Lake 133

N

Nahanni National Park 22,124-125
Nakusp Hot Springs 98
Nanaimo 46, 49, 53
Naramata 85
Neepawa 192
Nelson 96, 97
New Denver 97
New Hazleton 77
Newcastle Island 50
Nicola River 65
Ninstints 56
North Saskatchewan River 137
Northwest Territories 21-22, 28, 32, 114-125

O

Okanagan Mountain and Valley 27, 72, 81, 83, 83-84, 85, 86, 100
Oliver 83
Osoyoos 83, 100
Otter Lake 82

P

Paarens Beach 79
Pacific Crest Trail 82
Pacific Rim National Park 48, 50-51
Parksville 50
Pender Harbour 58
Pender Island 39
Pheasant Hills 176
Pilot Mound 183
Pine Lake 123
Pitt Lake and Polder 40, 41
Ponteix 153
Port Alberni 50
Port Edward 74
Port Hardy 53, 55
Port McNeill 54
Port Moody 27, 31, 40
Port Renfrew 50
Portage la Prairie 194
Portal Creek 138
Portland Canal 75
Powell River 53, 57
Prairies 142-158, 162-177
Prince Albert National Park 24, 169-170
Prince George 69, 79
Prince Rupert 53, 55, 74, 75
Princeton 82
Purcell Mountains 93, 96
Pyramid Mountain 70, 138

Q

Quadra Island 54
Qu'Appelle River and Valley 162, 164, 172-173, 176
Queen Charlotte Islands 19, 53, 56
Quesnel 67
Quesnel Forks 27

R

Radium Hot Springs 92, 131
Rae-Edzo 121
Red Bluff Provincial Park 79
Red Coat Trail 33, 150
Red Deer River 145
Red River 30, 182, 184, 199, 205
Red Rock Canyon 131
Regina 23, 31, 33, 172
Resolute Bay 115
Revelstoke 32, 88
Rhododendron Flats 81
Riding Mountain 25, 189-191
Roaring River 191
Rocher Déboulé Mountains 77
Rock Creek 86, 99
Rocky Mountain Trench 89
Rogers Pass 89
Round Lake 176

S

Sachs Harbour 125
Salmon Arm 72
Salt Spring Island 39
Saltery Bay 58
Sandon 98
Saskatchewan 23-24, 27, 153-177, 180
Saskatchewan Landing Park 165
Saskatchewan River 182
Saskatoon 166-167
Saturna Island 40
Sechelt 58
Selkirk Mountain 96
Seton Lake 63
Shell River 191
Shilo 188
Sicamous 72, 88
Silver Star Provincial Park 87

Similkameen River and Valley 82, 83
Singush Lake 192
Skagway 105
Skeena River 75, 77
Smithers 78
Snow Valley 94
Souris 186
South Moresby National Park 56
South Saskatchewan River 166
Spences Bridge 65
Spirit Sands 193
Spray Valley 133
Spruce Woods 193, 194
Spuzzum 64
Squamish 38, 61
St Elias Mountains 112
St François Xavier 195
St Victor 154
Steinbach 207-209
Steveston 38
Stewart 75
Stewart Canyon 134
Stewart Crossing 109
Strathcona Provincial Park 54
Stutfield Glacier 137
Sulphur Mountain 133
Summerland 85
Sun-Oka Beach 85
Susquatch Park 41
Swartz Bay 40, 46
Swift Current 165

T

Ta Ta Creek 94
Tagish Lake 106
Takhini Hot Springs 112
Telegraph Cove 54
Telkwa Mountain 78
Ten Mile Lake Park 67
Terrace 75
Tête Jaune Cache 69
Tetlin Junction 111
Thompson River 63
Tibbett Lake 119
Tofino 52
Topley 78, 79
Trail 99
Trans-Canada Hwy 42, 48, 53, 65, 72, 81, 131, 136, 146, 147, 180
Trophy Mountains 70
Tsawwassen 40, 46
Tuktoyaktuk 125
Tulameen River 82
Tunnel Mountain 133
Turtle Mountain 184-186
Tutshi Lake 106
Tweedsmuir Park 66
Tyhee Lake 78

U

Ucluelet 51
Upper Laird 75

V

Val Marie 151-153
Valemount 70
Valhalla Park 98
Vancouver 27, 35-37
- Capilano Suspension Bridge and Park 37
- Dr Sun Yat-Sen Classical Chinese Garden 36
- Granville Island 35
- Grouse Mountain 37
- Lynn Canyon Park 37
- Queen Elizabeth Park 36
- Stanley Park 35
- University of British Columbia 36

Vancouver Island 19, 26, 27, 38, 45-46, 53-56
Vanderhoof 79
Vaseux Lake 83
Vermilion Lakes 133
Vernon 87
Victoria 20, 27, 29, 39, 46, 46-47

W

Wakamow Valley 158
Wanuskewin Heritage Park 167-168
Waterton Lakes National Park 129-131
Watrous 170
Wellman Lake 192
Wells 67
Wells Grey Provincial Park 70
West Coast Trail 52
West Hawk Lake 211, 212
West Kettle River 100
Whistler 62
Whistler Mountain 139
White Horse Rapids 106
White Pass 106, 108
Whitehorse 107-108
Whiteshell Provincial Park 25, 210
Williams Creek and Lake 66, 67
Willow Bunch 154, 155
Windermere Valley 93
Windy Arm 106
Winnipeg 25, 26, 29, 198
- Assiniboine Park 202, 204
- Centre Culture Franco-Manitoban 202
- Chinatown 201
- Exchange District 200
- Forks Market 200
- Fort Garry 200
- Fort Whyte Centre 204
- Manitoba Children's Museum 200
- Manitoba Museum of Man and Nature 201
- Osborne Village 201
- Riel House 204-205
- St Boniface 202
- St Boniface Museum 202
- St Norbert Arts and Cultural Centre 205
- St Norbert Heritage Park 205
- Winnipeg Art Galley 201

Winnipeg River 210, 211
Wood Buffalo National Park 22, 115, 122, 123
Wood Mountain 152, 153, 154

Y

Yale 31, 64, 65
Yellowhead Hwy 69, 75, 140
Yellowknife 22, 114, 116-119
Yoho National Park 89
Yukon River 21, 104, 106, 108
Yukon Territory 20-21, 103-112

Discover a New World with

Off The Beaten Track

Travel Guides

Austria

Explore the quiet valleys of Bregenzerwald in the west to Carinthia and Burgenland in the east. From picturesque villages in the Tannheimertal to the castles north of Klagenfurt, including Burg Hochosterwitz standing on a 150ft high cliff and built by the man who brought the original Spanish horses to Austria.

Britain

Yes, there are places off the beaten track in even the more populated areas of Britain. Even in the heavily visited national parks there are beautiful places you could easily miss — areas well known to locals but not to visitors. This book guides you to such regions to make your visit memorable.

Czech and Slovak Republics

From the Alpine peaks of the High Tatras and the forests and lakes of the Sumava and the Krkonose Mountains, to remote hill-top castles and little-visited historic towns in Bohemia and Moravia, this book will take you to eleven different areas of the Czech and Slovak Republics and show you the lesser-known sights.

Greece

Brimming with suggested excursions that range from climbing Mitikas, the highest peak of Mount Olympus, the abode of Zeus, to Monemvassia, a fortified medieval town with extensive ruins of a former castle. This book enables you to mix a restful holiday in the sun with the fascinating culture and countryside or rural Greece.

Ireland

Ireland has a dramatic coastline, quiet fishing harbours and unspoilt rural villages, and friendly easy-going people. *Off The Beaten Track Ireland* will lead you to a memorable holiday where the pace of life is more relaxing and definitely not hectic.